Helping
At-Risk
Students

THIRTEENTH ANNUAL YEARBOOK
OF THE AMERICAN EDUCATION FINANCE ASSOCIATION
1992

Helping
At-Risk
Students

What Are the
Educational and
Financial Costs?

Edited by

Patricia Anthony
Stephen L. Jacobson

CORWIN PRESS, INC.
A Sage Publications Company
Newbury Park, California

To Hilary Jane and Jessica Anna Anthony

For information address:

Corwin Press, Inc.
A Sage Publications Company
2455 Teller Road
Newbury Park, California 91320

SAGE Publications Ltd.
6 Bonhill Street
London EC2A 4PU
United Kingdom

SAGE Publications India Pvt. Ltd.
M-32 Market
Greater Kailash I
New Delhi 110 048 India

Printed in the United States of America

Library of Congress Cataloging-in-Publication Data
Helping at-risk students: what are the educational and financial
   costs? / edited by Patricia Anthony, Stephen L. Jacobson.
       p. cm. — (Annual yearbook of the American Educational Finance
   Association : 13th)
   Includes bibliographical references and index.
   ISBN 0-8039-6032-8—ISBN 0-8039-6049-2 (pbk.)
   1. Special education—United States. 2. Socially handicapped
children—Education—United States. 3. Special education—
United States—Finance. I. Anthony, Patricia, 1948-   .
II. Jacobson, Stephen L.   III. Series.
LC3981.H45   1992
371.9'0973—dc20   92-26633
                                                                   CIP
The paper in this book meets the specifications for permanence of the American National Standards Institute and the National Association of State Textbook Administrators.

92 93 94 95 10 9 8 7 6 5 4 3 2 1

Corwin Press Production Editor: Tara S. Mead

Contents

Preface

In 1971, the day after Labor Day, I began teaching my first class of special education students. The class comprised 10 "trainable mentally retarded" youngsters between the ages of 7 and 11. We were housed in a little cottage located in a low-income neighborhood in Muskegon, Michigan. At that time in my life, my perceptions concerning special education, special student populations, and at-risk students were somewhat narrow and dogmatic. I was a neophyte in an emerging field. I had taken all the courses and had mastered working with all the disabilities, and I was fairly certain that whenever a child appeared who required special services, I would be able not only to identify the needs, but also to deliver what was needed.

More than 20 years later, I am no longer convinced that I could do either. Although the Individuals with Disabilities Education Act (IDEA) was passed by Congress in 1975, and although all of the 50 states mandate free appropriate public education for children with disabilities, the needs of students requiring services have blurred, overlapping previous categorical expectations. *Learning disabilities,* a category as yet unnamed when I initially began teaching, now claims the largest percentage of students with disabilities. Many of these students' specific disabilities are undefined, but their need for services is readily apparent.

And although there are Chapter 1 services for "disadvantaged" students, compensatory education for at-risk students, and federal programs for Native American students, demographic data reveal that out of the entire population in 1986, 13.9% of all students in the United States never finished high school. For minority student populations the proportions were even higher: 16.7% of African Americans and an astounding 41% of all Hispanic students (Ward, 1992). Other statistics are equally foreboding. *The New York Times* (1992) reports that as recently as 1990, 9.7% of all children lived in households not headed by either parent. The percentage of minority children living in poverty continues to increase, with 45% of all black children and 39.3% of all Hispanic children living in poverty (U.S. Department of Education, 1991).

Given these statistics, it is fitting that an edition of the American Education Finance Association Yearbook attend to this topic. This volume follows two previous yearbooks that, through thoughtful discourse and graphic statistics, have evoked provocative soul searching about educational equity for all students, particularly for those who are caught in the web of poverty and its ensuing strands of illiteracy, desperation, and powerlessness. This volume examines the educational and financial costs involved in educating at-risk students. When considering which students are at risk, the programs targeted for discussion in this text are those for students identified as requiring special education, federal programs directed toward disadvantaged children, students with limited English proficiency (LEP), and Native American students.

Overview of Contents

This book is divided into three sections: Part I addresses federal legislation's impact on education, Part II examines the funding of programs for at-risk students, and Part III discusses policies and issues concerning at-risk populations. The chapters in Part I discuss federal legislation that directly affects programs for specific at-risk student populations. Chapter 1 provides an overview of the evolving legislation for students with disabilities, presenting the changes in the federal special education law that was originally passed in 1975. The reader's attention is directed toward the effects of the most recent amendments to the law in 1986 and then again in 1990.

In Chapter 2, Riddle provides an extremely comprehensive examination of the federal laws relating to disadvantaged students. He examines recent legislative changes in relation to Chapter 1, and discusses policy issues surrounding the delivery of Chapter 1 services to parochial school students and within the regular classroom.

Sevilla chronicles the evolution of federal support for bilingual education in Chapter 3. Presenting both the current debate surrounding the delivery of bilingual education services to limited-English-proficient students and the cost figures for these programs, she articulates the federal government's weakening stand on LEP programs in this country.

In Chapter 4, Mueller and Mueller review past and current federal legislation affecting programs for Native American students. They provide cost data on programs for Native Americans as well as programmatic descriptions of the educational services currently available to Native American students.

McDonough and Jordan, in Chapter 5, discuss findings collected from a national study conducted on at-risk students. In surveying state administrators for at-risk student programs, they sought information on several issues: the criteria used by the states to identify at-risk students; the procedures states use to fund these programs; and the opinions and attitudes of the administrators concerning the delivery of services.

Lyons, in Chapter 6, explores several different options available to states for funding at-risk programs. Through a simulation program, she presents six different funding alternatives and then evaluates the effectiveness of each according to specific school finance evaluation criteria and program funding incentives and disincentives.

In Chapter 7, Verstegen and Cox provide cost data on special education programs for the 50 states. They describe the formulas utilized by the states and report for each state the approach used, as well as the funding provided.

Finlan and Hartman project future costs for the category of learning disabilities in Chapter 8. Basing their projections upon current and projected enrollment trends, they provide future cost data and examine relevant policy implications.

Thompson and Zabel report on the plight of at-risk programs in rural states, particularly the state of Kansas, in Chapter 9. They delineate the school funding wars existing between rural and urban areas in rural states and describe how funding formulas often favor some rural areas over others.

In Chapter 10, Rossman describes recent policy developments in several states for integrating special student populations into the regular classroom. She compares several states' policy initiatives that are currently under way and discusses their implications for the rest of the country.

In Chapter 11, Brown and her colleagues delve into the evolving role of personnel in meeting the needs of at-risk students. The authors provide cost data on personnel as well as a discussion concerning how personnel are currently being used.

Castle explores the emergence of tribal influence on the education of Native American students in Chapter 12. In his thoughtful discussion of the critical educational needs of Native American students, the confusing labyrinth of bureaucratic providers, and the press by Native American leaders to reclaim authority over directing their children's education, he presents a compelling portrait.

In the final chapter of this volume, Curley urges state policymakers to recognize the potential of the students they have and discusses the need for financing programs for gifted at-risk students. Citing relevant data on the numbers of capable at-risk students who drop out of school for lack of effective programs, Curley urges better financing of gifted programs, but only if there is a corresponding rigorous and equitable identification of gifted students, so that more students identified as at risk are included.

Acknowledgments

I would like to take this opportunity to thank all of the contributors of *Helping At-Risk Students*. It is their work and expertise that is reflected in these pages. It is their efforts and valuable knowledge that have borne this text to fruition. In addition, the authors' willingness to adjust their busy schedules so that my deadlines for the book could be accommodated was greatly appreciated.

I would also like to thank several individuals from Corwin Press whose assistance in producing the 1992 Yearbook was invaluable. I appreciate Gracia Alkema, President of Corwin Press, for her consistent graciousness and support throughout all of our meetings and phone conversations concerning the 1992 AEFA Yearbook. Changes Gracia recommended in the title of the Yearbook and the layout of the text have resulted in, I think, an improved Yearbook. I thank Ann McMartin for her excellent editing of the manuscript and for tracking down missing tables and copyright permissions. Such vigilance resulted in making this editor's job easier. Megan McCue and Tara Mead were of great assistance during the final stages of producing the book. Thank you for your fine work.

Finally, I would like to thank my two daughters, Hilary and Jessie, for being as they always are, avid supporters of their mom and the lights of my life.

PATRICIA ANTHONY

Reference

U.S. Department Of Education, Office of Educational Research and Improvement, National Center for Educational Statistics. (1991). *Digest of educational statistics 1990.* Washington, DC: Government Printing Office.

About the Contributors

Patricia Anthony is an Associate Professor of Educational Administration at the University of Massachusetts at Amherst. Prior to entering higher education, she was a special education teacher and curriculum specialist. From 1985 to 1989, she was editor of the *Journal of Education Finance,* and she now serves as a member of the Editorial Advisory Board. She received her doctorate from the University of Florida. Her primary research interests are in the areas of the interrelationship of law and finance in producing public funds for private schools and the funding of programs for special needs students. She has published widely in the fields of school law and school finance. She is coeditor, with James Gordon Ward, of *Who Pays for Student Diversity? Population Changes and Educational Policy,* the Twelfth Annual Yearbook of the American Education Finance Association.

Stephanie Brown is Director of Exceptional Children in Nash County Public Schools of North Carolina. She is currently completing a doctoral program in Educational Administration at North Carolina State University.

Sidney R. Castle received his Ph.D. in Educational Administration and Policy Studies from Arizona State University. He currently serves as Assistant Professor in the Department of Administrative and Foundational Services at Louisiana State University. While teaching master's and doctoral courses in educational administration, he specializes in school finance, school law, facility planning, and educational administration theory and works closely with the research staff of the Louisiana Legislature, as well as with Louisiana public school districts. His research interests focus on the design and implementation of innovative educational programs to meet the needs of minority and other special populations. He is currently faculty adviser for the LSU Fulbright Scholars Association. A former consultant to the Education Division of the Navajo Nation and the founding Executive Director of the Navajo Nation Public School Boards Association, he maintains a professional working association with the Navajo Nation and other southwestern Native American organizations.

Cynthia L. Cox, a native Virginian, has spent 15 years in the area of special education as a teacher, residential counselor, program director, supervisor, and professor. She earned all three of her degrees from the University of Virginia: a B.S. in 1977, an M.Ed. in 1980, and a Ph.D. in 1991. She taught previously at Minot State University in North Dakota. In 1990, she relocated to Glassboro State College in New Jersey, where she is currently an Assistant Professor in Special Education.

Marsha Craft-Tripp is Director of Pupil Personnel in Washington City Schools in North Carolina. Her current research examines the effects of collegial models of professional development on special education teachers.

Cathy Crossland is Head of the Department of Curriculum and Instruction in the College of Education and Psychology at North Carolina State University. Her research centers on policy and instructional issues pertinent to special populations of students.

John R. Curley is an Associate with the New York State Education Department. He received his Ed.D. in educational administration from the State University of New York at Albany and was an Education Policy Fellow with the Institute for Educational Leadership, Inc. His research interests are primarily in the areas of education finance and the politics of education. He conducted a study of the federal education block grant that appeared under the title *Federal Education Policy and the Block Grant* and has had work published in various professional journals, including the *Journal of Education Finance, Urban Review, Urban Education* and the *Irish Journal of Education.*

Thomas Gerald Finlan is currently Director of Special Education for Riverview Intermediate Unit in Shippenville, Pennsylvania. His previous professional experience includes 7 years as a school psychologist, 3 years as Director of Pupil Personnel, and 3 years as Assistant Director of Special Education, all with the Riverview Intermediate Unit. Previously, he was a teacher of high school English and reading for 5 years in the Elba Central School District in Elba, New York. He received his bachelor of science degree in Liberal Arts from the State University College at Buffalo, New York, and a master of arts degree in General-Experimental Psychology from the State University College at Geneseo, New York. He also received certification as a school psychologist from Indiana University of Pennsylvania. His Ph.D was awarded in Education Administration by the Pennsylvania State University in 1990.

Susan Gurganus is Assistant Professor of Special Education at the College of Charleston in Charleston, South Carolina. Her research theme concerns the personnel appraisal criteria and processes applied to special education teachers.

William T. Hartman is the Professor in Charge of the Educational Administration Program and an Associate Professor at The Pennsylvania State University. He is the author of *School District Budgeting* and a number of journal articles, chapters, and technical reports involving school finance topics. His research interests focus on special education finance, resource allocation, equity, and finance-based microcomputer models for application at state and local levels.

Stephen L. Jacobson is Associate Professor in the Department of Educational Organization, Administration and Policy at the State University of New York at Buffalo. He received his Ph.D. from Cornell University, and his dissertation was named cowinner of the AEFA's Jean Flanigan Award for Outstanding Research in the Field of Educational Finance in 1988. Prior to entering higher education, he was a special education teacher with the New York City Public Schools. His research interests focus primarily on the school workplace and rural education. He has published extensively in the areas of teacher compensation and educational reform and is coeditor, with James A. Conway, of *Educational Leadership in an Age of Reform* (1990).

K. Forbis Jordan is a Professor of Educational Leadership and Policy Studies in the College of Education at Arizona State University. He also has been Senior Specialist in Education with the Congressional Research Service in the Library of Congress, a faculty member at Indiana University and the University of Florida, Executive Secretary of the Commission on Schools of the North Central Association, and principal consultant in school finance studies in eight states. He is a member of the American Education Finance Association, American Educational Research Association, Association of School Business Officials, and Phi Delta Kappa. His teaching and research areas of interest include state school finance programs, school organization, and intergovernmental relationships. He has authored or edited 12 books and more than 80 monographs and articles. His bachelor's and master's degrees are from Western Kentucky University, and his Ed.D. was awarded by Indiana University.

Teresa S. Lyons is an Assistant Professor of Educational Administration and Higher Education at the University of Nevada, Las Vegas. She has been a public school administrator, teacher, and speech/language pathologist. Her primary research interests are in the areas of school finance, program development for special populations, and the impact of teacher belief systems on instructional decision making. Her Ph.D. was awarded by Arizona State University.

Bettye MacPhail-Wilcox is Head of the Department of Educational Leadership and Program Evaluation in the College of Education and Psychology at North Carolina State University. She conducts research in the areas of school finance, personnel administration, organizational theory, and critical thinking skills programs.

John T. McDonough is an Administrative Assistant for Curriculum and an Internal Facilitator for Strategic Planning in the Romeo Community School (Michigan). He has 20 years' experience as a high school English teacher and department chair. He has been an adjunct faculty member in the Division of Educational Leadership and Policy Studies at Arizona State University. In addition to issues related to at-risk students, his other research interests include school finance, school business management, and the educational change process. He is a member of the American Education Finance Association, American Educational Research Association, and Phi Delta Kappa. His B.A. was awarded by Central Michigan University, his M.A. is from Wayne State University, and his Ed.D. was awarded by Arizona State University.

Mildred I. K. Mueller is an Assistant Professor at Augsburg College in Minneapolis, Minnesota, and an enrolled member of the Sault Ste. Marie Band of Chippewa Indians of Michigan. She received a B.A. and an M.A. from Central Michigan University and an Ed.D. from the University of Minnesota. She has taught at the elementary, junior high, middle, and secondary levels in North Carolina, Michigan, and Minnesota. After receiving her doctorate in 1973, she spent a year on a special project to reduce racism in the Minneapolis Public School System. In 1974 she moved to the Minnesota Department of Education, where, over the course of 14 years, she served as Assistant Manager of Indian Education, Manager of Indian Education, and Director of Education Statistics. She has been at Augsburg College for 3 years and a member of AEFA for 15 years.

Van D. Mueller is Professor of Educational Policy and Administration at the University of Minnesota. Prior to receiving his doctorate from Michigan State University, he was a teacher, principal, and superintendent in Michigan. He has served two terms on the Board of Directors of the American Education Finance Association and in addition was President during 1991-92. He is coeditor, with L. Dean Webb, of *Managing Limited Resources: New Demands on Public School Management* (the 1984 AEFA Yearbook) and, with Mary P. McKeown, of *The Fiscal, Legal, and Political Aspects of State Reform on Elementary and Secondary Education* (the 1985 AEFA Yearbook). Recently, he has worked with the plaintiffs in school finance equity litigation in Minnesota, Missouri, and North Dakota.

Wayne Clifton Riddle is a Specialist in Education Finance at the Congressional Research Service, Library of Congress, which provides objective, nonpartisan, legislative research and policy analyses to the committees and members of Congress. Among his other responsibilities, he is the lead analyst of the federal Chapter 1 program for disadvantaged children. His other major areas of responsibility are school finance and comparative and international education. He has written numerous CRS reports for Congress on Chapter 1 and other national education policy issues, as well as several articles for the *Journal of Education Finance* and other publications. He holds a bachelor's degree in history from the University of Virginia and a master's degree in economics from George Washington University.

Gretchen B. Rossman is Associate Professor of Education and Coordinator of the Educational Administration Program at the School of Education, University of Massachusetts at Amherst. She received her Ph.D. in education from the University of Pennsylvania, with a specialization in higher education administration. Prior to taking her current position, she served as Senior Research Associate at Research for Better Schools in Philadelphia. Her research interests include the study of school cultures, school change, and policy implementation. She is Co-Principal Investigator, with Patricia G. Anthony, of a 5-year study, funded by the Massachusetts Department of Education, that is evaluating a Massachusetts program in which seven districts are experimenting with more fully integrating special needs, Chapter 1, and bilingual students into the regular classroom. She has published articles in several journals, and her books include *Change and Effectiveness: A Cultural Perspective* (with Dick Corbett and Bill Firestone) and *Designing Qualitative Research* (with Catherine Marshall). Her most recent book, *Courses, Credits, and the Curriculum: High School Responses to Mandated Curriculum Reform* (with Bruce Wilson), will appear in late 1992.

Jennifer Sevilla is a doctoral student at the University of Southern California. Her master's degree in business administration was granted by Pepperdine University. She is currently a Research Assistant in the Center for Research in Education Finance as well as a Title VII Bilingual Fellow. In addition to her work in education finance and bilingual education, her outside interests involve science and math curriculum development.

David C. Thompson is Associate Professor of Education Administration and Co-Director of the UCEA Center for Education Finance at Kansas State University. His professional career has spanned classroom teacher, elementary principal, high school principal, superintendent of schools, and currently the professoriate. A specialist in education finance litigation, he is currently involved in school finance lawsuits as expert counsel to plaintiffs and defendants representing approximately 500 school districts and more than one million students in nearly a dozen states. He has also served as consultant to blue-ribbon state legislative school finance task forces, including standing conferee to state legislatures and governors' task forces. His publication record exceeds more than 60 book chapters, monographs, and refereed journal articles, including the current NOLPE monograph, *Education Finance Law: Constitutional Challenges to State Aid Plans.* In addition to his own research in litigation and state school finance policy, he currently serves on several editorial review boards, including the Authors' Committee of West's *Education Law Reporter,* serves as book editor for the *Journal of Education Finance,* writes a regular finance/law/facilities column for the *Journal of the Council of Educational Facility Planners International,* and is an editor of *Educational Considerations.* His new textbook in school finance is scheduled to appear in early 1993.

Deborah A. Verstegen is Associate Professor of Education Policy and Finance in the Curry School of Education at the University of Virginia. She serves on the Board of Directors of the American Education Finance Association, the Advisory Board for the U.S. Department of Education's National Center for Education Statistics Technical Panel, the Finance Center of the University Council for Education Administration (UCEA), and various editorial boards. She is also editor of the *Journal of Education Finance.* She has received a distinguished service award from AEFA and UCEA and is active in school finance cases currently before state courts. Her research focus is on federal and state education finance policy. She has authored or coauthored more than 80 publications, including the recent book edited with James Ward, *Spheres of Justice in Education.*

Robert H. Zabel is a Professor of Special Education at Kansas State University. A former regular and special education teacher of students with behavioral and learning disorders, he received a Ph.D. in Educational Psychology from the University of Minnesota in 1977. His research has focused on teacher preparation, teacher stress and burnout, and supply and demand for special educators, as well as assessment issues in special education. He is coauthor, with Joseph Rizzo, of a textbook, *Educating Children and Adolescents with Behavioral Disorders: An*

Integrative Approach (Allyn & Bacon). He has been active in professional organizations such as the Council for Children with Behavioral Disorders and has been an associate editor for several special education journals. He is currently editor of the Forum section of *Behavioral Disorders*.

ONE

Individuals With Disabilities Education Act
THE LEGACY CONTINUES

PATRICIA ANTHONY

Students with disabilities constitute approximately 11% of the U.S. student population (U.S. Department of Education, 1988, 1991). Since the passage of P.L. 94-142 in 1975, Congress has consistently expanded federal legislative mandates safeguarding the educational rights of children with disabilities. Currently, more than 4 million students receive special education services, and this number is increasing given the enactment of the early childhood amendments in 1986 (P.L. 99-457) and the corresponding growth of an at-risk infant population due to alcohol and other drug abuse, AIDS, sexually transmitted diseases, and a decrease in prenatal care among groups at risk (i.e., teenage mothers and poor women) ("Tiny Miracles," 1989).

In 1990, the original name of P.L. 94-142 was changed from the Education for All Handicapped Children Act to the Individuals with Disabilities Education Act (IDEA). While most of the original act remains intact, several new provisions have been added, broadening the scope of the law. This chapter examines the broader reach of IDEA, and explains what IDEA does and does not mandate in regard to the educational rights of children with disabilities.

1

Continuance of the Original Mandates

All of the original guarantees accorded children with disabilities are present in IDEA:

- a free appropriate public education
- an individualized educational program
- special education services
- related services
- due-process procedures
- an individualized evaluation for placement
- placement in the least restrictive environment

Under IDEA, eligibility has become more inclusive. Any child with "mental retardation, hearing impairments including deafness, speech or language impairments, visual impairments including blindness, serious emotional disturbance, orthopedic impairments, autism, traumatic brain injury, other health impairments, or specific learning disabilities" who needs specialized educational programs is eligible for services (IDEA, sec. 1401[a][1], 1990). Two categories of disabilities, autism and traumatic brain injury, were added in 1990 (P.L. 101-476). Prior to that, children with these disabilities were subsumed under other categories, such as mental retardation or serious emotional disturbance. A third category, attention deficit disorder (ADD), was considered, but has not yet been designated as a category under IDEA. During 1990-1991, Congress sought input from the public concerning ADD being designated a category under IDEA, however, it has yet to be included (Ordover & Boundy, 1991).

All children with disabilities, ages 3 to 21, are eligible for educational services, unless providing services for populations 3-5 or 18-21 years old would be contradictory to a state's existing laws. IDEA has a zero-reject policy, which means that no child with disabilities, no matter how severe, can be denied services (*Timothy W. v. Rochester School District*, 1989).

Free Appropriate Public Education

All children with disabilities are afforded a free appropriate public education. Although IDEA fails to define what is meant by "appropriate," a 1982 Supreme Court decision, *Board of Education of the Hendrick Hudson Central School District v. Rowley*, interpreted *appropriate* to mean "access" to a free public education, consisting of specialized instruction and related services from which a student with disabilities derives educational "benefit." The Court defined *benefit* in terms of the child's ability to progress effectively along the educational spectrum, but noted that there could be no one standard for benefit. Cautioning that benefit did not mean maximizing a child's full potential, the Court, however, stipulated that the benefit derived could not be trivial.

The Individualized Education Program

IDEA stipulates that every child with disabilities must be provided an individualized education program, or IEP. The IEP is developed in a meeting at which the following individuals must be present: at least one parent, the teacher of the child, and an administrator or representative of the school district. The program that is written by this group must reflect the individual needs of the child, along with objectives and strategies for meeting those needs. Related services are included in the IEP to demonstrate how the child's needs will be met; the entire IEP must be an indication as to how educational benefit will occur.

The IEP is not synonymous with placement. In fact, IDEA mandates that placement for a child with disabilities can be discussed only *after* the IEP has been written; IEPs cannot be developed with specific placements in mind. IEPS must be reviewed at least once a year, and whenever a change in placement is being considered.

Related Services

IDEA defines *related services* as "transportation and such developmental, corrective and other supportive services . . . as may be required to assist a child with disabilities to benefit from special education" (sec. 1401[a][17]). The kinds of related services permitted under IDEA are as follows:

- speech pathology and audiology
- psychological services

- physical and occupational therapy
- recreation and therapeutic recreational services
- social work services
- medical and counseling services, including rehabilitation services

This list of services is by no means definitive. Any service that is defined as supportive, corrective, or developmental in nature is allowable under IDEA. In recent years, computers used by students who have severe disabilities have been designated as related services, as have one-on-one aides. The recreation, therapeutic recreation, rehabilitation, and social work services were stressed in IDEA in 1990 as related services deemed particularly necessary in serving the 18- to 21-year-old population of students with disabilities.

Medical services are acceptable only for diagnostic and evaluation purposes, and cannot be offered on a continuous, ongoing basis. However, some services that appear medical in nature are permissible as related services because they are not provided by doctors and are necessary if the child is to attend school. Examples of these health-related types of medical services are clean intermittent catheterization (*Irving Independent School District v. Tatro*, 1984) and the suctioning of tracheostomy tubes (*Department of Education, State of Hawaii v. Katherine D.*, 1983).

Although psychotherapy is not listed as a related service under IDEA, the courts have declared it to be similar to counseling, and therefore permissible (*T. G. v. Board of Education of Piscataway*, 1984). However, court decisions have been mixed regarding the use of psychiatrists to treat students (*Board of Education of the Town of Cheshire v. Department of Education*, 1991; *Darlene L. v. Illinois State Board of Education*, 1983; *McKenzie v. Jefferson*, 1983; *Metropolitan Government of Nashville and Davidson County v. Tennessee Department of Education*, 1989; *Tice v. Botentourt County School Board*, 1990). At least two courts have decided that the reason for providing the service is the determining factor as to whether psychotherapy is an excluded medical service or an allowable related service (*Tice* and *Town of Cheshire*, cited above).

Another controversial related service is psychiatric treatment. In order for it to be considered a related service, the child requiring the psychiatric treatment must first qualify as a child with a disability (sec. 1401[a][1]). Disputes most often arise over the question of who pays for residential psychiatric services—the school district, another state health agency, or the parents? Courts have interpreted this type of service in different ways. Some courts have ordered the school to pay for the entire cost of the program—both educational costs and room and board (*Papcoda v. State of Connecticut*, 1981). Other courts have ruled that school districts need only pay for those costs that are school related and are associated with assisting the child educationally, such as tuition and psychotherapy (*Darlene L., McKenzie, Tice*, cited above; *Taylor v. Honig*, 1990). In several cases, courts have ruled that school districts do not bear any costs for psychiatric placement (*Clovis Unified School District v. California Office of Administrative Hearings*, 1990; *Metropolitan Government of Nashville and Davidson County*, cited above).

Finally, students with substance abuse problems do fall under IDEA if they have been identified as having one of the disabilities specified by the law. For such students, residential placement in a substance abuse program can be a related service, provided that it has been ascertained that the placement will enable the student to receive benefit from an educational program (*Inquiry of Scariano*, 1988).

Special Education Services

IDEA defines special education services as

> specially designed instruction, at no cost to parents or guardians, to meet the unique needs of a child with a disability, including—
> (A) instruction conducted in the classroom, in the home, in hospitals and institutions, and in other settings; and (B) instruction in physical education. (sec. 1401[a][16][A][B])

IDEA does not mandate that this specialized education must occur in a particular setting; rather, the law stresses that these services and where they take place depend upon the individual needs of each child.

Education in the
Least Restrictive Environment

No matter what the student's needs are, IDEA also mandates that,

> to the maximum extent appropriate, children with disabilities, including children in public or private institutions or other care

facilities, are educated with children who are not disabled, and that special classes, separate schooling, or other removal of children with disabilities from the regular educational environment occurs only when the nature or severity of the disability is such that education in regular classes with the use of supplementary aids and services cannot be achieved satisfactorily. (sec. 1412[5][B])

The requirement that children with disabilities be educated in the least restrictive environment has been central to recent state policy initiatives to integrate children with disabilities back into the regular classroom (see Rossman, chap. 10, this volume). IDEA not only requires schools to educate children with disabilities in the most normal environment possible, it also mandates that these students be allowed and encouraged to participate to the fullest extent they are able in extracurricular activities, school mealtimes, and nonacademic periods of the day, such as recess and homeroom. However, education in the least restrictive environment cannot occur in lieu of meeting the individual needs of the child. In their headlong rush to become more cost-effective by placing children with disabilities in integrated programs, states need to exercise caution and first ascertain if such moves are in the best interests of the children involved.

Evaluation and Due Process

Fair and nondiscriminatory evaluation procedures are mandated by IDEA. These include the use of testing instruments that are not racially or culturally biased and that are administered in the child's native language and mode of communication. IDEA also requires that more than one criterion be used to determine whether or not a student is in need of specialized services (sec. 1412[5][C]). Evaluations must be conducted by a multidisciplinary team of specialists who are responsible for evaluating the child in every area that could be affected by the suspected disability, such as motor activities and academics.

The decision to evaluate a child suspected of having a disability sets in motion comprehensive due-process procedures. These procedures are delineated in the Code of Federal Regulations. The child's parents (or other legal guardians) must be notified that an evaluation is taking place (sec. 1415(b)(1)(C)). This also must occur each time there is a change in the program of a child with disabilities. The notice must be written in the parents' native language and must be in understandable terms (sec. 1415[b][1][D]). Generally, parents must consent before the child may be evaluated, although in some instances IDEA does allow students to be evaluated without parental consent; however, certain conditions must be met in such cases.

Parents also have the right to an independent evaluation, for which, depending upon the circumstances, the school district may bear the costs. In certain states—for example, Massachusetts—parents are permitted to seek an independent evaluation at the school district's expense.

Disciplinary Actions

One of the most controversial areas concerning students with disabilities has been discipline. Under IDEA, children with disabilities are assured of continuous services provided in the least restrictive environment. In the usual case of school suspension, a student is temporarily excluded from school and receives no educational services. If a student with disabilities is suspended, does the same hold true? According to the 1988 ruling in *Honig v. Doe*, it does not. No student with a disability can be excluded from school for disciplinary reasons for a period of more than 10 days. If such an exclusion takes place, then it is inferred that a change in placement has occurred, and all of the due-process, evaluation, and IEP procedures discussed above must again be set in motion. Although disciplinary measures involving lesser amounts of exclusion from school are permissible, courts have ruled that students who are suspended for fewer than 10 days still must be provided educational services (*Kaelin v. Grubbs*, 1982; *S-1 v. Turlington*, 1981).

Early Childhood Education

Recognizing the importance of early intervention for children with disabilities, Congress in 1986 amended IDEA by P.L. 99-457, which extended the act's reach to preschoolers, toddlers, and infants. Several states already had included preschoolers in their populations of children with disabilities, receiving federal funding for their efforts. However, as of the 1991-92 school year, states were required to serve *all* students in this age group or lose federal monies targeted toward these children.

A second part of P.L. 99-457, now incorporated into IDEA as Part H, is targeted toward children with disabilities who are in the age range of birth to 2 years. States that decide to offer services to infants and toddlers identified as having disabilities receive differing amounts of federal monies according to the state's infant and toddler population and the state's percentage of the national total of children within this age range. During the initial two years, the state receive funds from the federal government to establish a statewide system for early intervention. Third- and fourth-year funding is contingent upon the state's having in place the statewide early intervention system and actually implementing it. A state is eligible for fifth-year funding if the system is in place and the state can provide a description of its services.

There are two distinctive features to Part H of IDEA. First, as described above, it calls for states to "develop and implement a statewide, comprehensive, coordinated, multidisciplinary, interagency program of early intervention services for infants and toddlers" (sec. 1471[b][1]). Second, it mandates that an individualized family service plan (IFSP) be developed for each child suspected of having disabilities *and* the family of that child. The IFSP is similar to an IEP in that it requires that objectives be outlined, special services be described, and, if appropriate, plans be made for how to transition the child into special education services authorized under Part B of IDEA (sec. 1477[2][d]). However, it differs from the IEP in its emphasis upon the whole family. Objectives and special services must reflect family needs as they pertain to the child with disabilities. In regard to parental consent and evaluation procedures, states must comply with the same regulations currently required for the 3- to 21-year-old population. In June 1991, Congress approved a plan under which participating states could receive a one-year extension for meeting the requirement to serve all infants and toddlers with disabilities.

18- to 21-Year-Old Students
With Disabilities

IDEA provides a vital link for 18- to 21-year-old students with disabilities: transition from high school programs into postsecondary institutions. This is accomplished through

> grants to . . . state educational agencies, institutions of higher education, junior and community colleges, vocational and technical institutions, and other appropriate nonprofit educational agencies for the development, operation, and dissemination of specially designed model programs of postsecondary, vocational, technical, continuing, or adult education for individuals with disabilities. (sec. 1424a[a][1])

IDEA also stipulates that an IEP for a student who is 16 years of age or older must reflect the student's impending transition from high school to a postsecondary program (sec. 1401[20][D]). IDEA suggests that in some cases this should be written into the IEP when the child is younger, for instance, at age 14.

The types of services that fall into the realm of "transition services" include instruction, community experiences, development of employment and other postschool adult living objectives, acquisition of daily living skills, and functional vocational evaluation (sec. 1401[19]). With current statistics demonstrating that one-third of all students enrolled in special education programs drop out of high school prior to graduation (Gartner & Lipsky, 1987), the transitional services mandated under IDEA provide essential assistance to this population of students with disabilities for accessing appropriate vocational and postsecondary programs.

Attorneys' Fees

Until 1986, parents wishing to contest decisions reached by school officials often were unable to do because they lacked the money to expend on hearings or litigation. However, in 1986, Congress enacted the Handicapped Children's Protection Act (HCPA) (P.L. 99-372), which amended IDEA to include the awarding of attorneys' fees and other costs engendered by parents when they prevail either at administrative hearings or in court. Congress was responding to an earlier decision, *Smith v. Robinson* (1984), in which the Supreme Court ruled that under IDEA parents were not entitled to collect from school districts the cost of attorneys' fees if the parents had prevailed.

Under the HCPA, parents can recover fees and other costs if certain situations exist. First, if parents choose to accept a school district's offer to settle on placement or services prior to a ruling by the court, the offer must be accepted by the parents within 10 days. Second, if the parents reject the settlement offer, the final outcome of the litigation or hearing must be superior to the settlement offer.

Parents can also recover for fees encumbered in a dispute that was settled in their favor, prior to going to the due-process hearing stage. The passage of the Handicapped Children's Protection Act ensures that the ability of parents to obtain appropriate placement or services for their children will depend not so much upon their personal finances, but upon whether the placement or services they seek are really appropriate as defined by law.

Conclusion

The 1986 and 1990 amendments to P.L. 94-142 are positive additions to a landmark piece of federal legislation. Changing the name of the law to reflect independence rather than dependence, creating more definitive categories for those children whose lives are affected by autism or traumatic brain injury, enumerating the transitional services essential for shaping the future lives of children with disabilities, and providing incentives for states to initiate early intervention programs all result in a law that addresses the needs of students with disabilities more powerfully. In a time when, in some states, the number of children diagnosed as having disabilities approaches 20% of the student population, IDEA provides not only a guarantee of services for these children, but also funding for research and the development of programs that will intervene earlier and with greater impact.

References

Board of Education of the Hendrick Hudson Central School District v. Rowley, 458 U.S. 176, 102 S.Ct. 3034 (1982).

Board of Education of the Town of Cheshire v. Department of Education, 17 EHLR 942 (Conn. Super. Ct. 1991).

Clovis Unified School District v. California Office of Administrative Hearings, 903 F.2d 635 (9th Cir. 1990).

Darlene L. v. Illinois State Board of Education, 568 F. Supp. 1340 (N.D. Ill. 1983).

Department of Education, State of Hawaii v. Katherine D., 727 F.2d 809 (9th Cir. 1983), *cert. denied*, 471 U.S. 117 (1985).

Gartner, A., & Lipsky, D. K. (1987). Beyond special education: Toward a quality system for all students. *Harvard Educational Review, 57,* 367-395.

Honig v. Doe, 108 S.Ct. 592 (1988), *affirming as mod. Doe v. Maher,* 793 F.2d 1470 (9th Cir. 1986).

Individuals with Disabilities Education Act. (1990). 20 U.S.C. sec. 1400 et seq., P.L. 94-142, as amended by P.L. 99-372, P.L. 99-457, and P.L. 101-476.

Inquiry of Scariano (4/18/88). EHLR 213:133 (OSEP).

Irving Independent School District v. Tatro, 468 U.S. 883, 104 S.Ct. 3371 (1984).

Kaelin v. Grubbs, 682 F.2d 595 (6th Cir. 1982).

McKenzie v. Jefferson, 566 F. Supp. 404 (D. D.C. 1983).

Metropolitan Government of Nashville and Davidson County v. Tennessee Department of Education, EHLR DEC. 441:450 (Tenn. Ct. of App. 1989).

Ordover, E., & Boundy, K. (1991). *Educational rights of children with disabilities: A primer for advocates.* Cambridge, MA: Center for Law and Education.

Papcoda v. State of Connecticut, 528 F. Supp. 68 (D. Ct. 1981).

S-1 v. Turlington, 635 F.2d 342 (5th Cir. 1981), *cert. denied*, 454 U.S. 1030 (1981).

Smith v. Robinson, 468 U.S. 992 (1984).

Taylor v. Honig, 910 F.2d 627 (9th Cir. 1990).

T. G. v. Board of Education of Piscataway, 576 F. Supp. 420 (D. N.J. 1983), *aff'd.* 738 F.2d 420 (3rd Cir.), *cert. denied*, 469 U.S. 1086, 105 S.Ct. 592 (1984).

Tice v. Botentourt County School Board, 908 F.2d 1200 (4th Cir. 1990).

Timothy W. v. Rochester School District, 875 F.2d 954 (1st Cir. 1989), *cert. denied*, 110 S.Ct. 519.

Tiny miracles become huge public health problem. (1989, February 19). *The New York Times*, pp. 1, 44.

U.S. Department of Education, Office of Educational Research and Improvement, National Center for Educational Statistics. (1988). *Youth indicators 1988.* Washington, DC: Government Printing Office.

U.S. Department Of Education, Office of Educational Research and Improvement, National Center for Educational Statistics. (1991). *Digest of educational statistics 1990.* Washington, DC: Government Printing Office.

TWO

Federal Aid for the Education of Disadvantaged Children
FUNDING, PARTICIPATION, AND LEGISLATIVE TRENDS

WAYNE CLIFTON RIDDLE

This chapter provides an introduction to the status of, and trends related to, the largest program in the nation that addresses the needs of disadvantaged or "at-risk" children—the federal government's Chapter 1 program. This program was first enacted as Title I of the Elementary and Secondary Education Act (ESEA) of 1965; through various stages of legislative evolution it has become Chapter 1 of Title I of the ESEA, or simply Chapter 1.

Although the Chapter 1 program authorizes a number of different programs, in this chapter I will focus on its grants to local educational agencies (LEAs), because these funds constitute more than 90% of total program funding and dominate policy debates over the program. Appropriations for Chapter 1 LEA grants have exceeded $5 billion in recent years, and the program reaches approximately 90% of all LEAs in the nation. The chapter begins with a discussion of trends in funding and participation for Chapter 1 LEA grants, followed by a brief review of trends in policies and issues for the program. While I will consider the entire life of the Chapter 1 program,

AUTHOR'S NOTE: Views expressed in this chapter are my own, and should not be taken as reflecting the positions of the Congressional Research Service.

going back to 1965, my focus here is primarily on the period since 1980, especially the most recent amendments to the program in 1988.

Chapter 1 LEA grants serve "educationally disadvantaged" children—children whose educational achievement is relatively low, regardless of their family income level—who reside in relatively (in terms of the local context) low-income areas. Chapter 1 is a categorical program, with detailed provisions regarding such matters as fund allocation, yet has always provided a great deal of flexibility regarding such basic educational policies as the grade levels to be served, subject areas to be taught, and instructional techniques to be utilized. Policymakers are constantly attempting to strike the "right" balance between federal guidance on how to serve effectively the children most in need and flexibility for state and local officials and teachers to decide how best to serve them.

Funding Trends

Table 2.1 provides the Chapter 1 LEA grant appropriation for the program since its inception. Data are presented on the basis of program years—that is, the primary school years during which grants were allocated to states and LEAs. Appropriation amounts are shown in terms of current dollars and estimated dollars at 1990-91 price levels. The final column of the table expresses these estimated constant dollar amounts as an index, where the 1965-66 appropriation is the base year (100.0). Figure 2.1 illustrates the trend in constant dollar funding as well.

Brief Analysis

In constant (1990-91) dollars, Chapter 1 funding has exhibited three basic cycles over the program's lifetime. First, from 1965-66 through 1972-73, funding was relatively constant, falling within the index number range of 95.5 to 103.4 for all except one year (1968-69). The second cycle was the first of two periods when funding fell, then returned to approximately the same level in real terms—in this case, over the period of 1972-73 through 1979-80. The minimum funding during this period was for 1976-77 (80.7). The final cycle was a deeper decline and recovery over the period of 1979-80 through the present,

Table 2.1 ESEA Title I, Chapter 1, LEA Grant Appropriations, by Primary Program Year for Which Funds Are to Be Used

Program Year	Chapter 1 Appropriation in Thousands of Current Dollars	Chapter 1 Appropriation in Thousands of Estimated 1990-91 Dollars	Index Number for Appropriation in 1990-91 Dollars (1965-66 = 100.0)
1965-66	969,935	5,182,859	100.0
1966-67	1,015,153	5,083,835	98.1
1967-68	1,100,288	5,157,600	99.5
1968-69	1,020,439	4,483,100	86.5
1969-70	1,219,166	4,948,934	95.5
1970-71	1,361,261	5,132,223	99.0
1971-72	1,438,367	5,108,068	98.6
1972-73	1,614,238	5,358,113	103.4
1973-74	1,511,247	4,701,657	90.7
1974-75	1,638,793	4,699,315	90.7
1975-76	1,641,951	4,294,019	82.9
1976-77	1,745,654	4,184,787	80.7
1977-78	1,951,251	4,370,025	84.3
1978-79	2,355,708	4,925,642	95.0
1979-80	2,776,578	5,318,468	102.6
1980-81	2,731,651	4,793,705	92.5
1981-82	2,611,387	4,201,159	81.1
1982-83	2,562,753	3,845,961	74.2
1983-84	2,727,588	3,865,873	74.6
1984-85	3,003,680	4,008,300	77.3
1985-86	3,200,000	4,111,768	79.3
1986-87	3,062,400	3,747,692	72.3
1987-88	3,453,500	4,021,636	77.6
1988-89	3,829,600	4,246,125	81.9
1989-90	4,051,546	4,270,494	82.4
1990-91	4,806,484	4,806,514	92.7
1991-92	5,608,643	5,392,959	104.1
1992-93	6,200,179	5,788,304	116.8

NOTE: Chapter 1 has been a forward-funded program since fiscal year 1975. Therefore, beginning with the 1974-75 program year, these funds have been provided in appropriations acts for the preceding fiscal year (e.g., FY 1991 appropriations for the 1991-92 program year). The amounts shown include Chapter 1 basic and concentration grants, "capital expenses grants" for services to nonpublic school pupils, and program improvement grants. The price index used to calculate estimated 1990-91 dollar values of appropriations is the fixed weight deflator for state and local government purchases of services, published by the Bureau of Economic Analysis, U.S. Department of Commerce.

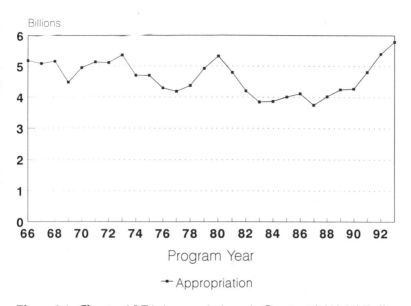

Figure 2.1. Chapter 1 LEA Appropriations, in Constant (1990-91) Dollars

when the real dollar index level fell to the 70s from 1982-83 through 1987-88, with the lowest at 72.3 for 1986-87.

The first dip in the real funding level for Chapter 1 coincided with the later Nixon and Ford presidencies, with the recovery occurring during the Carter presidency. The second, deeper, decline in the real value of Chapter 1 appropriations occurred during the early and middle years of the Reagan presidency, when the administration first proposed that Chapter 1 be absorbed into a block grant to the states, then proposed annual cuts in Chapter 1 appropriations of as much as one third in current dollar terms. Although the Congress maintained the basic nature of Chapter 1, and never cut funding as much as proposed by the administration, the legislators nevertheless agreed to funding levels that declined in real, and occasionally even in current, dollar terms during the early and middle 1980s. However, by the late 1980s, both congressional and administration support for Chapter 1 funding had increased, and relatively large annual increases in Chapter 1 appropriations have been adopted beginning with program year

1987-88 (budget fiscal year 1986). This trend has not yet shown signs of abating, although as of 1991-92 it had only raised Chapter 1 LEA grant appropriations to approximately the same level as 1965-66 in real terms.

There are several reasons for the late 1980s/early 1990s willingness on the part of Congress and the administration to support substantially increased Chapter 1 appropriations, in spite of general federal budgetary constraint. First, the continuing concern about educational quality that began with the publication of the National Commission on Excellence in Education's *A Nation at Risk* in 1983 and was boosted by adoption of the National Governors' Association's *National Education Goals* in 1990 has focused congressional attention on the need to raise achievement, especially among the disadvantaged. Second, demographic trends indicating that increasing shares of pupils are from disproportionately disadvantaged populations (e.g., African-American or Hispanic children, children from single-parent households, children from limited English-language backgrounds) have stimulated increased support for the major federal program intended to meet the needs of such children. Third, the relatively positive findings of the congressionally mandated National Assessment of Chapter 1, conducted from 1984 to 1987, also raised support for the program (U.S. Department of Education, 1987). Further, many individuals in Congress, corporations, and elsewhere have increasingly recognized the need to improve education of the disadvantaged, not only for the sake of the students involved, but in their own self-interest, for the sake of their businesses and the national economy. Finally, the amendments made to Chapter 1 in 1981 and 1988 helped to convince many in Congress and the administration that the program had developed a balanced mix of flexibility, targeting, and incentives for improvement and was therefore worthy of additional funding.

Participation Trends

Table 2.2 and Figure 2.2 show the number of children served by Chapter 1 during the period 1979-80 through 1988-89. These data are not shown for the entire life of the program because they are not available on a consistent basis for periods preceding 1979-80, when the TIERS/CHIERS data system was established.[1]

Table 2.2 ESEA Title I, Chapter 1, LEA Program Participating Pupils, 1979-80 Through 1988-89

Program Year	Total Participants	Index Number (1979-80 = 100.0)	Nonpublic School Participants	Index Number (1979-80 = 100.0)
1979-80	5,162,822	100.0	189,114	100.0
1980-81	5,075,807	98.3	213,499	112.9
1981-82	4,618,531	89.5	184,084	97.3
1982-83	4,447,634	86.2	177,210	93.7
1983-84	4,572,635	88.6	190,660	100.8
1984-85	4,712,709	91.3	184,532	97.6
1985-86	4,739,870	91.8	127,922	67.6
1986-87	4,732,661	91.7	137,900	72.9
1987-88	4,950,522	95.9	142,492	75.4
1988-89	5,046,873	97.8	—[a]	NA

SOURCE: For years through 1987-88, U.S. Department of Education (1989, p. 9). For 1988-89, data were provided by Office of Planning, Budget, and Evaluation (OPBE) staff from a forthcoming report.

a. Beginning with data for 1988-89, OPBE is reporting participation data in three categories: public schools, nonpublic schools, and institutions for neglected and delinquent children (which may be public or nonpublic). The disaggregation of neglected and delinquent participants between public and nonpublic institutions is not available. Thus total participant data for 1988-89 are comparable to those for previous years, but not the separate figures for public and nonpublic school pupils. The reported number of nonpublic participants for 1988-89, excluding those in institutions for the neglected and delinquent, is 137,656.

Brief Analysis

As illustrated in Table 2.2 and Figure 2.2, aggregate Chapter 1 participation fell, then rose, during the 1980s in a pattern similar to that of the real appropriation level. Under Chapter 1, LEAs have a great deal of flexibility to determine how many of their educationally disadvantaged children to serve and, consequently, the level of services provided to each participating child. They could respond to changes in the real level of their grants by changing either the number of children served or the amount spent per child served.

Nevertheless, during the 1980s, LEAs tended to adjust the number of children served by Chapter 1 directly and proportionally in response to changes in the constant dollar appropriation level. The correlation (Pearson's r) between the aggregate number of children served by Chapter 1 and the real appropriation level between 1979-80 and 1988-89 was a substantial 0.76. A study of Chapter 1 funding and

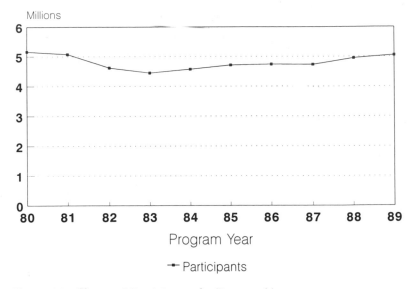

Figure 2.2. Chapter 1 Participants, by Program Year

participation trends in the early 1980s came to a similar conclusion, that reductions in the number of children served were proportional to reductions in the constant dollar level of program allocations. Thus, according to this study, the primary effect of reductions in Chapter 1 allocations was a decrease in the number of children served, not the level of services (or development of more cost-efficient ways of providing services) per child (Advanced Technology, 1983).

Of the participants in Chapter 1, the majority have always been in the elementary grades; in 1987-88, for example, 71% were in grades 1-6, and an additional 8% were in prekindergarten or kindergarten. Only 5% of participants were in senior high school. While Chapter 1 services may be provided to pupils at any level from prekindergarten through grade 12, LEA officials have usually focused on the early grades as part of a preventive strategy. While some have argued that services to secondary school pupils are equally important, and a separate Chapter 1 program specifically for secondary school pupils was authorized in 1988, as of fiscal year 1991 this program had not been funded.

Recent Legislative and Policy Trends

In the remainder of this chapter, I will review major legislative and policy trends regarding Chapter 1 in recent years, especially the period 1980-1991. This was a period during which Chapter 1's existence was seriously challenged by the Reagan administration and others who argued that such categorical, targeted federal education programs were inappropriate. However, instead of being absorbed into a block grant, as President Reagan proposed, Chapter 1 was first greatly simplified in 1981 (Education Consolidation and Improvement Act of 1981), then enhanced in terms of flexibility, targeting, and performance incentives in 1983 and 1988 (P.L. 98-211 and P.L. 100-297). Much of the following discussion focuses on the deliberation and results of the 1988 reauthorization of Chapter 1 by the Hawkins-Stafford Act, since this was the most recent comprehensive, national debate over Chapter 1 policy issues. Among the trends discussed are perennial Chapter 1 issues, such as the allocation formula, and newly developing issues, including a recent emphasis on the development of "higher-order" skills for the disadvantaged.

Allocation Formulas

In part because it is by far the largest program in the U.S. Department of Education, and one of the largest in the federal government, in which funds are allocated by formula to state and local agencies, the Chapter 1 allocation formula has always been the focus of substantial congressional interest and debate. Further, the formula uses proxy measures—poor children as a proxy for low-achieving children, state expenditures per pupil for costs of providing education—the appropriateness of which is always debatable. There is also frequent debate over the value of targeting limited funds at areas most in need versus distributing funds relatively broadly, to assure wider participation in and greater political support for Chapter 1. Also, the Chapter 1 LEA grant formula has been used to allocate funds under other programs—such as vocational education grants under the Perkins Act—and has been proposed for use in still other new programs. Finally, at least once each decade—when new decennial census data become available—there is the potential for large shifts in allocation patterns, heightening the interest in making formula modifications.

Current Formulas

Chapter 1 LEA grants are calculated by the federal government on a county basis. State education agencies (SEAs) receive the aggregate funds for counties in their state, then allocate the county amounts to individual LEAs. There are two LEA grant allocation formulas, for *basic* and for *concentration* grants. Each is based on each county's number of "formula children" multiplied by a state cost factor. The formula children are those ages 5-17 who are (a) in poor families, according to the latest decennial census, (b) in families receiving Aid to Families with Dependent Children (AFDC) payments above the poverty level for a family of four, and (c) in certain institutions for the neglected or delinquent. The number of poor children counted in the Chapter 1 allocation formula is much greater than the numbers found in the other two groups of children. For 1991-92 allocations, a national total of 7,734,343 (96% of total formula children) poor children were counted in this formula, compared with 80,336 (1%) AFDC children and 283,037 (3%) neglected and delinquent children. While the counts of children from poor families are available only from the decennial census, the other two formula child counts are updated annually.

The Chapter 1 "cost factor," by which formula child counts are multiplied to calculate maximum authorized Chapter 1 payments, is the state average per pupil expenditure (SAPPE), held to limits of 80% and 120% of the national average, and further multiplied by 0.4. Thus a payment goal of 40% of the SAPPE per child counted is established in the formula. While the formula child factor is assumed to measure need for Chapter 1 funds, the cost factor is intended to measure, within limits, variations among the states in the costs of delivering elementary and secondary education services.

The only threshold for Chapter 1 basic grant eligibility is that a county or LEA must have 10 formula children in order to participate in the program. However, the current statute requires that 10% of LEA grant appropriations be allocated using a different, concentration grant formula, under which only LEAs in counties where formula children equal either 6,500 children or 15% of the total population aged 5-17 are eligible to receive grants. The concentration grants are not a separate program from basic grants; rather, they are a supplementary fund distribution mechanism. The current concentration grant formula was adopted in 1988; there were previous Chapter 1 concentration grant formulas, intended to focus some of the funds on areas of greatest need, but this is the first for which appropriations have consistently been provided. Actually, the current concentration grant formula is not highly concentrated or focused. The 15% threshold is below the national average proportion of school-age children who are counted in the Chapter 1 formula (17% using 1991-92 data), and approximately two-thirds of all children reside in counties that meet one of the eligibility thresholds. Further, the current formula— unlike previous ones—provides the same relative gain, compared with distribution of an equal amount of funds under the basic grant formula, to LEAs in all counties meeting the 15% threshold, whether their "poverty rate" be 16% or 50% (Riddle, 1988).

Issues

Recent congressional interest in Chapter 1 allocation formulas has centered on possible effects of the 1990 census, marginally greater targeting on areas with concentrations of poverty, and the appropriateness of the formulas' cost factor. Interestingly, the more basic issue of whether poverty should be used as a proxy for educational disadvantage, and, if so, whether the current poverty measure is most appropriate, has not attracted much attention for at least a decade.

1990 Census

As noted earlier, the arrival of new census data to update the child poverty counts has in the past resulted in significant allocation shifts and renewed debate over the appropriateness of the Chapter 1 formula. These conditions are next scheduled to occur in late spring or early summer 1992. There is not yet available sufficient information from the 1990 census to predict which states or regions might be found to have relatively fewer, or more, poor children in 1990 compared with 1980. Also of interest may be the availability of LEA-level data from the 1990 census, so that basic and—especially—concentration grants may be determined by the federal government on an LEA, not county, basis.

Targeting

During the 1988 debate over Chapter 1 reauthorization, the question of whether Chapter 1 funds are appropriately targeted on areas most in need was at least temporarily settled by adoption of the current concentration grant formula and the requirement that 10% of funds be distributed under it, as described above. Nevertheless, there are some who feel that Chapter 1 basic grants are distributed too broadly, and that the concentration grant formula is not sufficiently "concentrated." No measure of state or local resources is considered in the formula except, indirectly, the cost factor (see below). With the only threshold for basic grant participation being the presence of 10 poor children in a county or LEA, areas with very low poverty rates and substantial ability to pay for education services can, and do, participate in Chapter 1.

Analyses published as part of the National Assessment of Chapter 1 in 1986 indicate that there is a statistically significant relationship between poverty and educational disadvantage in general, and there is a stronger relationship between concentrated poverty and educational disadvantage. In other words, the poverty of a child's family is more likely to be associated with educational disadvantage if the family lives in a geographic area with large numbers of poor families. One possible revision to deal with this would be an "absorption" factor whereby only LEAs or counties with poverty rates above some minimum level—perhaps at least 5%—would participate in the basic grant program. If it were also required that only formula children in excess of the absorption level were counted in allocating funds, then the formula would provide relatively more funds per child, the higher a locality's poverty rate.

Cost Factor

The appropriateness of the Chapter 1 cost factor may be questioned. While the purpose of taking into account differences in the cost of providing educational services is widely accepted, this may not be the best way to do so. First, this factor varies only by state, yet costs are likely to vary as much within as between states. Second, the SAPPE reflects not only differences in costs but also variations in ability and willingness to pay, extent of school employee unionization, and other factors. An examination of the relationship between the SAPPE for 1987-88 and state personal income per capita for 1988 reveals a very high correlation between these two measures (Pearson's *r* of 0.729). Unfortunately, a more direct measure of educational costs does not appear to be available nationwide, so the practical choice is between a flawed measure and no measure at all.

A General Theme: Increased Flexibility

Increased flexibility, often combined with new forms of accountability based on outcomes, is a relatively consistent theme running through many of the following discussions of Chapter 1 trends and issues. In part, this is a legacy of the Education Consolidation and Improvement Act of 1981, which simplified Chapter 1 and ultimately provided more explicit flexibility to state and local program administrators. Fiscal requirements (e.g., maintenance of effort, comparability) are often easier to meet, there are more options available for selection of schools and pupils to be served, and it is now possible to operate Chapter 1 programs on a schoolwide basis in high-poverty areas. In some cases, this process has consisted primarily of clarifying authority that already existed; in others, there has been a real increase in local flexibility. There has also been a partial change in approach in Washington, from primarily a reliance on regulatory mechanisms to somewhat more of a strategy mixing performance standards, incentives, and less regulation of processes.

In 1991, the Bush administration proposed carrying this strategy a step further by authorizing regulatory waivers for Chapter 1 and other federal education assistance programs in return for new forms of outcome-based accountability. Individual LEAs could negotiate for the waiver of virtually any current program regulation, in exchange for evidence of improved pupil performance. It remains to be seen whether such broad conditional deregulation authority will be granted, although a bill passed by the Senate in January 1992 (S. 2) would provide relatively broad regulatory waiver authority with respect to as many as 300 LEAs (Riddle, 1991).

Incentives for Accountability
and Improved Performance

Over most of Chapter 1's lifetime, there were neither financial incentives nor disincentives for improved pupil performance in Chapter 1 programs. Funds were usually allocated, and target areas selected, on the basis of counts of poor, not low-achieving, children. The one general exception to this pattern is in the distribution of Chapter 1 funds among target school attendance areas, after these have been selected (usually on the basis of poverty). Such allocation of funds among schools is typically based primarily on the number of educationally disadvantaged pupils to be served, not on poverty. At this stage, a school's success in raising pupil achievement might have a disincentive effect, in that it would reduce the school's share of the LEA's total Chapter 1 grant in the following year.

Beginning in the mid-1980s, the Department of Education has attempted to improve performance in Chapter 1 through the "Secretary's Initiative" to identify and disseminate information about exemplary Chapter 1 programs. Research on effective practices in Chapter 1 programs was also conducted as part of the 1984-1987 National Assessment of Chapter 1.[2]

Accountability Provisions

Chapter 1 now contains much more detailed provisions aimed at evaluating the performance of individual pupils, schools, and LEAs served by Chapter 1 and at providing technical assistance to those whose performance is not improving. Under current legislation, Chapter 1 evaluations must be conducted at least once every 3 years in each LEA, and at least once every 2 years in every state. Each LEA must also "review" its Chapter 1 program operations, particularly its parental involvement activities, every year. These evaluations are to be conducted in accordance with national standards established by the U.S. Department of Education regarding evaluation methods and are to be used to assess Chapter 1 program effects on individual pupils, as well as schools and LEAs as a whole.

The Secretary of Education must submit to the Congress at least once every two years a report on state and local Chapter 1 evaluations. The 1988 amendments to Chapter 1 also require the Department of Education to contract with an organization to conduct a national longitudinal study of the effects of Chapter 1 programs on participating children. This study must follow a nationally representative sample of Chapter 1 participants, and comparable nonparticipants, through the age of 25 years and must evaluate the effects of Chapter 1 participation on such characteristics as academic achievement, school dropout rates, delinquency, postsecondary education participation, employment, and earnings.[3] Subsequent legislation, adopted in 1990 (P.L. 101-305), has mandated that the U.S. Department of Education conduct a new national assessment of Chapter 1, with results to be available before the next scheduled program reauthorization.

Chapter 1 also provides grants to the states specifically for the development and implementation of Chapter 1 improvement programs. A total of $25.1 million was appropriated for this purpose for 1992-93. The state program improvement grants are to be used only for the direct costs of such plans, including technical assistance to LEAs.

A state survey of the early implementation of the 1988 program improvement provisions found that approximately 12% of Chapter 1 schools were in need of improvement in the initial year of application of this requirement, even though most states established minimal standards for determining program success (Council of Chief State School Officers, 1991). The report's authors anticipated that state standards might be raised in future years if larger appropriations were available for program improvement grants.

Another significant accountability provision is contained in Chapter 1's provisions regarding schoolwide plans, which are discussed later in this chapter. After 3 years of schoolwide plan implementation, such schools must demonstrate that the achievement of disadvantaged children enrolled in them is higher than either (a) the average for children participating in Chapter 1 in the LEA as a whole, or (b) the average for disadvantaged children in that school over the 3 years preceding schoolwide plan implementation.

Performance Incentives and Assistance

Along with the "stick" of additional accountability requirements, Chapter 1 has in recent years added the "carrot" of new authorities or grants intended to provide incentives for improved performance. In addition to removing certain barriers to adoption of schoolwide plans, the act authorizes LEAs, with SEA approval, to use up to 5% of their grants for "innovation projects." These projects may include several activities intended to reward high performance, such as incentive payments to schools that have demonstrated significant success in raising pupil performance and the continuation of Chapter 1 services to pupils who were eligible in any previous year, but whose achievement has increased so that they no longer meet the standard eligibility requirements.

A state survey of the initial implementation of this innovation authority (Council of Chief State School Officers, 1991) found that relatively few LEAs were using this option so far. Reasons offered for this low rate of use of the innovation authority were the relatively small size of the 5% authority, limited funds—relative to need—in the Chapter 1 grant overall, and the narrow range of activities for which the innovation funds could be used.

Technical Assistance and Research

Finally, increased support has been provided for technical assistance and research related to Chapter 1 in recent years. Technical assistance is provided not only by the regional technical assistance centers (TACs), but also by a recently established series of rural TACs. All of the TACs have attempted to shift their focus in recent years from primarily helping states and LEAs to meet statutory requirements, especially with respect to evaluations, toward efforts to improve the effectiveness of Chapter 1 programs.

In addition to national evaluations of Chapter 1 and related research described above, the U.S. Department of Education supports research and experimentation through the Center for Research on Effective Schooling for Disadvantaged Students, located at Johns Hopkins University. This center has initiated a range of activities intended to determine improved educational techniques for disadvantaged students and to apply those methods in schools.

The Center for Research on Effective Schooling for Disadvantaged Students has also implemented model programs in three Baltimore middle schools, based upon recommendations in the Carnegie Council report, *Turning Points* (Task Force on Eduction of Young Adolescents, 1989). In this and in all their work on the education of disadvantaged students, the Center is attempting to find ways to avoid tracking, retention, and special education assignments, which they consider to be key practices leading to low achievement for students.

Parental Involvement

Throughout the history of the Title I/Chapter 1 program, the active involvement of parents in the education of disadvantaged children has been considered by many observers to be important for program success. Under the current Chapter 1 statute, LEAs are required to implement procedures "of sufficient size, scope, and quality to give reasonable promise of substantial progress toward achieving the goals" of *informing* parents about the Chapter 1 program, *training* parents to help instruct their children, and *consulting* with parents. LEAs are required to do the following:

- Develop written policies for parental involvement in planning and implementing Chapter 1 programs.
- Convene an annual meeting of parents of all participating pupils at which parent activities are to be explained.
- Provide to each parent a report on his or her child's progress and, "to the extent practical," conduct an annual parent-teacher conference for each pupil.
- Provide program information and an opportunity for regular meetings for parents, if the parents so desire.

LEAs must also communicate with parents in a language and form of communication that the parents understand.

Several specific forms of parental involvement are listed in Chapter 1 as mechanisms that LEAs *may* adopt to meet their responsibilities in this area. Among these activities are parent training programs, the hiring of parent liaison workers, training of school staff to work with parents, use of parents as tutors or classroom aides, home-based education activities, and solicitation of parent suggestions on program operations or parental advisory councils.

Services to Nonpublic School Pupils

Since its initiation, Chapter 1 has provided aid to disadvantaged children attending both public and nonpublic schools. The legislation has required that educationally disadvantaged children attending nonpublic schools be served in an equitable manner in comparison with those attending public schools, taking into account the number of such children attending nonpublic schools and their particular educational needs. In cases where an LEA has not provided for such equitable participation in Chapter 1 by nonpublic school pupils, the U.S. Secretary of Education must arrange for a third-party organization to provide the services under a "bypass" mechanism. This situation usually occurs when there is a state constitutional limitation on aid to nonpublic schools. There has long been debate over whether nonpublic school pupils have actually been equitably served under Chapter 1, with some nonpublic school advocates arguing that public education authorities generally allocate a disproportionately small share of Chapter 1 funds to serving nonpublic school pupils (Vitullo-Martin & Cooper, 1987).

Aguilar v. Felton Decision

In 1985, the U.S. Supreme Court declared unconstitutional the practice of providing Chapter 1 services to pupils of religious institution-affiliated nonpublic schools by sending public school teachers into such schools (*Aguilar v. Felton*). A number of techniques for serving nonpublic school pupils under Chapter 1 were adopted by various localities in response to the *Aguilar* decision. These include using mobile classrooms or other "neutral sites" outside both public and nonpublic school property, serving nonpublic school pupils in public schools—either during or before/after regular school hours—or using microcomputers or other forms of electronic educational technology to provide instruction to nonpublic school pupils. These alternatives have tended to engender one or more of three types of problems. First, they often require additional costs (e.g., for mobile classroom rental), which, according to Education Department guidance, are to be paid from general Chapter 1 funds, not the funds set aside for aid to nonpublic school pupils. Second, these techniques may violate requirements that Chapter 1 services to nonpublic school pupils be equivalent to those provided to public school pupils. Finally, many advocates of nonpublic schools have considered the post-*Aguilar* methods of serving nonpublic school pupils in Chapter 1 to be unsatisfactory because of the time loss and inconvenience for some nonpublic pupils, who must often interrupt their school day to be transported to a "neutral" or public school site. As a result of these difficulties, nonpublic pupil participation in Chapter 1 has remained well below the level for 1984-85 (see Table 2.2).

During its consideration of the Hawkins-Stafford Act in 1987-88 and afterward, the Congress has attempted to find ways to resolve these difficulties without violating the Supreme Court's *Aguilar* decision. Some argued that the coalition of public and nonpublic interest groups and associations that had historically supported Chapter 1 and other federal aid to elementary and secondary education might be broken apart over the new barriers to serving nonpublic pupils in these programs (Cooper & Poster, 1986). Concern has been expressed over the reduction in nonpublic school pupils served under Chapter 1, as well as the increased costs of serving these pupils, with those cost increases reducing the funds available to serve all pupils, public and nonpublic.

During the mid-1980s, the Reagan administration proposed that these problems be resolved by authorizing the provision of Chapter 1 services in the form of vouchers. Proponents of the voucher proposal argued that it would be a constitutional means to serve all eligible children equitably under Chapter 1 and would improve education for disadvantaged children by expanding their range of educational services. Opponents of Chapter 1 vouchers argued that their constitutionality was dubious and untested and that the relatively low value of the vouchers—combined with the lack of a market for supplementary educational services for the disadvantaged—would provide more of an illusion than a reality of increased choice of educational service providers to the recipients. A somewhat similar proposal for Chapter 1 vouchers (although without use of that term) was included in the Bush administration's America 2000 strategy, introduced in April 1991.

The most significant new provision for serving nonpublic pupils that was adopted in the 1988 Hawkins-Stafford Act was the authorization of specific appropriations to pay the additional so-called capital expenses of serving nonpublic school pupils under Chapter 1 as a result of the *Aguilar* decision. *Capital expenses* are defined as including costs for purchasing, leasing, or renovating facilities; transportation; insurance; maintenance; or similar goods and services. These funds are to be allocated to the states in proportion to their relative number of nonpublic pupils served under Chapter 1 in school year 1984-85. State education agencies are then to distribute these funds to their LEAs with greatest need for assistance. Funds have been appropriated for such capital expenses beginning with FY 1989; the FY 1992 level is $40.1 million.

Emphasis on Higher-Order Skills
and Other Forms of "Restructuring"
for the Disadvantaged

There appears to be a growing consensus that certain instructional techniques, methods of school organization, and curricula could be especially effective in helping disadvantaged children to succeed academically. Many have called for a restructuring of school programs in line with this new consensus, incorporating the findings of recent research and other concerns.[4]

The current status of much of this activity is summarized in a recent U.S. Department of Education report, *Better Schooling for the Children of Poverty: Alternatives to Conventional Wisdom*[5] (Knapp & Turnbull, 1990); in *Effective Programs for Children at Risk*, by Slavin, Karweit, and Madden (1989); and in the "accelerated schools" strategy developed by Henry M. Levin and others. The Department of Education report is part of the ongoing Study of Academic Instruction for Disadvantaged Students, which attempts to determine what approaches are most effective in serving these students by documenting and evaluating curriculum and instructional practices in a number of high-poverty schools. Several similar themes are echoed in three recent reports on the educational status of minority children: *A Common Destiny*, edited by Jaynes and Williams (1989); *Visions of a Better Way*, by the Committee on Policy for Racial Justice (1989); and *Education That Works*, by the Quality Education for Minorities Project (1990). Common themes of all of these reports and strategies are discussed below.

Some of these restructuring themes relate specifically to Chapter 1 and other supplementary programs for the disadvantaged, while others relate to the overall school program. In general, analysts have increasingly emphasized improving the general school program as the most effective way to increase educational performance of disadvantaged children, rather than relying primarily on part-time, supplementary services. Children spend only a few hours per week in a typical Chapter 1 program, and the time frequently replaces regular instruction, rather than providing a net increase in instructional exposure. Further, the quality of categorical programs, such as Chapter 1, may depend primarily on the quality of the *core* curriculum and how well the categorical programs are aligned with it (Odden, 1987).

Chapter 1 itself has been amended to increase opportunities to use its funds to improve overall programs in schools with high poverty rates. Both before and after enactment of the Hawkins-Stafford Act, LEAs have been authorized to conduct Chapter 1 programs on a schoolwide basis—that is, without limiting services to the specific pupils determined to be most educationally disadvantaged—in certain schools where 75% or more of the pupils are from low-income families. The 1988 legislation modified this provision to remove a local fund matching requirement, but added new accountability requirements (discussed above) for schools allowed to use the schoolwide option.

In several ways, these restructuring techniques build upon the "effective schools" model developed by Ronald Edmonds and others (Stedman, 1985). This model has emphasized strong leadership by the principal and other school staff; high and well-communicated expectations for pupil achievement; frequent monitoring and feedback on performance; a high degree of agreement on, and commitment to, academic goals; and a disciplined atmosphere. The new restructuring techniques focus on particular methods of instruction, classroom and school management, and curriculum.

Common Restructuring Themes

A common theme underlying all of the proposals for restructuring schools serving the disadvantaged is that attention should be shifted away from supposed "deficiencies" of disadvantaged pupils and their families and toward removing structural barriers to academic achievement for these children. Thus the argument is that the problem with achievement for disadvantaged children lies in the school structure and instructional methods, not the pupils and their families. A second common theme is that the traditional "remedial" approach should be replaced with an "accelerated" approach, as the only realistic strategy that will help disadvantaged pupils catch up with their more advantaged peers.

The main features of the conventional wisdom that are challenged by these alternative approaches are the emphasis on the "deficits" that disadvantaged children bring to school, their lack of certain forms of knowledge or experience; the curricular focus on basic skills broken into discrete, sequential topics; relatively long-term grouping or tracking of pupils by ability or achievement; and the usually heavy reliance on strictly managed classroom environments and instruction that is closely directed by the teacher.

Proponents of alternative methods hypothesize that, as alternatives to such conventional approaches, schools should attempt to emphasize the knowledge, abilities, and cultural heritages that disadvantaged pupils do bring to school and build upon those, rather than focusing on supposed deficits of the children or their families. While the school's culture and expectations should be explicitly taught and communicated, there should be more respect for the children's backgrounds and cultures, as reflected in such things as curricular materials and teacher attitudes. The fact that virtually all young children, whatever their backgrounds, are active and sophisticated learners should be recognized and built upon.

A central tenet of these alternative approaches is that academic expectations for all pupils should be high. According to this emerging consensus, basic skills must be taught, but should be combined with instruction in higher-order and more challenging skills whenever possible, to reduce repetition and pupil boredom, especially for older pupils. Currently, more challenging and interesting work is postponed too long, perhaps forever, for compensatory education students. This practice can place an unintended ceiling on learning. Alternatives such as the accelerated schools strategy mix basic skill learning with more complex tasks as early as possible, including more meaning and context in the instruction, such as the application of mathematics to "real-world" problems.

The Chapter 1 statute has recently addressed this concern that disadvantaged pupils be taught higher-order skills. A requirement that pupils be taught, and evaluated for gains in, "more advanced" or "higher-order" skills was added to Chapter 1 by the 1988 Hawkins-Stafford Act. Local Chapter 1 programs are not to be considered successful unless they effectively instruct pupils in more advanced, as well as basic, skills. The statute defines these skills as including "reasoning, analysis, interpretation, problem-solving, and decisionmaking" (sec. 1471[13]). Program regulations specify that examinations in "reading comprehension" and "mathematics problems and applications" would cover these skills.

Regarding assignment of pupils to Chapter 1 or other special programs, as well as tracking in general in the "regular" school program, it is argued that there should be more flexibility in pupil grouping arrangements, that such arrangements should be changed over time, and that many instructional groups should include pupils of mixed achievement levels. Deadlines should be placed on assignments to compensatory programs—it should never be assumed that pupils will be permanently in need of supplementary services; rather, it should be assumed that they can be "mainstreamed" at some point, at least by the end of elementary school. This is a theme found in several recent critiques of current educational practices for the disadvantaged. The conventional wisdom that pupils should be grouped by ability level, in order to match students with learning tasks most appropriately, may primarily reduce the learning of disadvantaged students without significantly improving that of more advantaged students. It can lead to relatively long-term segregation, stigma, and a more limited curriculum, shaping and limiting students along race and class lines ("Teaching Inequality," 1989).

Proponents of this emerging consensus argue for more use of mixed ability groups, greater use of such cooperative learning techniques as peer tutoring and team reading, and assignment to groups, when necessary, on an explicitly temporary basis as alternatives to tracking and other forms of ability grouping. Regarding Chapter 1, they favor providing supplementary services in the regular classroom, or on a schoolwide basis, rather than the more typical "pullout" method. Where pullout methods are used, they should be intensive and brief, such as the one-to-one tutoring in the Success for All program. And in all cases, there should be greater coordination and consistency between Chapter 1 and the regular program's instructional methods and curriculum.

Finally, proponents of alternative methods for educating disadvantaged children believe that there should be greater variety in classroom management techniques, depending on the type of classroom work being done, including such unconventional methods as cooperative learning techniques that might involve substantial movement and "noise."

Applying these general hypotheses to specific subject areas, Knapp and Turnbull (1990) argue that in mathematics there should be less emphasis on mechanical computation and less repetition of topics in different grades. They favor more emphasis on understanding the context, meaning, and application of mathematical concepts. In reading, the authors recommend less focus on discrete skills, more reading for meaning, and use of a wider variety of texts, including more use of texts that emphasize the cultures and contributions of ethnic and racial minorities. For writing instruction, less emphasis on the mechanics of writing and more emphasis on meaningful communication are recommended. Further, all of these reports agree on the importance of more substantial parental involvement and an emphasis on prevention, such as through prekindergarten programs.[6]

Reconsideration of the Role of Testing

In the early 1990s, several analysts and educators have expressed concern that the norm-referenced tests, with results that can be aggregated, that are required by Chapter 1 are not necessarily good for Chapter 1 participants. They worry that the required tests and their results are overemphasized, that they absorb too many resources, that they do not provide useful guidance for improving instruction, and that, since they are required, they "drive out" alternative forms of assessment because of time and resource limitations. The significance of testing in Chapter 1 has also been amplified by the 1988 amendments (discussed above) requiring the identification of schools and pupils in need of additional assistance and establishing program improvement procedures.

Partially in response to these concerns, the U.S. Department of Education established in 1991 an Advisory Committee on Testing in Chapter 1 (*Federal Register*, February 4, 1991, p. 4272). This committee has just begun its deliberations, and this issue area is at an early stage of development, but some issues and questions have recently been considered in a report by Brenda Turnbull (1991). Turnbull and others have recommended consideration of alternative assessment methods to meet many of the Chapter 1 purposes for which norm-referenced tests are now used in Chapter 1. Such assessments might include use of criterion-referenced, rather than norm-referenced, tests; performance assessments; review of student portfolios; tests in a broader range of subject areas; or a focus on student achievement gains for periods longer than 1 year. Undoubtedly, assessment issues will be a focus of substantial deliberation in the next reauthorization of Chapter 1.

Concluding Remarks

Interest in and support for the Chapter 1 program have grown recently, following a period in the early 1980s when the existence of the program, or at least the continuation of substantial support for it, was threatened. Nevertheless, real funding levels and participation have returned approximately to their levels of the late 1970s.

There is a great deal of ferment in the development of new approaches for educating disadvantaged children. Attention has focused on ways to make Chapter 1 and related programs more effective. The program improvement and innovation provisions added to Chapter 1 in 1988 are supporting these trends, to at least a limited extent, as well as a variety of research and development efforts.

An unresolved issue is how Chapter 1 fits into the variety of comprehensive reforms in general school policies and programs being developed in many states. That is, how does Chapter 1 support the core program, including its curriculum, instructional strategies, and assessment methods, rather than being an unrelated, or even contradictory, adjunct to that program? One possibility is expansion of Chapter 1's schoolwide plan authority so that it might be available in a wider range of circumstances.

Notes

1. TIERS/CHIERS stands for the Title I/Chapter 1 Evaluation and Reporting System, under which Chapter 1 participation and achievement are reported annually by the states to the U.S. Department of Education. This system was initially developed as a result of requirements in the Education Amendments of 1978 (P.L. 95-561). Participation data were collected for earlier years, but are not generally considered to be comparable to the data collected under TIERS/CHIERS.

2. Features that were found by National Assessment of Chapter 1 staff to be characteristic of effective Chapter 1 programs were small instructional group size, well-qualified instructors, increased instructional time, direct instruction (i.e., instruction with active teacher involvement, as opposed to independent "seatwork" by the pupil), and instruction in higher-order academic skills (e.g., problem solving, analysis, or interpretation) (U.S. Department of Education, 1987).

3. The first data collection for this study—now named Prospects: The Congressionally Mandated Study of Educational Growth and Opportunity—took place in the spring of 1991. An interim report is due to be provided to the Congress in January 1993.

4. I use the term *restructuring* to refer specifically to changes in instructional techniques, curriculum, and occasionally finance or governance that are intended to help improve the achievement of disadvantaged pupils. This should be distinguished from the use of this term by others to refer primarily to proposed changes in educational governance, such as *school-based management,* or incentives, such as *merit pay* for teachers, or public school *choice,* that do not directly address the special needs of disadvantaged children.

5. In a supplementary report, Knapp et al. (1991) describe current practices in classrooms serving children from poor families.

6. Means and Knapp (1991) have recently published a companion report providing additional recommendations in specific subject areas.

References

Advanced Technology, Inc. (1983). *Local operation of Title I, ESEA 1976-1982: A resource book.* McLean, VA: Author.

Aguilar v. Felton, 473 U.S. 402, 105 S. Ct. 3232 (1985).

Committee on Policy for Racial Justice. (1989). *Visions of a better way: A black appraisal of public schooling.* Washington, DC: Joint Center for Political Studies Press.

Cooper, B., & Poster, J. (1986, May 21). Breakdown of a coalition. *Education Week,* p. 28.

Council of Chief State School Officers. (1991). *Chapter 1 program improvement and innovation across the states.* Washington, DC: Author.

Education Consolidation and Improvement Act, part of the Omnibus Budget Reconciliation Act of 1981, P.L. 97-35.

Education Consolidation and Improvement Act Technical Amendments Act of 1983, P.L. 98-211; Augustus F. Hawkins-Robert T. Stafford Elementary and Secondary School Improvement Amendments of 1988, P.L. 100-297.

Jaynes, G. D., & Williams, R. M., Jr. (Eds.). (1989). *A common destiny: Blacks and American society.* Washington, DC: National Academy Press.

Knapp, M. S., & Turnbull, B. J. (1990, January). *Better schooling for the children of poverty: Alternatives to conventional wisdom.* Washington, DC: U.S. Department of Education, Office of Planning, Budget and Evaluation.

Knapp, M. S., Adelman, N. A., Needels, M. C., Zucker, A. A., McCollum, H., Turnbull, B. J., Marder, C., & Shields, P. M. (1991, March). *What is taught, and how, to the children of poverty.* Washington, DC: U.S. Department of Education, Office of Planning, Budget and Evaluation.

Means, B., & Knapp, M. S. (Eds.). (1991). *Teaching advanced skills to educationally disadvantaged students.* Menlo Park, CA: SRI International.

National Commission on Excellence in Education. (1983). *A nation at risk: The imperative for educational reform.* Washington, DC: Government Printing Office.

National Governors' Association. (1990). *National education goals.* Washington, DC: Author.

Odden, A. (1987). Education reform and services to poor children: Can the two policies be compatible? *Educational Evaluation and Policy Analysis, 9,* 231-243.

Quality Education for Minorities Project. (1990). *Education that works: An action plan for the education of minorities.* Cambridge: MIT Press.

Riddle, W. (1988). Chapter 1 concentration grants: An analysis of the concept and its embodiment in federal elementary and secondary education legislation. *Journal of Education Finance, 14,* 285-303.

Riddle, W. (1991). *Conditional deregulation of federal elementary and secondary education programs: The AMERICA 2000 proposal.* Washington, DC: U.S. Library of Congress, Congressional Research Service.

Slavin, R. E., Karweit, N. L., & Madden, N. A. (1989). *Effective programs for students at risk.* Boston: Allyn & Bacon.

Stedman, J. (1985). *The effective schools research: Content and criticisms.* Washington, DC: U.S. Library of Congress, Congressional Research Service.

Task Force on Education of Young Adolescents. (1989, June). *Turning points.* Washington, DC: Carnegie Council on Adolescent Development.

Teaching inequality: The problem of public school tracking. (1989). *Harvard Law Review,* pp. 1318-1341.

Turnbull, B. J. (1991). *Testing in Chapter 1: Issues and options.* Washington, DC: Policy Studies Associates.

U.S. Department of Education, Office of Educational Research and Improvement, National Assessment of Chapter 1. (1987). *The current operation of the Chapter 1 program.* Washington, DC: Government Printing Office.

U.S. Department of Education, Office of Planning, Budget, and Evaluation. (1989). *A summary of state Chapter 1 participation and achievement information for 1987-88.* Washington, DC: Government Printing Office.

Vitullo-Martin, T., & Cooper, B. (1987). *Separation of church and child: The constitution and federal aid to religious schools.* Indianapolis: Hudson Institute.

THREE

Bilingual Education
THE LAST 25 YEARS

JENNIFER SEVILLA

As the United States nears the year 2000, the year set for achievement of national educational goals, educators are focusing on the special needs and methods of instructing the increasing numbers of children in U.S. schools who are limited in English proficiency. National statistics show that there are between 1.5 and 2.2 million limited-English-proficient (LEP) schoolchildren in the United States between the ages of 5 and 17 (U.S. Department of Education, 1991). In California alone, there are currently 986,462 students in grades K-12 whose native tongue is not English (D. Dolson, California State Department of Education, Bilingual Office, personal communication, August 1991). LEP children have not only changed the racial/ethnic composition of the schools in the United States, they have presented an overwhelming challenge for teachers to find effective methods of educating these special needs children. Pallas, Natriello, and McDill (1989) predict that by the year 2020 the population of Hispanic children (to 17 years old) will more than triple, so that 25.3% of the nation's children will be Hispanic. Unfortunately for Hispanic children, their educational attainments do not match the success of their numbers. Hispanic students have long had lower scores on achievement tests and higher dropout rates in comparison with white students (Carter, 1970; Crawford, 1989; Flax, 1991; Melesky, 1985; Rumberger, 1987) and are more likely to be placed in special education classes (Crawford, 1989; Pearson & Agulewicz, 1987).

Two of the major issues regarding bilingual instruction for LEP children, and the focuses of this chapter, are (a) the shaded past of bilingual education policy and (b) cost-effectiveness. However, before discussion is presented on either issue, a definition of *bilingual education* is necessary. Bilingual education encompasses a wide range of programs, goals, and outcomes. Local factors such as languages spoken, resources available, and geographic dispersion play a primary role in the definition of programs. According to Fillmore and Valadez (1986, p. 654), there are two defining goal and outcome characteristics of truly bilingual education programs:

(1) Instruction is given in two languages; in the United States, English is one and the home language of the LEP students served by the program is the other.

(2) Instruction in the language of the school is given in a way that permits students to learn it as a second language.

The definition of *bilingual education* used for this chapter and by most organizations in the United States is that offered by the Bilingual Education Act 1974 reauthorization (which is not discernibly different from that of Fillmore & Valadez, 1986): a program that instructs a child in his or her native language as well as English so that the child can effectively progress through the school system (Stewner-Manzanares, 1988).

Effectiveness Studies and Findings

This chapter focuses on three of the most common types of programs used to instruct LEP students: (a) English as a second language (ESL) or English speakers of other languages (ESOL), (b) transitional bilingual education (the native language is provided until the child is able to participate in academic subjects in English), and (c) sheltered English (instruction in simplified English). ESL/ESOL programs rely exclusively on English for instruction and student learning and thus are not bilingual programs by definition. However, they are used so extensively as the sole method for instructing LEP students that they are included in this section.

According to Ulibarri (1985), an effective ESL program includes the following elements: theoretically based second-language instructional strategies, relative instruction pertinent to the all-English curriculum, and the inclusion of social, academic, and content skills. ESL/ESOL programs are offered by most states with the reasoning that transitional bilingual programs require bilingual certification of teachers. Many states, such as California, have several languages spoken in the schools and have found that there are shortages of credentialed bilingual teachers (California State Department of Education, 1991; Macias, 1989). As a result, states have had difficulties serving all LEP students. The second argument for ESL/ESOL is that self-contained bilingual education classes cost considerably more than ESL classes, an argument often refuted and discussed later in this chapter.

Transitional bilingual education programs are the most common type of programs in use now in the United States; these teach English through the use of both English and the native language of the child. The goal is the provision of assistance in the child's native language only until the child can effectively learn in English. One instructional strategy is to find commonalities between the two languages and use the commonalities as a means of transfer to English-speaking classes.

A variation on the transitional bilingual program is the two-way bilingual education program, which is designed to place bilingual children with native English speakers. In such programs, both languages are taught to both groups of children simultaneously. According to federal guidelines for desegregation regulations, up to 40% of the children in these classes can be native English speakers.

In the sheltered approach, English instruction is modified so that it is understandable to the LEP student. Students generally begin sheltered classes in less language-based courses, such as mathematics, and then move to more language-dependent courses, such as science and social studies. Some states provide teachers in these programs with instructional aides; others do not.

Which type of program works best? Fully bilingual programs appear to be the most effective, based on language-acquisition research and numerous case studies (Krashen & Biber, 1988, p. 63). However, the programs that have surfaced in the public schools are seldom fully bilingual. Instead, programs tend to take whatever form the schools are able to sustain, in terms of staffing, funding, and state legislation regarding the establishment of bilingual programs (Crawford, 1989).

English-only proponents argue that bilingual education is divisive, and if earlier groups of immigrants "sank or swam" in the educational system and were able to learn English through "immersion," why not the newer immigrants (Crawford, 1989)? What this argument fails to address is that this country was founded on the concept of freedom, and language diversity is one of those freedoms. Furthermore, about 87% of early immigrants did not "swim" in the education system, and a mere 13% were left to go on to high school (Crawford, 1989). Additional research by Lambert and Tucker (1972) and Swain (1984) has found that immersion programs have been successful only if the following conditions exist: Students are from good educational backgrounds, have strong proficiency in their non-English language, have strong self-concepts, have middle-class orientations toward education, and are members of the majority culture in their own countries attempting to learn English (Crawford, 1989).

Research conducted in the late 1970s provided support for the argument that bilingual education has no benefit over the immersion method of language instruction. The results of these studies led to changes in the reauthorization of the Bilingual Education Act. A federally funded evaluation of bilingual education that took place in 1977, conducted by the American Institute for Research (AIR), found that bilingual education offered no additional benefits to students learning English (see Danoff, 1977, 1978). The AIR study also found that many teachers in bilingual programs were not qualified to teach in the native language of the student.

The research team reported to the federal government that bilingual programs had no effect on Spanish-speaking children. Gray (1977) challenged the AIR study findings, arguing that there were methodological problems with the research design that included the following: (a) a mere 5 months between pre- and posttests, (b) use of inappropriate and/or unreliable tests, and (c) testing of students who had received more than just bilingual education. Gray (1977) and Cardenas (1977) also point out that many of the programs designated bilingual were not, and other programs employed substandard methods or lacked additional necessities.

In 1980, the Office of Planning and Budget commissioned another study of the effectiveness of transitional bilingual education, which was conducted by Baker and de Kanter (1981). After a review of more than 300 cases, they selected just 28 for study, one of which was the controversial AIR study. Excluded were 12 bilingual programs found effective by Troike (1978). Baker and de Kanter concluded that there was no evidence to support the effectiveness of transitional bilingual education. Criticisms of Baker and de Kanter's study abound, as evidenced in publications by Hernandez-Chavez, Llanes, Alvarez, and Arvizu (1981) and Yates and Ortiz (1983).

The results of the AIR and Baker and de Kanter studies were a setback for bilingual education both in the reauthorization of the Bilingual Education Act in 1978 and in desegregation litigation. The 1978 reauthorization excluded funds for the maintenance of native languages and provided programs solely for transitional bilingual education (Crawford, 1989).

The federal courts began adjudicating bilingual education programs in the schools on the basis that they were a form of segregation on the part of school districts. Many justices argued that bilingual students were being segregated from the mainstream through bilingual classes at a time when the courts were trying to desegregate the public schools. The 1978 amendments to the Bilingual Education Act addressed the issue of segregation by allowing for 40% English speakers in bilingual programs (Crawford, 1989), thereby further diluting the maintenance of native language and culture in favor of the assimilation of LEP students.

The argument for bilingual education goes beyond teaching children English, the only goal of some bilingual programs. Researchers argue that true bilingualism can allow development of cultural self-esteem (Krashen, 1982) and superior cognitive development (Hakuta & Diaz, 1986; Ianco-Worrall, 1972; Kessler & Quinn, 1980) while preparing children for future careers (Krashen & Biber, 1988).

Research on bilingual education has identified specific instructional practices that are deemed effective for bilingual students (Carter & Chatfield, 1986; Krashen & Biber, 1988). Krashen and Biber (1988, p. 25) suggest three requirements for a successful bilingual program:

(1) high-quality subject-matter teaching in the first language, without translation
(2) development of literacy in the first language
(3) comprehensible input in English (ideally, provided directly by high-quality classes in English as a second language, supplemented by comprehensible or sheltered subject-matter teaching in English)

Carter and Chatfield (1986) further note that effective programs include bilingual education as an integral part of the school, not isolated from the mainstream. To avoid isolationism, a school should have an integrated language curriculum, a system for carefully monitoring the progress of students, and teachers in the program who are involved with the community and who seek to include parental input. In a study of a Head Start program, Macias (1976) found that 83.9% parents in Chicano neighborhoods of East Los Angeles supported bilingual education for their children as well as the preservation of their Mexican heritage.

Krashen and Biber (1988) suggest that all programs that enhance the LEP child's ability and meet the three criteria for effective programs are beneficial, but that full bilingual programs are more effective. Their study of bilingual education in California revealed that bilingual children took between 3 and 5 years to reach grade level in properly designed bilingual programs (p. 63). Comparisons of scores on the California Test of Basic Skills between bilingual and native English speakers indicated that students in full bilingual programs scored at or about national norms (p. 58).

Research has shown that the most effective programs for LEP students are those that are fully bilingual and taught by qualified educators. Why is it, then, that many LEP students are served by ESL or not at all? One reason is the evolving nature of the reauthorization of the Bilingual Education Act of 1968.

Politics and Policy-Making at the Federal Level

The federal government became involved in the financing of bilingual education with the passage of the Bilingual Education Act of 1968, an amendment to Title VII of the Elementary and Secondary Education Act (ESEA) of 1965. However, despite its passage, the act did not specifically mention whether schools receiving funding were required to use a language other than English in the instruction of children or whether the purpose of the act was to make children bilingual or fluent in English (Bilingual Education Act, 1968; Crawford, 1989). The compensatory nature of the Bilingual Education Act was obvious in that school districts receiving money had to have a proportionate number of students whose family incomes were below $3,000 (Crawford, 1989).

During the early 1970s, politically motivated demands for bilingual instruction were heard, but the arguments approached the issue as less one of language than of civil rights. The Civil Rights Act of 1964 had ensured protection for African Americans from discrimination but had not addressed the situation and needs of Mexican Americans and other language-minority groups. Until the 1970s, the federal government had ignored language as a possible source of discrimination. A response to demands for bilingual instruction was issued by the director of the Office of Civil Rights, advising school districts that they had a responsibility to provide language instruction to students who were limited English proficient under Title VI of the Civil Rights Act of 1964 (U.S. Department of Education, 1991); the director further indicated that students were not to be placed in special education programs based on tests given to them in the English language (Crawford, 1989).

Many states, however, did not take the director's memo seriously (Crawford, 1989). Litigation began during the 1970s, partly because of the sluggishness of the states but also because of that on the part of the executive branch of government. The most important outcome of these lawsuits was the U.S. Supreme Court ruling in the *Lau v. Nichols* decision of 1974.

In the *Lau* case, the attorney argued that language-minority children, specifically 1,800 Chinese students in San Francisco, were being denied equal opportunity of education. In essence, Chinese students were failing in school because they could not speak the English language. The school district argued that the Chinese students were not segregated from other students and were given identical instruction and materials offered to all students. According to the school district, it was the child's responsibility to enter the classroom with the ability to comprehend English. The Supreme Court ruled that children who do not understand English cannot possibly gain any meaningful education and that the Chinese children were entitled to special instruction. As Teitelbaum and Hiller (1979) note, the *Lau* decision was critical in raising the public's consciousness concerning the need for bilingual education within the nation.

As with any court decision, the problem of enforcement became the issue, and the Office of Civil Rights developed the "Lau remedies" to spell out to school districts how to assess LEP students, which programs were appropriate, and the professional standards teachers had to meet (U.S. Department of Health, Education and Welfare, 1975).

The Lau remedies were guidelines, not mandates, but they served to prompt states to establish ESL and bilingual programs for fear of losing federal funding.

In 1974, the Bilingual Education Act was up for reauthorization, and Congress dropped the poverty aspects of the act and included the requirement for language instruction in the native language and in the culture of the student (Crawford, 1989). This was the first attempt to treat bilingual education as an instructional method to promote language and culture rather than a compensatory program to correct for deprivation.

In 1980, Congress further amended the Bilingual Education Act to require bilingual education in schools where at least 25 LEP students of the same language group are enrolled (Crawford, 1989). Many states reacted negatively to this requirement because they had several languages spoken in schools and a shortage of bilingual teachers.

The early 1980s brought unfounded criticism of bilingual education from a lobby of "English-only" promoters. These groups wanted and still want to make English the official language of the nation. Coupled with this nativistic attitude toward language is the promotion of the preservation of "American culture" and what Americans should share as a common thread, whatever that may be. For instance, E. D. Hirsch, Jr. (1989) has compiled a dictionary for children based upon what he and his colleagues feel are the cultural aspects of American society all children should learn. The dictionary, and the Cultural Literacy Foundation founded by Hirsch, emphasizes not diversity and acculturation, but commonality and assimilation into the dominant culture.

To counter these political pursuits in favor of diversity and maintenance of language and culture, the League of United Latin American Citizens and the Spanish American League Against Discrimination began a lobby for English Plus, a campaign to save the diversity of America's languages (Crawford, 1989). However, language diversity is losing the battle. So far, 16 states have adopted English as their official language: Nebraska, Illinois, Virginia, Indiana, Kentucky, Tennessee, California, Georgia, Arkansas, Mississippi, North Carolina, North Dakota, South Carolina, Arizona, Colorado, and Florida (Crawford, 1989).

The last major change to the Bilingual Education Act was made in 1988, when the U.S. Senate proposed the following changes: additional funding for English-only instructional strategies, a decrease in funding for bilingual instruction, and a limit on student participation in bilingual programs to 3 years. According to Crawford (1989), the 3-year rule was passed without hearings or bilingual expert testimony. The next reauthorization of the Bilingual Education Act will take place in 1993.

Bilingual Education: Cost-Effectiveness

Federal Funding

The federal financial commitment to education in general has always been proportionately small. Recent trends in financial stability of school districts and National Assessment of Educational Progress (1990) data reflecting student achievement indicate that if national goals are to be achieved, the federal commitment in terms of dollars for education must increase. However, both federal and state commitments to LEP children have traditionally been lower than their commitments to other special needs groups (U.S. Department of Education, Office of Bilingual Education and Minority Languages Agency [OBEMLA], 1991).

There are several ways to address funding and the costs of programs. One method is to look at the cost-effectiveness of programs themselves. Another is to look at categories of costs required for program design. Odden and Picus (1992) discuss three particular cost categories for program design that are useful here: state eligibility for federal funds, types of services offered at the federal level, and determination of the state and local share of the costs. This section addresses federal funding for LEP students using the conceptual framework developed by Odden and Picus, followed by a discussion of federal funding objectives and overall implications for the 1993 reauthorization of the act.

Eligibility

In order to be eligible for Title VII funding for a demonstration program, states must apply for grants by providing information on students enrolled in the district who will receive instruction in the proposed program. Such information includes the number of LEP students in the district, how the state arrived at the determination, qualifications of the personnel who will serve the LEP students, and so on (Bilingual Education Act, 1968). Further, the state applications must be developed in coordination with an advisory council comprising LEP parents and other qualified personnel.

Grants are awarded based on a proposed program's meeting the following requirements: Qualified personnel are used to instruct children; the needs of underserved students are considered; federal funds are to supplement, not supplant, state and local funds; the district trains bilingual personnel; the district continues the program at the end of the 3-year grant; and the program is evaluated and meets federal regulations (Bilingual Education Act, 1968). Additionally, priority goes to those states with greater numbers of LEP students and those in greater need of program assistance. Hence states such as Arizona, California, New Mexico, and New York receive the majority of Title VII funding. In turn, the states pass the funds on to the districts having the greatest needs.

Types of Services Offered
at the Federal Level

The Office of Bilingual Education and Minority Languages Agency is responsible for administering the programs authorized under two statutes: the Bilingual Education Act of 1968 and the Emergency Immigrant Education Act of 1984. Part A grants are designed to assist LEP students in English achievement, grade promotion, and graduation requirements; Part B funding is used for data collection, research, and evaluation; and Part C grants are awarded for training of personnel.

Title VII A grants allow states to choose among several programs: transitional bilingual education programs, developmental bilingual programs, special alternative instructional programs, academic excellence programs, family English literacy programs, and special population programs, but not maintenance programs. The U.S. Department of Education (1991) states that the purpose of the grants is to provide grantees with development and instructional support for instructional programs for LEP students and that 60% of Title VII funds go to these programs. Table 3.1 indicates the number of awards and expenditures for fiscal year 1990 across all grant areas. The

Table 3.1 Federal Title VII Programs by Numbers of Awards Granted and
Funding Amounts Fiscal Year 1990

Program	Number of Awards	Funding Amount ($)
Transitional bilingual education programs	515	80,176,000
Developmental bilingual education programs	17	2,789,000
Special alternative instructional programs	171	17,940,000
Academic excellence programs	12	2,127,000
Special population programs	49	7,493,000
Family English literacy programs	37	4,994,000
Totals	801	115,519,000

SOURCE: Data from U.S. Department of Education, OBEMLA (1991).

transitional bilingual programs receive the majority of funding in
both the number of grants and award amounts (64% of the grants and
69% of the total amount).

Table 3.2 indicates the number and award amounts of Title VII A
grants per state. California, New York, Texas, and Arizona receive 62%
of the total funding for all Title VII A grants. Under Part B of the
Bilingual Education Act (1968), contracts and grants are awarded for
data collection, evaluation, and research to improve education for LEP
students. Also included is support for the National Clearinghouse for
Bilingual Education, the establishment of at least two evaluation
assistance centers (Georgetown University for eastern states and the
University of New Mexico College of Education for western states),
and a state educational agency (U.S. Department of Education, 1991).

The federal government spent $2.6 million in fiscal year 1990 for
research in the following areas under Part B of the Bilingual Education
Act: assessment of instructional materials/strategies, characteristics
and outcomes of students enrolled in Title VII and other LEP programs, effectiveness of personnel training programs, improvement of
existing programs, and research and development of educational
materials (U.S. Department of Education, 1991). Research for Part B
grants is 3% of the total $80,176,000 spent for transitional bilingual
education programs under Title VII.

OBEMLA funds training programs under Title VII, Part C, as well
as 16 multifunctional resource centers. The training programs include
short-term training, educational personnel training, a training devel-

Table 3.2 Federal Title VII, Part A, Grants by State and Award Amounts
Fiscal Year 1990

State	Number of Grants	Award Amount ($)	State	Number of Grants	Award Amount ($)
Alabama	1	161,700	Montana	18	1,716,154
Alaska	8	949,004	Nebraska	3	255,632
Arizona	41	5,586,542	Nevada	1	203,529
Arkansas	0	0	New Hampshire	0	0
California	272	40,574,928	New Jersey	5	613,961
Colorado	12	1,175,473	New Mexico	35	5,734,964
Connecticut	2	206,612	New York	109	17,623,834
Delaware	0	0	North Carolina	0	0
Dist. of Columbia	6	793,009	North Dakota	8	1,086,563
Florida	14	1,819,324	Ohio	5	540,142
Georgia	1	68,260	Oklahoma	39	5,126,273
Hawaii	5	932,734	Oregon	16	1,992,924
Idaho	1	83,948	Pennsylvania	4	543,258
Illinois	24	3,459,741	Rhode Island	0	0
Indiana	4	477,578	South Carolina	1	40,440
Iowa	6	825,005	South Dakota	6	695,378
Kansas	1	175,000	Tennessee	1	83,435
Kentucky	1	70,518	Texas	54	7,768,839
Louisiana	8	879,404	Utah	5	569,685
Maine	2	332,147	Vermont	0	0
Maryland	4	453,158	Virginia	1	56,919
Massachusetts	17	2,792,844	Washington	13	1,940,848
Michigan	17	2,341,545	West Virginia	0	0
Minnesota	8	1,094,160	Wisconsin	0	0
Mississippi	4	956,030	Wyoming	5	607,712
Missouri	2	358,614	Totals	790	115,483,922

SOURCE: Data from U.S. Department of Education, OBEMLA (1991).
NOTE: American Samoa, Guam, Northern Marianas, Palau, Puerto Rico, and the U.S. Virgin Islands have been omitted.

opment and improvement program, a bilingual education fellowship program, and multifunctional resource centers. Table 3.3 shows the numbers and the total amounts of awards granted under Title VII, Part C, in fiscal year 1990.

Short-term training programs are designed to improve the skills of teachers who educate LEP students. The educational personnel training program grants are awarded to universities to train teachers/

Table 3.3 Federal Title VII, Part C, Grants by Number and Amount
Fiscal Year 1990

Program	Number of Awards	Amount of Award ($)
Short-term training	18	1,887,081
Educational personnel training	15	16,927,051
Bilingual fellowships	178	1,956,000
Multifunctional resource centers	16	10,200,000
Totals	327	30,970,132

SOURCE: Data from U.S. Department of Education, OBEMLA (1991).

personnel to work with LEP students. The federal government provides a total of 33 grants and $18 million to states and universities to
train bilingual teachers. Training development and improvement
programs are designed to improve bilingual education programs at
the university level. Bilingual education fellowship programs were
not offered in 1988 or 1989 but were granted in 1990 for 178 fellows at
30 universities in 16 states. The multifunctional resource centers are
designed to provide assistance and to disseminate information on
bilingual programs (U.S. Department of Education, 1991).

Awards are granted to state education agencies based on a formula
for the numbers of eligible students under the Emergency Immigrant Education Act. In 1989, the federal government also funded
the Transition Program for Refugee Children in the amount of
$15,808,000, which was granted to SEAs based on the number of
eligible refugee children enrolled in the schools. However, Congress
did not fund the program in 1990 or 1991. Table 3.4 shows the total
award amounts by state as well as the numbers of children served by
EIEA in 1990 and TPRC in 1989. Some of this funding may be spent
on LEP children providing they qualify.

State and Local Share of the Costs

The federal government is explicit regarding the role of state and
local agencies in the funding of Title VII programs:

Funds made available under this section for any fiscal year shall
be used by the State educational agency to supplement and, to

Table 3.4 Emergency Immigrant and Transition Programs for Refugee
Children: Students Served and Award Amounts

State	EIEA Award Totals FY 1990 ($)	TPRC Award Totals FY 1989 ($)	Students Served EIEA	TPRC
Alabama	0	14,510	0	68
Alaska	0	0	0	0
Arizona	574,169	102,420	11,470	480
Arkansas	0	28,600	0	134
California	13,438,398	5,492,580	268,455	25,742
Colorado	67,328	75,960	1,345	356
Connecticut	205,740	189,690	4,110	889
Delaware	0	55,480	0	260
District of Columbia	310,912	45,240	6,211	212
Florida	935,940	2,150,350	18,697	10,078
Georgia	151,773	115,010	3,032	539
Hawaii	145,820	44,390	2,913	208
Idaho	0	16,650	0	78
Illinois	1,550,055	697,510	30,965	3,269
Indiana	0	23,260	0	109
Iowa	31,987	102,850	639	482
Kansas	61,722	223,190	1,233	1,046
Kentucky	0	43,750	0	205
Louisiana	187,769	226,390	3,751	1,061
Maine	0	37,560	0	176
Maryland	508,843	105,200	10,165	493
Massachusetts	846,135	1,006,680	16,903	4,718
Michigan	95,762	254,130	1,913	1,191
Minnesota	113,132	480,730	2,260	2,253
Mississippi	0	5,340	0	25
Missouri	54,013	88,770	1,079	416
Montana	5,206	8,750	104	41
Nebraska	0	93,460	0	438
Nevada	0	34,360	0	161
New Hampshire	0	13,660	0	64
New Jersey	922,324	174,970	18,425	820
New Mexico	156,482	0	3,126	0
New York	5,044,324	589,550	100,769	2,763
North Carolina	0	57,190	0	268
North Dakota	0	10,670	0	50
Ohio	72,334	220,420	1,445	1,033
Oklahoma	33,940	72,240	678	339
Oregon	111,780	107,760	2,233	505

(Continued)

Table 3.4 (Continued)

State	EIEA Award Totals FY 1990 ($)	TPRC Award Totals FY 1989 ($)	Students Served EIEA	Students Served TPRC
Pennsylvania	181,962	289,970	3,635	1,359
Rhode Island	351,159	323,900	7,015	1,518
South Carolina	0	5,130	0	24
South Dakota	0	4,910	0	23
Tennessee	76,139	194,600	1,521	912
Texas	2,400,946	564,160	47,963	2,644
Utah	319,172	100,930	6,376	473
Vermont	0	4,270	0	20
Virginia	490,571	379,590	9,800	1,779
Washington	481,711	641,400	9,623	3,006
West Virginia	0	0	0	0
Wisconsin	102,970	289,330	2,057	1,356
Wyoming	0	0	0	0
Totals	30,030,518	15,807,460	617,971	74,084

SOURCE: Data from U.S. Department of Education, OBEMLA (1991).

the extent practical, to increase the level of funds that would, in the absence of such funds, be made available by the State for the purpose described in this section, and in no case to supplant such funds. (sec. 7031[e])

Over the last 25 years, the federal commitment to bilingual education has increased from zero funding for the first year (1968) of Title VII (Crawford, 1989), to 76 programs serving 25,521 students at a cost of $7.5 million in 1969 (Baca & Cervantes, 1984), to $156,349,000 for 290,000 children in most of the continental United States, American Samoa, Guam, Northern Marianas, Palau, Puerto Rico, and the U.S. Virgin Islands in 1991 (U.S. Department of Education, 1991). Although this seems to be a substantial amount of money, in comparison with other programs for special needs children, the amount is minimal. For example, compensatory education Chapter 1 funds are 97.7% higher than Title VII A grants, and those for Head Start are 94% higher (U.S. Department of Education, OBEMLA, 1991).

Federal Funding Objectives

Guthrie, Garms, and Pierce (1988) found that federal funding has been directed at the accomplishment of two objectives: equalization of educational opportunity and enhancement of educational productivity. Although the *Lau* decision indicated that LEP students were not receiving equal educational opportunities in public schools, the direction of federal spending to equalize that educational opportunity has not been toward support of research-based fully bilingual programs, but, instead, toward minimal funding of transitional bilingual programs that require state support.

In terms of educational productivity, states receiving federal funds for LEP students are reluctant to assess academic progress for reclassification purposes because they would lose funding, and others terminate LEP services after a certain number of years regardless of the child's progress (Council of Chief State School Officers, 1991). Currently, fewer than five states require monitoring data about LEP students once they exit language programs.

Implications for the 1993 Reauthorization

The federal role for the 1993 reauthorization of the Bilingual Education Act must be restructured if national goals are to be achieved for all children. Odden (1991) indicates that national and state goals may differ over the next decade, but the two levels are aligning themselves on the following: (a) Increase the high school graduation rate to 90% or above, (b) provide for demonstration of student competency, and (c) improve student proficiency in mathematics and science (National Governors' Association, 1990).

If these are to be the goals of both state and federal education policy, local school districts need to find ways to pay for these base programs, providing that the goals apply to all students. Odden (1991) suggests that the development of financial formulas for the next decade needs to include both program and financial analysts so that the programs that produce the highest student achievement gains are coupled with the most cost-effective methods of producing these gains. Further, Odden (1991) predicts that federal funding will increase at least 30% over the next decade. If this is the case, the dollars need to be spent in a manner that will produce achievement gains for all students at the levels stated by the national goals.

Currently, Title VII grants are categorical, competitive grants designed for the purpose of providing transitional bilingual instruction and are accompanied by strict application and reporting requirements (Picus, 1991). Districts that wish to participate must file the appropriate applications and compete for funding with other states. Picus (1991) argues that categorical grants stimulate local districts to spend more than the amount of the grant. However, the current procedures are contradictory in terms of rewards for student achievement and, in fact, deter districts from reporting student progress because funding ceases when students progress.

The 1993 reauthorization of the Bilingual Education Act is an opportunity to link policy, program, and finance to achieve these goals specifically for LEP students. Further, the categorical grant needs to be reworked so that districts have an incentive to strive for student achievement with respect to bilingual education.

State Commitment

Education is a state responsibility under the Constitution; therefore, it is not surprising that many states have enacted legislation to deal with their special needs populations over and above federal legislation. Regarding linguistically special needs students, Massachusetts was the first state to enact a law mandating bilingual education in 1971 (Crawford, 1989). Today, 22 states have state-funded bilingual education programs (Sevilla, 1991). However, of the remaining 28 states, 5 have banned bilingual education through legislation: Alabama, Arkansas, Delaware, Nebraska, and West Virginia (Baca & Cervantes, 1984).

This section addresses state funding of LEP programs utilizing the conceptual framework developed by Odden and Picus (1992): eligibility, types of services offered at the state level, and determination of state and local share of the costs.

Eligibility

Eligibility for bilingual instruction in most states is determined by state statutes and/or regulations, with school districts using their own criteria for the identification of LEP students. A total of 30 states have laws that determine how students are to be identified (Council of Chief State School Officers, 1991). The most common methods of determining eligibility are as follows:

(1) language assessment tests
(2) parent information
(3) assessment of achievement level
(4) evaluation of student records
(5) teacher information and/or referral
(6) home language surveys

Most states use more than one method of assessment. The most commonly used language assessment tests are the Oral Proficiency Test, California Achievement Test, Language Assessment Scales, Bilingual Syntax Measure, and Iowa Test of Basic Skills. The cutoff marks for scores on the standardized tests to determine eligibility differ from state to state. Several states use the test publishers' cutoff marks; others develop their own cutoff points. Michigan and New Mexico, for example, have a 40% cutoff mark, while Hawaii uses a 25% cutoff point. States with higher cutoff marks have higher percentages of eligible students (Odden & Picus, 1992).

Many states use the Lau remedies suggestion of 20 students as the cutoff number of students in a district before the establishment of a bilingual program. Alaska, however, uses a standard of 8 students per district for the establishment of a bilingual program. Obviously, Alaska has proportionally more students who qualify for program funding than would, say, Michigan, which uses a cutoff of 20 students. Additionally, some states give school boards the right to determine whether or not the number of students below 20 per district warrants some type of bilingual program. The determination for establishing a program, ESL or other, is generally based upon program cost-effectiveness and whether or not alternative measures can be provided for LEP children, such as part-time instruction.

Types of Services Offered
at the State Level

Services offered to LEP students vary from state to state; for example, 43 states have implemented transitional bilingual education and

2 states have developmental bilingual programs under Title VII (U.S. Department of Education, 1991). Most states offer English as a second language instruction either along with a bilingual program or as the only program serving LEP children.

In California, for example, three programs are available at the elementary school level: ESL, fully bilingual classrooms, and English only. Parents are allowed to choose what they feel is best for their children at this level of schooling (California State Assembly Office of Research, 1986). However, at the secondary level, bilingual classrooms are not required in California, limiting students to English-only or ESL classrooms.

Determination of State and Local Share of the Cost

States deal with added costs in a variety of ways; for example, five states fund through excess costs, eight use pupil weighting, four fund through flat grants, one fully funds bilingual education programs, two use block grants, and four fund through other methods (Sevilla, 1991). The two most popular methods are excess costs and per pupil weighting.

Excess cost reimbursement is a local-state cost-sharing program in which the state reimburses a percentage of the excess local costs of the program. The rationale behind this method is that the local district needs to control program costs or face the financial increases in terms of the match. One difficulty of this approach is that many of the state matches are legislatively bound, and when excess costs exceed the percentage allotted by law, local districts are responsible for the added costs, further straining their budgets. Another difficulty is that, for property-poor districts that raise taxes to generate additional funds, the match requires higher and higher tax rates to make up the difference in cost (Odden & Picus, 1992).

Pupil weighting involves a fiscal capacity equalization element in which each LEP student receives an extra weight, relative to some norm expenditure, as to how much additional funding is needed to service one student (Odden & Picus, 1992). The advantage to this type of funding is that it is simple to use and easy to adjust for high and low property wealth districts. Further, the weighted pupil count can be used for all state aid to local districts, so only one state aid formula is needed (Odden & Picus, 1992).

The difficulty of pupil weighting, according to Odden and Picus (1992), is that states that base the pupil weights on foundation programs set below costs will provide fewer resources than are required. Additionally, those states that fund under a guaranteed tax base and use pupil weights might find that districts taxing at or above average levels will have expenditures above the state average, thereby causing districts to generate more funds than are needed to pay for the excess costs of the programs (see Odden & Picus, 1992, pp. 208-241).

Despite the difficulties associated with excess cost and pupil weighting approaches to financing bilingual education, they are the most widely used methods among the states, as can be seen in Table 3.5. This table also shows that most states do have populations of LEP students as well as some types of programs to serve them.

Implications for the 1990s

Several states have undergone major education finance reform in the 1980s in response to litigation over within-state disparities in per pupil expenditures (Odden & Picus, 1992). If this trend continues, coupled with an emphasis on the achievement of national educational goals, it seems that future litigation and policies may involve intrastate per pupil expenditure and policy disparities as well as expenditure and policy disparities involving special needs children.

The problem with equalizing intrastate expenditure disparities in programs for special needs children is that states are affected differently by LEP students and have unequal abilities to provide substantive, effective programs to produce achievement gains at levels advocated by national goals. Additionally, states are not subject to equal pricing standards. Odden and Picus (1992) indicate that a high-cost district in California may have to pay 25% more for materials than a low-spending district within the state. States in other parts of the country with lower prices will be able to provide additional services/materials for fewer dollars.

Determining the actual dollar amounts in terms of cost for state-funded bilingual programs is difficult. Odden and Picus (1992) found that in studies of the extra costs associated with bilingual programs, the additional funding did not exceed 35%, except in cases where class size was dramatically reduced. They found that increased costs, excluding class size reduction, were in the areas of teachers, staff

Table 3.5 State Programs and Funding for LEP Students

State	LEP Program	Number of Students	Total $	$ per Pupil	Method of Funding
Alaska	5 categories of bilingual instruction, per state code AS 14.17.041	11,183	15,708,600	1,404	foundation program with weights based on ADM as follows: Category A, 1; Category B, 1; Category C, .2; Category D, .2; Category E, .1
Alabama	ESL	1,600	0	0	NA
Arizona	bilingual	52,632	23,341,236	443	funds added to base for non-LEP students based on group B weight .060
Arkansas	ESL with 1 bilingual district	2,000[a]	0	0	NA
California	bilingual and ESL	950,000	96,000,000	101	flat grant based on formula
Colorado	bilingual/ESL/tutorial	9,445	2,601,598	275	block grant 75% to Lau Categories A and B, 25% to Category C
Connecticut	ESL	15,885	12,380,000	779	flat grant
Delaware	ESL with 1 bilingual district	1,470	0	0	recently added an LEP unit to a block grant
Florida	bilingual	83,937	132,662,216	1,580	weight applied as follows: K-6, 1.734; 7-8, 1.727; 9-12, 1.692
Georgia	ESOL	5,882	4,270,346	726	formula based on the number of segments a child is enrolled in ESOL
Hawaii	bilingual	9,654	6,142,024	636	full state funding

Idaho	ESL	3,253	0	0	NA
Illinois	bilingual	79,000	49,000,000	620	reimbursement of excess cost; currently at 72% of excess cost
Indiana	ESL	5,000	0	0	NA
Iowa	not available				
Kansas	bilingual	4,339	650,850	150	flat grant
Louisiana	ESL	7,841	0	0	NA
Maine	ESL	1,800	0	0	NA
Maryland	ESL	NA	0	0	NA
Massachusetts	bilingual	42,296	95,000,000	2,246	scale 1 is based on local aid and FTE; added weight per LEP student, 2.0
Michigan	bilingual	20,462	4,212,000	205	flat grant
Minnesota	bilingual	11,831	3,500,000	295	salary reimbursement based on a pupil/teacher ratio of 45/1 for full-time and 22/1 for half-time; currently, reimbursement set at 55% of the salary cost, with a cap of $15,000
Mississippi	ESL	1,609	0	0	NA
Missouri	ESOL				
Montana	ESL				
Nebraska	not available				

(Continued)

59

Table 3.5 (Continued)

State	LEP Program	Number of Students	Total $	$ per Pupil	Method of Funding
Nevada	ESL	9,500	0	0	proposal for pupil weighting
New Hampshire	ESL	1,164	0	0	NA
New Jersey	bilingual	43,500	52,687,609	1,211	state categorical aid and state competitive grants
New Mexico	bilingual	71,266	17,850,622	250	formula based on weights with a base of $1,866 for 1991 as follows: 1989-90, .3; 1990-91, .35; 1991-92, .40; 1992-93, .45; 1993-94, .50
New York	bilingual	122,041	32,361,300	265	competitive grants through categorical aid; formula-based aid dependent on local effort at a weight of 13% for LEP students
North Carolina	ESL	4,586	0	0	NA
North Dakota	not available				
Ohio	ESL	8,526	0	0	NA
Oklahoma	bilingual	9,392	3,581,812	381	formula based on local revenue with a .25 weight for LEP students
Oregon	ESL	9,607	0	0	additional .5 FTE for each student eligible for and enrolled in ESL added to state grant of $4,500; weight to begin in 1992-93
Pennsylvania	ESL	15,000	0	0	NA

State	Program				Notes
Rhode Island	bilingual	6,447	1,022,291	158	formula based on incentive program; currently funded at 80% of total cost
South Carolina	ESL	1,146	0	0	NA
South Dakota	ESL				
Tennessee	ESL	4,000	152,000	38	
Texas	bilingual	154,568	205,602		10% added to the basic allotment of $2,200/student and adjusted by cost-of-education index based on number of bilingual students enrolled
Utah	bilingual	14,310	416,380	29.10	
Vermont	ESL				
Virginia	ESL, 1 district has a bilingual program	15,133	1,700,000	$112	funds based on the numbers of identified students and a composite index based on each locality's ability to pay for education
Washington	bilingual	23,504	11,992,000	510	based upon eligible numbers of students
West Virginia	not applicable				
Wisconsin	bilingual	13,325	7,273,200	545	reimbursement mandate at 63%, but state currently reimburses at 52.9%
Wyoming	ESL	2,106	0	0	NA

SOURCE: Data collected by the author from individual state surveys, followed up by telephone interviews with officials in each state. Confirmed through checking against tables in Verstegen (1990).
a. Not based on survey data.

development, and additional materials. Carpenter-Huffman and Samulon (1981) determined that self-contained bilingual classrooms were the most cost-effective method of providing bilingual education because no extra personnel beyond the teacher were required to staff them; the additional cost amounted to about 5%. However, Chambers and Parish (1983) indicate up to a 100% increase for bilingual education in Illinois, where the state reduced class size and costs varied by the specific program adopted.

The issue for states will be, then, given unequal inputs, how to achieve equal outputs with respect to achieving the nation's educational goals for special needs students. More specifically, each state must find a way to assure that all local districts can meet these goals through linking specific programs, such as bilingual education, to the school finance formula (Odden, 1991). Suggestions for linking programs to finance formulas at the state and local levels include site-based management and budgeting, accountability systems, and district-level input incentive systems (Odden, 1991; Picus, 1991).

Conclusions

The Bilingual Education Act is approaching its 25th year of enactment in a country supposedly founded to be accepting of diversity. Originally enacted as a compensatory program, the act has evolved into a program designed to assimilate children into a world intolerant of linguistic diversity. The national goals set forth for the year 2000 are optimistic for English-speaking children, let alone LEP students. If the goals are to be achieved, the 1993 federal reauthorization of the Bilingual Education Act must do the following:

- Link policy, program, and finance components.
- Design categorical grants that will produce achievement gains for LEP students at national goals levels.
- Develop accountability measures that do not deter student achievement.
- Promote research in effective bilingual instruction.

In addition, states must accomplish similar aims:

- Link policy, program, and finance components.
- Develop accountability measures in terms of student outputs.

- Study and consider site based management and budgeting.
- Study incentive systems specifically related to bilingual students.
- Study specific bilingual programs to determine effectiveness and actual dollar costs.

Together, states and the federal government should, as in other countries, promote pride in the ability of citizens to speak more than one language. Multilingualism will not only promote pride; it will allow this country to compete in the global marketplace with greater understanding. Our linguistic special needs children are a resource to be tapped and respected.

References

Baca, L., & Cervantes, H. (1984). *The bilingual special education interface.* Santa Clara, CA: Times Mirror/Mosby College Publishing.

Baker, K. A., & de Kanter, A. A. (1981, September). *Effectiveness of bilingual education: A review of the literature.* Washington, DC: U.S. Department of Education, Office of Planning, Budget and Evaluation.

Bilingual Education Act. (1968). (Title VII, ESEA 1974, August 21). P.L. 93-380, 20 U.S.C. 1, 800b.

California State Assembly Office of Research. (1986). *Bilingual education: Learning English in California.* Sacramento: Joint Publications Office.

California State Department of Education. (1991). *Remedying the shortage of teachers for limited-English proficient students: A report to the superintendent from the Task Force on Selected LEP Issues.* Sacramento: Author.

Cardenas, J. A. (1977). *An IDRA response with summary: The AIR evaluation of the impact of ESEA Title VII Spanish/English Bilingual Education Program.* San Antonio, TX: Intercultural Development Research Associates.

Carpenter-Huffman, P., & Samulon, S. (1981). *Case studies of delivery and cost of bilingual education programs.* Santa Monica, CA: RAND Corporation.

Carter, T. P. (1970). *Mexican Americans in school: A history of educational neglect.* New York: College Entrance Examination Board.

Carter, T. P., & Chatfield, M. L. (1986). *Bilingual education that works: Effective schools for Spanish speaking children* (Report submitted to California State Department of Education). Sacramento: California State Department of Education.

Chambers, J., & Parrish, T. (Eds.). (1983). *The development of a resource cost model funding base for education finance in Illinois.* Stanford, CA: Associates for Education Finance and Planning.

Council of Chief State School Officers. (1991). *Summary of state practices concerning the assessment of and the data collection about limited English proficient (LEP) students.* Washington, DC: Author.

Crawford, J. (1989). *Bilingual education: History, politics theory and practice.* Trenton, NJ: Crane.

Danoff, M. (1977). *Evaluation of the impact of ESEA Title VII Spanish/English bilingual education programs: Vol. 1. Study designs and interim findings.* Washington, DC: Government Printing Office.

Danoff, M. (1978). *Evaluation of the impact of ESEA Title VII Spanish/English bilingual education programs: Vol. 3. Year 2 impact data: Educational progress and in-depth analysis.* Washington, DC: Government Printing Office.

Fillmore, L., & Valadez, C. (1986). Teaching bilingual learners. In M. Wittrock (Ed.), *Handbook of research on teaching* (3rd ed., pp. 648-685). New York: Macmillan.

Flax, E. (1991, September 25). First national study of young dropouts finds 6.8% leave before 10th grade. *Education Week,* p. 21.

Gray, T. (1977). *Response to the AIR study.* Arlington, VA: Center for Applied Linguistics.

Guthrie, J. W., Garms, W. I., & Pierce, L. C. (1988). *School finance and education policy* (2nd ed.). Englewood Cliffs, NJ: Prentice-Hall.

Hakuta, K., & Diaz, R. (1986). The relationship between degree of bilingualism and cognitive ability: Some longitudinal data. In K. E. Nelson (Ed.), *Children's language* (Vol. 6). Hillsdale, NJ: Lawrence Erlbaum.

Hernandez-Chavez, E., Llanes, J., Alvarez, R., & Arvizu, S. (1981). The federal policy toward language and education: Pendulum or progress? (Monograph No. 12). Sacramento: Cross-Cultural Resource Center.

Hirsch, E. D., Jr. (1989). *A first dictionary of cultural literacy.* Boston: Houghton Mifflin.

Ianco-Worrall, A. (1972). Bilingualism and cognitive development. *Child Development, 43,* 1390-1400.

Kessler, C., & Quinn, M. (1980). Positive effects of bilingualism on science problem-solving abilities. In J. E. Alatis (Ed.), *Current issues in bilingual education: Georgetown University Round Table on Languages and Linguistics 1980.* Washington, DC: Georgetown University Press.

Krashen, S. (1982). *Principles and practice in second language acquisition.* Hayward, CA: Alemany.

Krashen, S., & Biber, D. (1988). *On course: Bilingual education's success in California.* Sacramento: California Association for Bilingual Education.

Lambert, W., & Tucker, G. (1972). *Bilingual education of children: The Saint Lambert Experiment.* Rowley, MA: Newbury House.

Lau v. Nichols, 414 U.S. 563 (1974).

Macias, R. (1976). Opinions of Chicano community parents on bilingual preschool education. In A. Verdoodt & R. Kjolseth (Eds.), *Language in society.* Louvain: Institut de Linguistique de Louvain.

Macias, R. (1989). *Bilingual teacher supply and demand in the United States.* Los Angeles: University of Southern California Center for Multilingual, Multicultural Research.

Melesky, T. (1985). Identifying and providing for the Hispanic gifted child. *Journal of the National Association for Bilingual Education, 9*(3), 43-56.

National Assessment of Educational Progress. (1990). *Accelerating academic achievement: A summary of findings from 20 years of NAEP.* Princeton, NJ: Educational Testing Service.

National Governors' Association. (1990). *National education goals.* Washington, DC: Author.

Odden, A. (1991). *School finance in the 1990s* (Working Paper No. 1). Los Angeles: University of Southern California, Center for Research in Education Finance.

Odden, A., & Picus, L. (1992). *School finance: A policy perspective.* New York: McGraw-Hill.

Pallas, A., Natriello, G., & McDill, E. (1989). The changing nature of the disadvantaged population: Current dimensions and future trends. *Educational Researcher, 18*(5), 16-22.

Pearson, C., & Agulewicz, E. (1987). Ethnicity as a factor in teachers' acceptance of classroom intervention. *Psychology in the Schools, 24,* 385-389.

Picus, L. (1991). *Using incentives to stimulate improved school performance: An assessment of alternative approaches* (Working Paper No. 4). Los Angeles: University of Southern California, Center for Research in Education Finance.

Rumberger, R. (1987). High school dropouts: A review of issues and evidence. *Review of Educational Research, 57*(2), 101-121.

Sevilla, J. (1991). [Survey of state-funded bilingual education programs]. Unpublished raw data.

Stewner-Manzanares, G. (1988). *The Bilingual Education Act: Twenty years later.* Rosslyn, VA: National Clearinghouse for Bilingual Education.

Swain, M. (1984). French immersion programs across Canada: Research finding. *Canadian Modern Language Review, 31,* 117-129.

Teitelbaum, H., & Hiller, R. (1979). Bilingual education: The legal mandate. In H. Truega & C. Barnett-Mizrahi (Eds.), *Bilingual multicultural education and the professional: From theory to practice.* Rowley, MA: Newbury House.

Troike, R. (1978). *Research evidence for the effectiveness of bilingual education.* Rosslyn, VA: National Clearinghouse for Bilingual Education.

Ulibarri, D. (1985). Complementary ESL/mainstream instructional features for teaching to limited English proficient students. In S. Jaeger (Ed.) *Educating the minority language student: Classroom and administrative issues* (Vol. 2). Rosslyn, VA: National Clearinghouse for Bilingual Education.

U.S. Department of Education. (1991). *The condition of bilingual education in the nation: A report to the Congress and the President.* Washington, DC: Government Printing Office.

U.S. Department of Education, Office of Bilingual Education and Minority Languages Agency (OBEMLA). (1991). *Title VII reports for fiscal years 1988-90.* Washington, DC: Government Printing Office.

U.S. Department of Health, Education and Welfare, Office of Civil Rights. (1975). *Task force findings specifying remedies available for eliminating past educational practices ruled unlawful under Lau v. Nichols.* Washington, DC: Government Printing Office.

Verstegen, D. (1990). *School finance at a glance.* Denver: Education Commission of the States.

Yates, J., & Ortiz, A. (1983). Baker-de Kanter review: Inappropriate conclusions on the efficacy of bilingual education. *Journal of the National Association for Bilingual Education, 7*(3), 75-84.

FOUR

Federal Legislation Affecting American Indian Students

MILDRED I. K. MUELLER

VAN D. MUELLER

This chapter focuses on the unique manner in which Indian children and youth are at risk. This condition persists in spite of a congressional declaration that states:

> A major national goal of the United States is to provide the resources, processes, and structures which will enable tribes and local communities to effect the quantity and quality of educational services and opportunities which will permit Indian children to compete and excel in life areas of their choice. (U.S. Senate, Select Committee on Indian Affairs, 1988c)

The introductory section of this chapter describes the unique nature of the relationship between Indian people and the federal government. This special relationship confounds the normal expectation that the responsibility for education resides with the respective states. The next section draws attention to trends in major federal budget items affecting the American Indian population. Federal outlays for education, health, housing, and other human services are found in the budgets of numerous departments and agencies (Office of Management and Budget, 1991).

In the third section, we provide an overview of four major federal programs that support the education of American Indian students, describing each program's intent, level of participation, funding level, and impact on Indian students. In addition to the major program areas, we provide descriptions of specific set-aside programs for Indian education, the availability of financial support for Indian postsecondary students, and other supportive and supplementary programs. A brief description of the nature and funding arrangements for Bureau of Indian Affairs-operated schools is included.

A following section provides a short description of the impact of the major federal educational programs on Indian students of Minnesota. Also included is a summary of the initiatives that have been created in Minnesota to complement as well as extend the education services available to American Indian students. Finally, we close the chapter with some conclusions, policy implications, and targets of opportunity for improving the educational condition of Indian children and youth.

The location of authority and responsibility for the education of Indian students is important. The conditions of the indigenous peoples of the United States are at a critical stage. Will Indian children continue to be at risk? Will the states continue to hide behind the special treaty relationships between the federal government and Indian peoples? The objective of this overview is to increase awareness of a very unique condition in education funding and service delivery.

America's Native Population: Uniquely at Risk

The financing of educational services for American Indian students has always been a patchwork quilt, or a maze, or a disgrace—depending on one's perspective or locale. American Indian tribes were treated as independent nations (which they were) in the Constitution of the United States, but reduced to "subject" nations by a proliferation of wars and treaties that ended in the 1860s. Since that time, American Indians have been legally tied to the federal government, with the expectation (by states and others) that the federal government is totally responsible for *all* services to tribal members.

This unique relationship between American Indian tribes and the federal government has caused confusion in many states. The states have constitutional responsibility for the education of all of their youth, but have often inferred that this responsibility does *not* include American Indian youth who reside on reservations. The concept of triple citizenship for American Indians—as legal citizens of the United States, of their tribes, and of their particular states—did not enter the bureaucratic consciousness until late in the twentieth century.

Because of the unique relationship of American Indian persons with the federal government, funding for the education of Indian youth has been the shared responsibility of the federal government, state governments, and tribal governments. Sometimes this shared responsibility has been coordinated effectively, but often one or more parties in the partnership have failed to cooperate or coordinate, and Indian students have been the losers.

In spite of the planned 1992 celebrations, Columbus did not discover a continent or found any nations. He stumbled upon a pristine wilderness that was populated by a variety of anthropologically related peoples who were fiercely independent, deeply religious, environmentally astute, and politically sophisticated. The native peoples probably numbered 10 million or more, and they were members of more than 200 distinct nations, or tribes, as they were labeled by the European invaders. While these indigenous peoples were reduced to fewer than 1 million in a process of planned genocide that current Americans rarely wish to acknowledge, at least 1 million descendants of America's original people still exist, with at least 400,000 currently in U.S. K-12 school systems.[1]

As settlers descended on the East Coast of what is now the United States, they were often befriended and assisted by American Indian individuals or groups. Without exception, relationships soon deteriorated and animosity or hostility resulted. The white settlers' obsession with owning land, or their exploitation of natural resources, or their rigorous attempts to Christianize all the "savages," inevitably led to unfriendly or hostile relationships. In the early days, Indian groups were either massacred in totality or persuaded to move into other "unsettled" areas.

Between 1790 and 1830 the European population of the United States grew from 3.9 million to 13 million, putting horrendous pressure on American Indian nations to find any land that was not claimed or settled by whites. The prior policy of removal (to areas not desired by European settlers) was invigorated after the Louisiana Purchase, since this provided the opportunity to remove all the Indian people from east of the Mississippi to land west of the Mississippi. When western lands were found to have fertile soil or abundant natural resources, removal ceased to be a viable option. A new policy of establishing reservations, based on treaties with Indian nations, was instituted in order to "open" western lands for settlement.

A cynic might conclude that treaties were a subversive tactic used by the U.S. government to get Indians out of the way or to buy them off in order to provide land and safe passage to white settlers. When Andrew Jackson instituted the treaty period (from 1814 to 1865) in U.S.-Indian relations, the government provided a legal basis for Indian-federal relations that persists to the present and into the future. By recognizing Indian tribes as nations, by negotiating with them as sovereign nations, by signing treaties authorized or legalized by Congress, the United States, knowingly or unknowingly, solidified a legal responsibility to the American Indian population that is unlike any other relationship of our nation to its subgroups. First, American Indians are noted in the U.S. Constitution in conjunction with apportionment and in the regulation of commerce, but most important is Article VI, which states: "All Treaties made, or which shall be made, under the Authority of the United States, shall be the Supreme Law of the land; and the Judges in every State shall be bound thereby, any Thing in the Constitution or Laws of any State to the Contrary notwithstanding."[2] No other minority or subgroup has a treaty (legal) relationship with the U.S. government like that of the American Indian tribes.

Whether to gain land or access to natural resources legally, or to be fair to the original inhabitants, or to preserve peace and order, treaties proliferated between 1814 and 1865. In most of these legal documents the United States set aside certain areas (reservations) for the Indian group, offered or promised payment for the lands ceded, and guaranteed services in the areas of health, housing, technical assistance, and *education*. In grandiose fashion, many of the treaties promised these services "as long as the grass shall grow and the rivers flow" or in other such terms meant to designate perpetuity.

Although most Americans, in the 1880s or now, are unfamiliar with treaty language, treaties are nonetheless legal entities. Therefore, a promise to provide educational services in the context of a treaty invokes a legal obligation that does not exist for other groups. States of the United States are not promised, much less guaranteed, educational services from the federal government. While most of the federal framers of the U.S.-Indian treaties had little knowledge of how the various guarantees would be implemented, they should have been aware that they were creating legal documents that would steer relations between the United States and American Indians for centuries to come.

The U.S.-Indian treaty relationship also caused some additional problems for states, as alluded to in the opening paragraphs of this section. If the U.S. government guaranteed educational services to American Indians, did that mean *all* educational services? Did educational service mean K-8 education, or K-12 education, or did it include postsecondary education? Did such guarantees relieve the states of some or all of their responsibility to American Indians? With the advent of universal education as administered by state governments (and usually decreed by state constitutions), how were "regular" education and "Indian education" to be coordinated?

Answers to these questions have been slow in coming and vague in nature. Since 1924, when American Indians were made citizens of the United States and of their respective states,[3] the usual response has been that states must provide the same or equivalent education services to American Indian youth as are available to all other youth. The role of the federal government is to provide for additional services needed because of cultural differences, isolation, linguistic differences, or previous deprivation. However, states often interpret their roles differently and fail to provide Chapter 1, special education, free or reduced-price lunches, or other services to Indian youth under the belief that such services fall under the responsibility of the Johnson O'Malley Act, the Indian Education Act, or the Bureau of Indian Affairs (BIA) (Alexander & Salmon, 1976). Consequently, American Indian youth continue to fall between the cracks, educationally, socially, and psychologically.

It is interesting (and depressing) to note that three recent publications that deal with youth at risk or with current trends in education fail to include American Indians. None of the recent reports by the National Commission on Children (1991) or the U.S. Department of Education (1990b, 1991) includes American Indians in its charts and graphs relative to at-risk factors, retention, employment, health, academic progress, and so on. The charts and narratives invariably list white, black, and Hispanic, or just white and black. We find this trend discouraging, given that American Indian youth have the highest dropout rates (Chavers, 1991), the highest suicide rates, the lowest family incomes, and the most serious health problems of all groups of youth in the United States. That they are nonexistent in national studies speaks volumes about the status of concern for American Indian youth.

While American Indians try to affirm their treaty rights in courtrooms and hearing rooms, they also must continue to negotiate with state boards and school boards to secure what most Americans consider their just due in the classrooms of America. American Indians do *not* receive regular stipends from the federal government, nor do they receive any huge amount of educational services from the federal government. In the next section, we describe the programs and dollars currently available from the federal government and the kinds of programs they support.

Trends in Major Federal Budget Items Affecting the U.S. Indian Population

The Indian-related budget items in this section include the Bureau of Indian Affairs in the Department of the Interior, the Indian Health Service (IHS) and the Administration for Native Americans (ANA) in the Department of Health and Human Services, Indian education in the Department of Education, and Indian housing in the Department of Housing and Urban Development. According to the Office of Management and Budget, these agencies accounted for about 75% of Indian-related spending governmentwide in FY 1990.

Education data from Table 4.1 show that the Department of Education budget has averaged $15.2 billion in constant 1982 dollars during the period 1975-1991 (Walke, 1990). In contrast, Office of Indian Education programs have averaged $70.4 million a year and have fallen by $2.4 million. These data also show that BIA education funding has fallen by $11.3 million a year. This pattern of constant dollar decline is repeated in most Indian-related budget areas.

Federal health outlays, as shown in Table 4.1, averaged $30.9 billion a year, for a change ratio of 4.09%. Indian health service appropriations in constant dollars also increased during FY 1975-1991, but at a lower rate of 2.58%. Housing expenditures for the entire United States and for Indians have been significantly different. Table 4.1 shows the

Table 4.1 Trends in Selected Elements of the Federal Budget in Constant
1982 Dollars, FY 1975-91

	Average Level ($)	Annual Change ($)	Change Ratio[a] (%)	R^2
Education				
U.S. Department of Education	15,206.2	193.2	1.27	.332
education function	29,880.0	–378.5	–1.27	.180
Indian education (in Department of Education)	70.4	–2.4	–3.44	.713
BIA education	280.3	–11.8	–4.21	.898
Health				
U.S. Department of Health and Human Services	108,096.1	5,140.5	4.76	.975
health function	30,874.2	1,262.0	4.09	.839
Indian Health Service	763.8	19.7	2.58	.625
Housing and economic development				
U.S. Department of Housing and Urban Development[b]	14,612.1	401.1	2.74	.240
Indian housing[b]	392.1	–36.0	–9.18	.246
economic development function	8,343.6	–464.2	–5.56	.454
Administration for Native Americans	34.4	–2.3	–6.59	.805
BIA economic development	64.1	–4.9	–7.59	.767
Natural resources				
U.S. Department of the Interior	4,460.7	–22.3	–.50	.053
Fish and Wildlife Service	345.6	5.7	1.66	.277
Bureau of Land Management	834.2	–11.6	–1.39	.065
Forest Service	2,096.0	5.6	.27	.019
natural resources function	13,257.8	–129.5	–.98	.202
BIA natural resources	97.1	3.2	3.35	.462
Overall				
BIA total	1,053.0	–27.8	–2.64	.726
BIA: Indian services	228.2	.1	.04	.000
overall Indian budget	2,313.6	–48.8	–2.11	.285
federal nondefense budget[c]	478,982.7	9,611.1	2.01	.928

SOURCE: Walke (1990, p. 8).
NOTE: Constant dollars are based on implicit price deflator for GNP. Dollar figures are in millions.
a. Annual change as percentage of average level.
b. Covers only 1978-1991.
c. Excludes national defense and net interest payments on national debt.

Department of Housing and Urban Development budget averaged $14.6 billion in constant dollars from FY 1978 to FY 1991 and increased at an annual rate of 2.74%. Indian housing, on the other hand, decreased at an annual rate of $36 million or a negative 9.18%. Economic development budgets have lost ground in constant dollars during the FY 1975-1991 period, but Indian-related economic development programs (BIA and ANA) that provide funding for social and economic development projects to Indian tribal governments and nongovernment Indian organizations have fallen faster. Table 4.1 shows that the decline has been most consistent for the Indian-related programs.

The final part of Table 4.1 examines trends over time for the total BIA budget, overall Indian-related spending, and the federal nondefense budget as a whole in constant dollars. Federal nondefense spending went up at a rate of 6.62%, while overall Indian-related budgets declined at a rate of 2.11% a year and the BIA budget declined by 2.64% annually for this period.

Per capita federal spending comparisons between the overall U.S. population (average level of 234,292,824 people) and the American Indian populations (average number of persons, 885,751 during FY 1975-1991) illustrate a similar trend. The overall U.S. population grew at .97% annually, while the Indian population grew much faster, at 3.79% per year. Figure 4.1 illustrates the per capita spending trends. It shows that during the first 10 years of the period the federal government spent more per capita on Indians than on the population as a whole. After 1985, however, Indians received less expenditure per capita. The per capita spending level declined from 1979 until 1990.

Indian-related federal spending, corrected for inflation, has been declining in almost all areas. Among Indian-related items, only Indian health and BIA natural resources spending have avoided this trend. When one looks not only at overall Indian spending, but also at its major parts as illustrated in Figure 4.2, it is clear that all Indian-related spending areas have lagged behind their equivalent spending areas.

Major Federal
Indian Education Programs

Four major federal education programs serve Indians: the Indian Education Act of 1972 (P.L. 91-318), the Johnson O'Malley Act (1934),

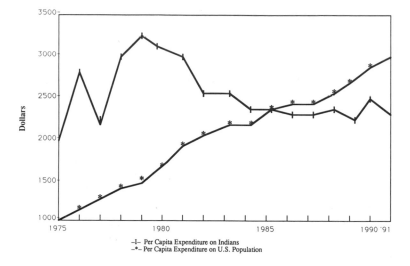

Figure 4.1. Per Capita Expenditure: U.S. Population and Indian Population
          FY 1975-FY 1991, in Current Dollars
SOURCE: Walke (1990, p. 29).

Federal Impact Aid (P.L. 81-874 and P.L. 81-815), and the Indian
Self-Determination and Education Assistance Act of 1975 (P.L. 93-
638). Indian-funded programs are administered through the U.S.
Department of Education, Office of Indian Education, and through
the Bureau of Indian Affairs in the U.S. Department of the Interior. A
brief description of each major program is provided below, including
intent, level of participation, funding level, and impact on Indian
students.

Indian Education Act of 1972

   This program was originally funded in 1972 and reauthorized in
1988 (P.L. 100-297). The act authorizes a variety of programs to supplement state, local, and tribal education efforts to improve educational opportunities for Indian children, college students, and adults.
These programs include supplementary programs in schools of local
education agencies and BIA-operated or BIA-contracted schools; enrichment programs in Indian-controlled schools; special education

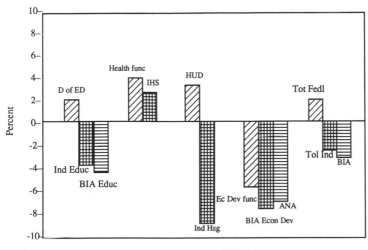

o Based on Constant 1982 Follars

Figure 4.2. Comparison of Real Change Ratios[a] (in percentages) in Federal and Indian Budget Areas, FY 1975-1991
SOURCE: Walke (1990, p. 31).
a. Based on constant 1982 dollars.

services to Indian children, including gifted and talented; training for Indian education personnel; fellowships for postsecondary Indian students; adult education; and regional technical assistance centers. To ensure Indians a voice in all of these programs, parental and community participation is required.

Over the last 15 years, more than $900 million has been available to support Indian Education Act programs. About 1,000 school districts and 100 Indian organizations and tribes receive federal contributions each year. Federal support, in combination with much larger sums provided by state and local governments, has had a positive effect on the educational progress of American Indian students. Between 1970 and 1980 the proportion of Indian adults age 25 and over who are high school graduates increased from 33% to 55.8%. The median years of school completed for the Indian population aged 25 and older increased from 9.8 to 12.2 years.

Despite this progress, Indians, as a group, still lag behind the national average in such areas as years of school completed, high school retention rates, and median family income. For example, more

Table 4.2 Indian Education Act Appropriations (in millions of dollars)

Part	1989	1990	1991
(1) Grants to local education agencies and Indian-controlled schools (Subpart 1)	52.7	54.3	56.6
(2) Special programs for Indian students (Subpart 2)	12.3	12.6	12.0
(3) Special programs for Indian adults (Subpart 3)	4.0	4.0	4.2
(4) Program administration and National Advisory Council	2.5	2.7	2.9
Total	71.5	73.6	75.7

SOURCE: U.S. Department of Education (1990c, p. 11).

than 25% of American Indian children aged 5 to 17 live in poverty, and almost 24% of American Indian youth 16 and 17 years old do not attend school (Hodgkinson, 1990).

Tables 4.2 and 4.3 provide trend data on spending and participation levels for Subpart 1 of the Indian Education Act, the largest of the programs of this act. It can be seen that almost 85% of Indian children and youth are served in local education agencies, while a much smaller number are served in BIA-contracted or BIA-operated schools. In 1991, Subpart 1 formula grants amounted to an average of $154.00 for each Indian child involved. In contrast, payments under the discretionary program average $588.00 per child in Indian-controlled schools (U.S. Department of Education, 1990c).

Federal Impact Aid

This federal program was enacted in 1950 and consists of general funds (P.L. 81-874) and facility construction and repair funds (P.L. 81-815). The purpose of general impact aid is to compensate school districts for the cost of educating children when enrollments and the availability of revenues from local sources have been adversely affected by federal activities. Impact aid funds are general funds that

Table 4.3 Indian Education Act Grants to LEAs and Indian-Controlled Schools

Impact Data	1989	1990	1991
Funding (in millions of dollars)			
LEAs	45.4	46.0	48.5
BIA-controlled schools	1.5	1.6	1.7
BIA-operated schools	2.3	3.1	3.3
Number of awards			
LEAs	1,023	1,020	1,020
BIA-controlled schools	58	60	60
BIA-operated schools	81	80	80
Number of states in which awards were made			
LEAs	41	41	41
BIA-controlled schools	17	17	17
BIA-operated schools	9	9	9
Number of eligible children			
LEAs	314,367	314,400	314,400
BIA-controlled schools	11,300	11,300	11,300
BIA-operated schools	21,523	21,500	21,500
Estimated number of students served	270,800	270,800	270,800
Average payment per eligible student	$143	$146	$154

SOURCE: U.S. Department of Education (1990c, p. 16).

can be used for current expenditures, except that increased payments received for children with disabilities must be used for programs and projects designed to meet the special education needs of these children. Entitlement for impact aid is based on children residing on Indian lands or on parental employment in federally funded activity. The FY 1990 appropriation for the P.L. 81-874 component was $717,354,000. About $230 million of this appropriation was spent for children residing on Indian lands. Funding was received by 674 school districts serving approximately 106,000 Indian children.

The impact aid construction program component (P.L. 81-815) had a FY 1990 appropriation of $22,929,000. The purpose of this program is to provide assistance to school districts for the construction and repair of urgently needed minimum school facilities in areas affected by federal activities, including school districts that comprise mainly Indian lands or that educate children who reside on Indian lands. In FY 1989, of the 24 construction awards made, 3 went to Indian districts. The total funding for all awards was $18 million, of which $7 million went to Indian districts. The availability of impact aid (either general or construction) to serve Indian children has been contingent on their attendance in public schools. Indian students who attend BIA schools, tribal contract schools, or other alternative schools do not contribute to the eligibility of the public school district and not only create a loss of funding on a per pupil basis but also lower the entitlement rate for the entire program if the required minimum number of students is not met.

Johnson O'Malley Act

Federal programs to help finance Indian education in the public schools began in 1934 with the enactment of the Johnson O'Malley (JOM) Act. Congress granted the Secretary of the Interior broad authority to contract with individual states for the education of Indian children. JOM funds initially compensated public school districts for the absence of property tax revenues from tax-exempt reservation lands that lay within a school district's boundaries. When federal impact aid began to fulfill this purpose in the 1950s, Johnson O'Malley funds were used to develop supplemental programs for eligible Indian children attending public schools.[4] Education contracts under JOM are now authorized and funded under P.L. 93-638, the Indian Self-Determination and Assistance Act of 1975 as amended.

Tribal organizations, Indian corporations, public school districts, or states that have eligible Indian children attending public schools and that have established Indian education committees to approve supplementary programs beneficial to Indian students are eligible for funding. Annual contracts and awards are administered by the Bureau of Indian Affairs.

During FY 1990, $20,351,000 was appropriated for this supplemental program. The formula for distribution of funds is dependent on the number of eligible students served, state average per pupil costs, and the amount of federal funds appropriated for the program. In FY 1990, the JOM program served approximately 217,000 Indian students in 31 states under 325 separate contracts. Examples of funded programs include home school coordinators, remedial tutoring, educational field trips, and cultural programs.

Indian Self-Determination and Education Assistance Act of 1975

The Indian Self-Determination and Education Assistance Act (P.L. 93-638) was enacted in 1975. It was designed to strengthen tribal governments and to increase Indian participation in the education of Indian children and youth. Financial assistance to governing bodies of federally recognized Indian tribes provides for improving their capacity to (a) plan, conduct, and administer federal programs; (b) improve tribal government fiscal and managerial capabilities; (c) exercise self-determination; and (d) provide supplemental education programs for eligible Indian students.

Only governing bodies of federally recognized Indian tribes are eligible to apply for self-determination grants (U.S. Senate, Select Committee on Indian Affairs, 1988a). The program funding was suspended for FY 1990. The estimated funding for FY 1991 is $2,754,000. The distribution formula is based on tribal priority-setting procedures. A total of 480 tribes were eligible for grants in FY 1991.

A second program component focuses on self-determination training and technical assistance. For FY 1991 a total of $1,750,000 was available for grants and contracts.

The third component of P.L. 93-638 as amended provides for the funding of education contracts under the Johnson O'Malley Act. For FY 1991, $20,351,000 was available for direct payments to eligible public schools. The impact of this program for supplementary education programs for Indian children was described in the previous section.

Other Department of Education Programs

In addition to the major funding programs focused on American Indians, many other programs provide educational funding and services to Indians. Indian students participate in most of these programs on the same basis as the rest of the population, to the extent that they meet eligibility criteria related to educational need. The programs are generally targeted to public schools and include, for example, the Chapter 2 block grants, the Drug-Free Schools state grant program, Education for Homeless Children and Youth, bilingual education, Magnet Schools Assistance, migrant education, the Chapter 1 LEA grants program, many of the special education programs, and a host of small discretionary programs.

In addition, several federal education funding programs contain set-asides of funds specifically for Indian students—usually those attending Bureau of Indian Affairs schools. Programs that include such set-asides include vocational education, compensatory education, Chapter 1, mathematics and science education, library programs, the Drug-Free Schools and Communities program, and programs funded through the Individuals with Disabilities Education Act (IDEA). Table 4.4 provides an overview of several of the federal set-aside programs that provide financial assistance to special categories of Indian students, primarily those attending schools operated by or contracted by the Bureau of Indian Affairs (U.S. Senate, Select Committee on Indian Affairs, 1988a).

Bureau of Indian Affairs-Operated Schools

The U.S. Department of Interior's Bureau of Indian Affairs has the primary responsibility for Indian education in the BIA-funded schools system. The majority of Indian children attend public schools, although the BIA school system enrolled 39,856 students in 180 schools in FY 1990. The system encompasses 23 states, with 80% of the enrollment from Arizona, New Mexico, North Dakota, and South Dakota (U.S. Senate, Select Committee on Indian Affairs, 1989).

The legislative direction for BIA education efforts is found in Title XI of P.L. 95-561, the Education Amendments of 1978. The BIA has several different types of schools, including day schools, boarding schools, contract schools (with tribal organizations), and cooperatively operated schools (with public schools). In FY 1990, the BIA provided a total of $316 million to support these schools. Most of the funding that totaled $201 million in FY 1990 was allocated to the schools through a formula called the Indian School Equalization Formula and was intended for basic instruction and residential programs (U.S. Department of the Interior, Office of Inspector General, 1991). The detailed funding pattern is outlined in Table 4.5.

Table 4.4 Illustrative Special Federal Programs Serving Indian Students

Program and FY 1990 Appropriation	Awards
Library Services for Indian Tribes $1,703,250	196 basic and special grant awards
Indian Vocational Education Program $11,073,333	50 grant awards
American Indian Vocational Rehabilitation Services Grants $3,875,000	14 grant awards
Dwight D. Eisenhower Mathematics and Science Education State Grants $128,440,000 $686,600 BIA set-aside	discretionary grants to BIA-operated schools
Drug-Free Schools and Communities Programs for Indian Youth $3,583,150	182 schools served
Minority Science Improvement Program $5,487,000	37 grants to postsecondary institutions where minority enrollment exceeds 50%
Aid for Institutional Development (Title III) $198,747,000	613 grants to IHEs with high minority enrollments (mostly historically black colleges)
Education for the Handicapped Grants to States $1,564,017,000	1.25% of this amount to BIA for education of handicapped children on reservations
Education for the Handicapped Grants for Infants and Families $80,624,000	1.25% set-aside for BIA-operated or contract schools
Bilingual education (projects that serve Indian students) $10,729,000	60 discretionary grants serving about 14,000 Indian students

SOURCE: U.S. Department of Education (1990c, pp. 20-26).

Table 4.5 BIA Education Funding, FY 1990

Program Element	Amount ($)	
Office of Indian Education programs		
education administration	12,591,000	
Indian school equalization formula	169,003,900	
director's contingency	1,707,100	
transportation	12,489,000	
school program adjustments and special programs	4,495,000	
management information system	320,000	
subtotal		$200,606,000
Department of Education flow-through funds		
supplemental education (Chapter 1)	25,217,025	
education of the handicapped	17,778,580	
drug and alcohol abuse	3,653,000	
Title IV formula grants	2,576,368	
math and science programs	598,375	
subtotal		49,823,348
Facility management funds		
operation and maintenance funds	65,349,787	
subtotal		65,349,787
Total		315,779,135

SOURCE: U.S. Department of the Interior, Office of Inspector General (1991, p. 16).

The second funding source in support of BIA schools is that of transfers from the U.S. Department of Education. These supplemental funds provide for services such as Chapter 1 and special education. Table 4.5 provides some detail on the source of some $50 million in transfer funds. A third funding allocation, which totaled $65 million in FY 1990, is for operating and maintaining BIA-operated school facilities and equipment.

The Office of the Inspector General of the U.S. Department of the Interior, in an audit report issued in June 1991, found that the BIA was not providing the kind of quality educational opportunity needed by Indian children. In a review of the principal provisions of the Education Amendments of 1978, 10 of the 17 provisions were found to be inadequately implemented. The report notes that achievement test scores for Indian children in only 2 of 153 BIA schools were greater than the fiftieth percentile, and that most test scores were near the thirtieth percentile. The report describes BIA school conditions as inadequate, ill conceived, inequitable, deplorable, unsafe, unhealthy, and a failure.

Postsecondary Support Programs for American Indians

In addition to the numerous categorical and set-aside programs that focus on the education of K-12 Indian children and youth, the federal government has established several programs that assist Indian students in the pursuit of postsecondary education (U.S. Senate, Select Committee on Indian Affairs, 1988b, 1988c). These include the following:

(1) *Indian Education/Higher Education Grant Program.* This program is authorized by the Snyder Act of 1921, P.L. 67-85, and provides financial aid to eligible Indian students to enable them to attend accredited institutions of higher education. It is administered by the BIA and had $26,314,000 in funds available for FY 1990. In FY 1990 and FY 1991 an estimated 14,800 students were assisted, with grants averaging $1,800 per year per student.

(2) *Pell Grant Program.* This program is authorized by the Higher Education Act of 1965, Title IV, Part A, and provides grant assistance to undergraduate postsecondary students with demonstrated financial need. This program is administered by the U.S. Department of Education and had available $4,804,478,000 for all students for FY 1990. The average award was estimated at $1,515 for the 3,420,979 participants in the program. A specific breakdown of recipients by race for FY 1990 is not available.

(3) *Fellowships for Indian Students.* Under the Indian Education Act of 1988, Title V, Part C, P.L. 100-297, the U.S. Department of Education provides fellowship support to Indian students pursuing undergraduate or graduate degrees in selected fields. For FY 1990 a total of $1,578,000 in financial assistance was available. The program made awards to 128 applicants in 1990, with the average financial assistance being $12,000.

Federal Indian Spending
Impact on Minnesota

What is the impact of the four major federal Indian education laws on the state of Minnesota? The descriptions, appropriation levels, and general impact assessments for the following fiscal programs have been presented in preceding sections: Indian Education Act of 1972 (P.L. 92-318), Johnson O'Malley Act (1934), Federal Impact Aid (P.L. 81-874, P.L. 81-815), and Indian Self-Determination and Education Assistance Act of 1975 (P.L. 93-638). In addition to presenting the brief impact statement for each federal program, we will describe in this section how the state of Minnesota has created an extensive and complementary structure of financial support for Indian education programs (Minnesota Department of Education, 1991; Minnesota Department of Finance, 1991).

Indian Education Act of 1972

The Federal Indian Education Act of 1972 has funded supplementary programs in Minnesota public schools since its inception in 1972-73. From 10 grants in that school year, the program has grown to include 50 to 60 school districts each year since. In 1991-92, 53 public schools in Minnesota received $1,846,189 in Part A grants. Since these are entitlement grants for each district that meets the criteria (10 or more American Indian students) and fulfills the required prerequisites (a parent committee, a needs assessment, and so on), districts receive a prescribed amount per eligible student, usually about $155.

These grants constitute a supplement program, so regulations prohibit their supplanting other programs (Chapter 1, Handicapped Education, free and reduced-price lunches, and so on), and funds are usually directed toward cultural priorities. Many grants are coordinated with other American Indian funding sources to better serve the students. A few Part B or Part C grants have been received by Indian-operated alternative schools, tribes, or Indian nonprofit agencies. Since these are competitive on a national basis, the amounts vary from year to year.

Johnson O'Malley Act

For FY 1991, $899,500 was appropriated for 36 eligible Minnesota school districts serving 8,590 Indian students. The average funding available from JOM was $104.71 per student. All JOM contracts and awards in Minnesota are managed by the Minneapolis office of the Bureau of Indian Affairs. School districts receiving JOM in Minnesota are located near reservation lands in rural areas of the state. JOM funds are not received by the four largest school districts in Minnesota: Minneapolis, St. Paul, Anoka-Hennepin, and Rosemount.

Federal Impact Aid

For FY 1991, 33 public school districts received general fund impact aid. No construction funds under P.L. 84-815 were received by Minnesota school districts. Of these districts, 22 (66.7%) claimed eligibility due to Indians living on reservations. The total impact aid received for FY 1991 was $5,535,590. A total of 95% of this funding, or $5,266,387, was directed to school districts eligible because of the presence of Indian students. Grants ranged from $10,752 to $2,014,446. The largest grant went to the Red Lake School District, a public school district located on the Red Lake Indian Reservation.

Indian Self-Determination and
Education Assistance Act of 1975

The Bureau of Indian Affairs contracts with four tribally operated schools in Minnesota (Chief Bug-O-Nay-Ge-Shig, Fond du Lac Ojibwe, Circle of Life, and Nay Ah Shing). These schools are located on reservations and serve approximately 500 students, predominantly in grades 7-12. JOM funding for these four contract schools was $1,087,604 in FY 1991. For FY 1991 the total self-determination and assistance act funding for Minnesota tribes was $2,393,242. These funds include programs in support of the education of Indian students.

Other Federal Programs

Additional federal funding for the four BIA contract schools during FY 1991 included $48,373 from the set-aside for Drug-Free Schools and Communities, $361,257 for Chapter 1, and $303,188 for IDEA. Higher-education scholarship set-asides totaled $23,659. The FY 1991 BIA funding level for the operation of the contract schools was $3,817,700.

Minnesota has developed a comprehensive program in Indian education to supplement federal efforts; its various components include the following:

- *American Indian Language and Culture Education Program.* This program seeks to make curriculum more relevant to the needs, interests, and cultural heritage of Indian students and to develop cultural awareness among public, parents, and staff. Grants are awarded on a competitive basis. For FY 1992, 14 grants totaling $590,000 have been made. This program was initiated in 1979.

- *Minnesota Indian Scholarship Program.* This program provides supplementary financial assistance to American Indian students who are state residents and who are accepted for enrollment in postsecondary institutions. The scholarships are "need based" and were first offered in 1955. Approximately 1,600 postsecondary students currently receive financial assistance, with an annual appropriation level of $1,600,000.

- *Indian Adult Basic Education.* With the help of federal grants, programs are offered at Indian reservations and rural sites to assist Indian adults with literacy skills and GED preparation classes. Participation annually involves 300-400 Indian adults who have not completed high school.

- *Indian Social Work Aide Training Program.* Persons from school districts with concentrations of Indian students are recruited and trained to work with Indian youth and parents. Currently, 44 aides from 55 school districts are involved in training in a program that began in 1974.

- *Johnson O'Malley Basic Support Replacement Aid.* State funds are allocated to six school districts that lost operational support under the federal JOM program between 1977 and 1979. Funds are expended only for Indian student programs and services. In FY 1991 the appropriation was $176,000.

- *American Indian Post-Secondary Preparation Program.* This Minnesota program provides grants to schools to serve Indian students in grades 7-12 to enable them to prepare for successful enrollment and attendance in Minnesota postsecondary education institutions. The program was enacted in 1984 and had a 1991 appropriation level of $857,000. Grants were made to 29 public and tribally operated schools.

- *Tribal School Equalization Act of 1989.* The state tribal contract school aid is used to supplement the funds for Indian education programs provided by the federal government. The goal is to provide tribal schools with access to the same spending level as the public schools.
- *Indian Teacher Training Grants.* This grant program was established to assist American Indian people to become teachers. Grants are actually loans available to American Indian education majors. The loans are "forgiven" if recipients teach in schools with significant American Indian populations for 4 years after licensure. Joint grants are made to four teacher training institutions and four public school districts. The FY 1991 appropriation was $150,000.

Conclusions: Policy Implications and Targets of Opportunity

The legacy of inconsistent and historically conflicting public policies toward Indian people is evident in the confusing pattern of educational services provided for American Indian children and youth. In the 1950s, federal budget cuts shifted emphasis from boarding schools to public schools. Numerous tribes and communities contracted with Bureau of Indian Affairs schools, establishing local school boards and setting up alternative schools. Again the federal budget cuts of the late 1970s and 1980s eliminated or weakened many of these self-determination initiatives.

Dropout rates for American Indian high school students are currently near a shameful 50%. Teenage pregnancy and alcoholism rates among American Indians exceed national averages. Unemployment of Indians on reservations and in urban centers is always in double figures. Adult illiteracy among Indian parents creates difficult problems for educating the young. The social, economic, and political ills that plague Indian communities, both reservation and urban, suggest that American Indians have many educational needs that differ from those of the mainstream society (Center for Demographic Policy, 1990).

The overview presented in this chapter of federal initiatives in support of the education of American Indian children and youth provides the basis for several conclusions:

- The U.S. government has a unique responsibility to guarantee the education of Indian children and youth.
- Existing federal funding for Indian students can be characterized as cumbersome and lacking in coordination between and among separate agencies such as the BIA and the Office of Indian Education.
- The federal approach to supporting Indian children and families treats various needs, such as housing, jobs, health, and education, as separate issues requiring discrete solutions.
- Existing federal programs for Indian students do not reflect the demographic shift from reservations to urban areas that has occurred for about half of the Indian population.
- The conflict between goals of assimilation and cultural preservation is reflected in the ambiguity of federal financing initiatives and programs.
- The relationship of the federal government to the states in providing and funding the education of Indian students lacks definition and clarity.
- The provision of substantial school choice—public schools, tribal schools, BIA schools, alternative schools, and so on—has not provided strong motivation and commitment to high-quality educational programs and student outcomes.
- Data gathering on schooling, student performance, and funding of educational programs and services for Indian students is inadequate and incomplete.
- The planning, implementation, and evaluation of all federal Indian education programs lack Indian involvement. The 1992 White House Conference on Indian Education (see Martin, 1991) and the final report of the Nations at Risk Task Force of the U.S. Department of Education (1990a, 1990b) may provide badly needed evaluation data.

Several targets of opportunity for new federal policy initiatives could lead to the improvement of education for Indian children and youth. An underlying premise upon which most of these initiatives are based is that schools alone cannot resolve the multitude of issues that stand as obstacles to the success of Indian students. Nor can the federal government, acting in a unilateral manner, without the cooperation and collaboration of state and local agencies, effect substantial improvement in the education of Indian youth. Some examples of policy initiatives include the following:

- Collaboration—between the public and private sectors; between schools and the many child, youth, and family service agencies; and between and among the various levels of government—is a necessary strategy for improving conditions for Indian students. Improvements in health, housing, and family stability would have positive effects on the capacity of Indian children to learn. Since the federal government bears a unique responsibility for Indian education, it also bears a major responsibility for leadership in implementing a strategy of collaboration.

- In concert with the collaboration initiative, the federal government should establish a national Indian school board with sufficient authority, staffing, and funding to bring into being a common vision and common goals for Indian education. Implicit in this policy initiative would be the aggregation of all federal Indian programs under a single umbrella agency and the development of responsible leadership to create inter-agency and cross-sector collaboration. Education cannot be viewed as an institution separate from the broader community.

- The federal role in the education of Indian children and youth should be limited to assurance of high-quality education outcomes for all students and the assurance of sufficient resources to supplement state and local finances. The federal government should not continue to direct the operation of Indian schools. This responsibility should be transferred to the tribes.

- The shared responsibility of federal, state, and local agencies meeting the common goals for Indian children and families requires that organization and agency performance be monitored and measured. The assumption by Indian people of the education of their young is essential. Therefore, all federal, state, and local education efforts should provide for not only Indian voice, but Indian control of the process.

- The geographic locations of Indian children and their families (e.g., reservation, urban, or rural setting) should not be a determinant of education quality or access. Federal financial support programs for Indian children and families should identify and serve those in need without discrimination.

- The U.S. government should use its fiscal resources and judicial authority to assure that inequities in financial support programs for Indian education within and among the states are not allowed to continue. The federal role should be to address the disparities of financial support created by each state's ability to fund public education.

- The National Indian Policy Planning Office established by P.L. 101-301 and located at George Washington University has been charged with becoming an "Indian think tank." Seven task forces have been formed to facilitate policy development in the areas of education, economic development, health and human services, natural resource management and environmental protection, law and the administration of justice, tribal governance, and cultural rights and responsibilities. This activity holds promise as a framework for analyzing issues, developing policy, and writing authorizing legislation to meet critical Indian needs (Tallbear, 1991; West, 1991).

The current fragmented and uncoordinated federal funding of Indian education does not meet the needs of the 1990s and beyond. A holistic approach to funding education and human services is needed. The unique federal responsibility for the well-being of Indian families and children and for their education is apparent. What is needed is strong collaborative leadership and the will to develop a plan for improving educational and human service programs that are relevant to the needs of Indian people. The confusion and complexity that have characterized federal Indian education and financing policy must give way to clear and concerted efforts to meet the needs of Indian children. The proliferation of federal grant and aid programs, the overorganized bureaucracies at all government levels, and the insensitivity and uncaring delivery of schooling to Indian children must give way to efficient, effective, and caring systems.

They made us many promises, more than I can remember, but they never kept but one; they promised to take our land, and they took it. (Red Cloud, quoted in Brown, 1970, p. 449)

Notes

1. Total Indian population figures range from 885,000 in U.S. Department of Education reports to an estimate of 1,700,000 from the U.S. Bureau of the Census. Figures for American Indian school-age children also vary widely.
2. Article VI of the U.S. Constitution provides the primary context for Indian treaty conditions.
3. This was six years after women were granted the franchise, making American Indians the last group to be given voting rights.
4. *Eligible* has several meanings for American Indian persons. Within the BIA it often means one-fourth Indian ancestry in order to receive services. In tribes it may mean being on the tribal rolls, having a parent(s) or grandparent(s) on the tribal rolls, or otherwise meeting the criteria to be recognized as a tribal member.

References

Alexander, M. D., & Salmon, R. G. (1976). Financing Indian education. *Journal of Education Finance, 2*, 33-49.

Brown, D. (1970). *Bury my heart at wounded knee.* New York: Henry Holt.

Center for Demographic Policy. (1990). The demographics of American Indians. *CDP Newsletter—Demographics for Education, 2*(1).

Chavers, D. (1991). *The Indian dropout: An annotated bibliography.* Albuquerque, NM: Coalition for Indian Education.

Hodgkinson, H. L. (1990). *The demographics of American Indians: One percent of the people; fifty percent of the diversity.* Washington, DC: Institute for Educational Leadership/ Center for Demographic Policy.

Martin, B. (1991, July 31). *Projected goals: The White House Conference on Indian Education* [Unpublished memo]. White House Conference on Indian Education, Washington, DC.

Minnesota Department of Education. (1991). *Minnesota Indian education: State laws and statutes.* St. Paul: Author.

Minnesota Department of Finance. (1991). *1992-93 proposed biennial budget: Education finance.* St. Paul: Author.

National Commission on Children. (1991). *Beyond rhetoric: A new American agenda for children and families.* Washington, DC: Government Printing Office.

Office of Management and Budget. (1991). *1991 catalog of federal domestic assistance.* Washington, DC: Government Printing Office.

Tallbear, L. (1991). Special report: The national Indian policy center. *Communicator, 10*, 1-2.

U.S. Department of Education. (1990a, April 5). *Cavazos appoints Bell, Demmert to head Indian Nations at Risk Task Force* [News release]. Washington, DC: Government Printing Office.

U.S. Department of Education. (1990b). *The condition of education 1990: Vol. 1. Elementary and secondary education.* Washington, DC: Government Printing Office.

U.S. Department of Education. (1990c). *Indian education: Justifications of appropriation estimates for committees on appropriations FY 1991.* Washington, DC: Government Printing Office.

U.S. Department of Education. (1991). *Youth indicators 1991: Trends in the well-being of American youth.* Washington, DC: Government Printing Office.

U.S. Department of the Interior, Office of Inspector General. (1991). *Audit report: Implications of the Education Amendments of 1978, Bureau of Indian Affairs* (Report No. 91-I-941). Washington, DC: Government Printing Office.

U.S. Senate, Select Committee on Indian Affairs. (1988a). *Hearing on Indian self-determination and Education Assistance Act amendments.* Washington, DC: Government Printing Office.

U.S. Senate, Select Committee on Indian Affairs. (1988b). *Hearing on S. 1645 to reauthorize certain Indian educational programs* (Senate Hearing 100-429). Washington, DC: Government Printing Office.

U.S. Senate, Select Committee on Indian Affairs. (1988c). *Hearing on S. 1645 to reauthorize certain Indian educational programs* (Senate Hearing 100-429, Part II). Washington, DC: Government Printing Office.

U.S. Senate, Select Committee on Indian Affairs. (1989). *Hearing to review the programs of the principal recipient of federal funds for Indian education* (Senate Hearing 100-429). Washington, DC: Government Printing Office.

Walke, R. (1990, March). *Trends in Indian-related federal spending: FY 1975-1991.* Washington, DC: Congressional Research Service, Library of Congress.

West, P. (1991). Task force to propose new Indian education post. *Education Week, 11*(1), 36, 43.

F I V E

State Funding for At-Risk Programs and Services
OPINIONS AND PRACTICES

JOHN T. McDONOUGH

K. FORBIS JORDAN

The rationale for state funding of programs and services for at-risk youth is that the cost to society is too great to permit the present situation to continue. Levin (1989) asserts that the social benefits of investing in at-risk programming are likely to be well in excess of the costs of providing such programs. He projects that a serious effort would require an additional annual expenditure nationally in excess of $25 billion. However, the annual cost of the current dropout problem on the national level has been estimated at $71 billion in lost tax revenues, $3 billion in increased welfare and unemployment, and $3 billion in crime-related costs (Grossnickle, 1986; Hodgkinson, 1985; Kunisawa, 1988; Natriello, Pallas, & McDill, 1987). Such high social and economic costs suggest that it would be cost-effective to invest in programs for students at risk of dropping out of the educational system.

The state, as the level of government with the primary responsibility for ensuring that children have access to an adequate education, has a special interest in identifying methods for allocating funds to support such programs. The project reported in this chapter was part of a larger research effort, Project FAIR, which focused on identifying and evaluating alternative state funding mechanisms for allocating resources to support programs and services for at-risk youth (Jordan, Lyons, & McDonough, 1990).

Defining At-Risk Youth and Identifying State Programs

Given the apparent increase in the numbers of students identified as at risk and the potential human, social, and economic costs associated with student dropouts, there appears to be sufficient justification for programs and funding to stem and eventually eliminate this loss. This need, coupled with the legal principle that education is primarily a state function, has resulted in states and local educational units addressing the issue of at-risk youth. In spite of the increased attention being given to responses to the needs of at-risk youth, information is limited on these issues. Therefore, this study was conducted to determine (a) the criteria used by the 50 states to define or identify at-risk youth, (b) the procedures used by the states to fund programs and services for these youth, and (c) the opinions and attitudes of the survey population regarding the focus, delivery, and funding of at-risk programs.

The baseline data for this chapter came from a national survey of state at-risk program administrators, state school finance officers, legislative liaisons for members of the Council of Great City Schools, and selected national experts on at-risk programming and funding.

Focus of the Activity

Following field testing and preliminary analysis, data were collected through a direct-mail questionnaire. In the first component of the survey, respondents were asked for their states' definitions of *at-risk youth* and for information regarding programming and funding for at-risk youth.

The survey was conducted in the spring of 1990, and responses were received from all 50 states. As discussed in the following section, responses from the states have been summarized to indicate general patterns.

Definitions of At-Risk Youth

According to the survey responses, 29 states have no official definition of at-risk youth (see Table 5.1 for a complete list of states). Of those 29 states, 10 indicated their method of defining and/or determining youth at risk. In Delaware, Hawaii, Indiana, New York, and Ohio, the state departments of education have developed lists of characteristics that are indicators of a youth's "at-riskness." In some of these states, the characteristics are limited to school performance. In others, the list also includes socioeconomic conditions. Using the characteristics developed by the state, local school districts identify their at-risk populations when applying for competitive grants to underwrite their designed programs.

In New York, in addition to the state's list of characteristics, local districts may develop their own lists of characteristics. In Illinois, local applicants define at-risk youth when writing competitive grants for funding. Also in Illinois, intermediate units and community college districts, in addition to local educational agencies (LEAs), are eligible to submit grant requests for funding. In Mississippi, each LEA is required to define its at-risk youth and then to develop and implement a program to meet the needs of those identified. Kentucky has no official definition of at-risk youth but does target programming toward youth with a pattern of academic failure and/or unsatisfactory social behavior. Finally, the Colorado Department of Education has developed a list of characteristics that indicate an increase in a youth's at-riskness; the state targets programs for preschool services for 4- and 5-year-old children in need of language development.

Limited definitions for at-risk youth were reported by 13 states (these states are listed in Table 5.1). In this context, a limited definition is one that keys primarily on factors or characteristics of youth relative to their academic performance.

The definitions used in Alabama, Connecticut, Tennessee, and Washington classify as at risk those youth who are likely to drop out or have dropped out of school before graduation. The definition used in Texas does not specifically mention dropping out of school, but instead enumerates poor academic performance criteria that place a student at risk, including retention, reading two or more years below grade level, and failure on sections of the state standardized test. Wisconsin's definition is similar to that of Texas, with the addition of student attendance criteria.

Table 5.1 State Definitions of At-Risk Youth

State	No State Definition	Limited Definition	Comprehensive Definition	LEA's Definition
Alabama		X		
Alaska		X		
Arizona		X		
Arkansas			X	
California			X	
Colorado	X			
Connecticut		X		
Delaware	X			X
Florida	X			
Georgia			X	
Hawaii	X			
Idaho	X			
Illinois	X			
Indiana	X			X
Iowa			X	
Kansas			X	
Kentucky	X			
Louisiana	X			
Maine	X			
Maryland	X			
Massachusetts	X			
Michigan	X			
Minnesota	X			
Mississippi	X			X
Missouri		X		
Montana	X			
Nebraska	X			
Nevada	X			
New Hampshire	X			
New Jersey	X			
New Mexico		X		
New York	X			X
North Carolina			X	
North Dakota	X			
Ohio	X			
Oklahoma			X	
Oregon	X			
Pennsylvania			X	
Rhode Island	X			
South Carolina	X			

(Continued)

Table 5.1 (Continued)

State	No State Definition	Limited Definition	Comprehensive Definition	LEA's Definition
South Dakota		X		
Tennessee		X		
Texas		X		
Utah		X		
Vermont	X			
Virginia	X			
Washington		X		
West Virginia	X			
Wisconsin		X		
Wyoming		X		

The definitions of Arizona and Missouri refer to unspecified factors that impede educational development and increase the likelihood of students dropping out before graduation. Alaska, New Mexico, South Dakota, Utah, and Wyoming define as at risk those youth who are in danger of not graduating or not attaining the skills, knowledge, and social skills necessary to achieve personal, economic, and social sufficiency in society.

According to the survey responses, eight states have comprehensive definitions for at-risk youth (see Table 5.1). A comprehensive definition is *one that enumerates both academic performance and socioeconomic factors and characteristics that place a youth at risk of not graduating from high school or not attaining the skills, knowledge, and attitudes necessary to function successfully in society.* The definitions from the states typically mention progress in school, but key on social factors that hamper or preclude success in school. Examples of the cited factors or characteristics include poverty, substance abuse, health, nutrition, limited English proficiency, pregnancy and parenthood, minority status, unstable home environment, delinquency, and attempted suicide. Two states (California and Iowa) listed a characteristic that was unique to their particular definition. California includes membership in a gang as a characteristic of at-riskness; Iowa cites cultural isolation as a characteristic.

State At-Risk Programming

Survey responses indicate that 33 states do not specifically provide funding for programs to serve at-risk youth (see Table 5.2). Of these 33 states, 21 do not provide funds for at-risk programs, but do provide funds that target particular segments of the youth population considered to be at risk. Of those 21 states, 7 fund programs through competitive discretionary grants. The types of programs funded include academic remediation, counseling, life skills curriculum, peer tutoring and mentoring, parenting programs, career educations, and dropout and suicide prevention programs. Through competitive grants, Maryland and Illinois fund locally designed programs that target particular segments of the at-risk student population.

The remaining 14 states in this group of 21 fund programs aimed at particular at-risk populations through a variety of formula-based funding mechanisms. Florida and New Jersey fund programs through a pupil weight. The types of programs funded in these two states include academic remediation, dropout prevention, compensatory education, and bilingual education. Virginia funds remediation programs based upon a local district's "economic index of need." The remaining 11 states that do not specifically fund programs to serve at-risk youth, but rather fund programs for particular segments of the at-risk population, do so through categorical grants to school districts.

The types of programs funded by formulas are much like those funded by competitive grants; the difference is that funds are available to all school districts that qualify. Additional program examples mentioned in these states include early childhood development programs, youth employment programs, learning centers, research and development grants for at-risk programs, latchkey programs, and substance abuse programs.

A total of eight states indicated that they fund various at-risk programs through competitive discretionary grants. Arizona provides 4-year funding for 55 at-risk pilot projects that focus on academic remediation, alternative and vocational programs, and support services for at-risk youth. Colorado's at-risk grants are targeted specifically at language arts development programs for 4- to 5-year-olds. The remaining states that fund at-risk programs through competitive grants are Delaware, Indiana, Kansas, New York, Oklahoma, and South Dakota. In each of these states, local school districts develop at-risk programs and submit grant proposals for funding. The variety

Table 5.2 State Funding of At-Risk Programs

State	No At-Risk Specific Funding	At-Risk Funding	Funding Special Groups	Competitive Grants	Formula-Based Funding
Alabama	X				
Alaska	X		X	X	
Arizona		X		X	
Arkansas	X				
California		X	X	X	X
Colorado		X		X	
Connecticut		X			X
Delaware		X		X	
Florida	X		X		X
Georgia	X		X		X
Hawaii	X		X		X
Idaho	X		X		X
Illinois	X		X	X	
Indiana		X		X	
Iowa		X		X	X
Kansas		X		X	
Kentucky	X		X	X	
Louisiana	X				
Maine	X				
Maryland	X		X	X	
Massachusetts	X		X	X	
Michigan	X		X		X
Minnesota	X		X		X
Mississippi	X		X		X
Missouri	X				
Montana	X				
Nebraska	X				
Nevada	X				
New Hampshire	X				
New Jersey	X		X		X
New Mexico		X		X	X
New York			X	X	
North Carolina		X			X
North Dakota	X				
Ohio	X		X		X
Oklahoma		X	X		
Oregon			X	X	
Pennsylvania	X		X	X	
Rhode Island		X			X
South Carolina	X		X		X

(Continued)

Table 5.2 (Continued)

State	No At-Risk Specific Funding	At-Risk Funding	Funding Special Groups	Competitive Grants	Formula-Based Funding
South Dakota		X		X	
Tennessee	X		X		X
Texas		X			X
Utah		X			X
Vermont	X		X		X
Virginia	X		X		X
Washington	X				
West Virginia	X		X		
Wisconsin		X			X
Wyoming	X		X		

of programs is generally the same in these states; the list of state programs typically includes all-day kindergarten, summer school, preschool, parent education, tutorial and mentoring programs, family-based services, counseling, substance abuse programs, and dropout prevention and awareness. Oklahoma's program also permits school districts and nonprofit organizations to submit cooperative proposals for funding.

According to the responses, six states fund at-risk programs through their state aid formulas. North Carolina, Rhode Island, and Utah make categorical grants to eligible school districts. The largest share of North Carolina's at-risk funding is for two categorical programs. The first is an in-school suspension program that operates in every high school in the state. The second program provides counseling services for at-risk students. Rhode Island, through categorical grants, funds programs to address the academic, social, and personal needs of potential dropouts. Connecticut funds various at-risk programs through a combination of categorical grants, pupil weights, and an index of need to target funds to districts with a high incidence of at-risk youth. Utah provides funds to local school districts based upon the number of at-risk students they service.

At-risk funding is based on pupil weights in the state school aid formulas in Texas and Wisconsin. Texas funds a state compensatory education program through a pupil weight based upon a school district's free/reduced-price lunch population. Wisconsin provides criteria for identifying at-risk youth and then funds programming through a pupil weight for students so identified. Programs in Wisconsin focus on academic remediation, parent/community involvement, and development of community support services.

Of the 50 states, 3 fund at-risk programs through two or more funding mechanisms. The types of programs funded in these states are very similar to those already cited. California funds programs through a combination of competitive and categorical grants. Iowa funds programs through a combination of competitive discretionary grants and limited categorical funding. Finally, New Mexico funds its at-risk programming through a combination of pupil weights and competitive grants.

Major Findings

For the 50 states, the following major findings on state definitions and funding practices were identified:

- In 29 states, no official definition exists of *at-risk youth*.
- In 13 states, limited definitions of at-risk youth focus on students' academic performance.
- In 8 states, comprehensive definitions of at-risk youth are in use; these include academic performance criteria but are keyed on socioeconomic characteristics.
- In 33 states, there is no funding specifically for at-risk programs; however, in 21 of those states, funding is available for programs aimed at segments of the at-risk population. Funds are provided primarily through competitive or categorical grants.
- In 17 states, specific funding is available for at-risk programs. In 8 of these states, funds are allocated through competitive grants; in 6, through formula-based mechanisms; and in 3, through a combination of formula-based mechanisms and competitive grants.

Preferred Focus, Delivery, and Funding

The focus, delivery, and funding of at-risk programming differ greatly from state to state. Even further, programs are implemented and delivered at individual sites. Various researchers have attempted to identify successful at-risk programs. Davis and McCaul (1990) and Slavin and Madden (1989) have asserted that classroom change programs are most effective and that pull-out and in-class interventions are less effective. Other research has focused on academic interventions to help youth succeed in the existing school culture (Brodinsky, 1989; Orr, 1987; Pellicano, 1987). Typically, programs have been designed to address only a specific portion of the school population (Center for Research on Elementary and Middle Schools, 1987; Durian & Butler, 1988; Wehlage, 1983).

From a survey of the states, Coley and Goertz (1987) have identified four elements of effective strategies for meeting the needs of at-risk youth:

(1) collaboration and coordination
(2) staff and parental involvement in program planning and implementation
(3) emphasis on prevention and early intervention
(4) opportunities for nontraditional education experiences

Their survey results also indicate that the most prevalent programs had an academic focus and were delivered either in classes or small groups. However, they caution that state program restrictions and prescriptions may not be advisable because of the lack of an information/research base about "what works" in terms of effective programs for at-risk youth. Coley and Goertz are in agreement with other researchers in contending that pull-out programs may be detrimental because they tend to disrupt the basic instructional program of the pulled-out students.

Building upon this research base, the second part of this national survey was used to determine the attitudes and opinions of national experts about at-risk programs. Several issues were addressed in this portion of the survey. Given the diversity in the proportion of the school population that is at risk among local school districts and other differences among school districts, the objective of this component was to identify preferred target group(s) for programming, preferred method(s) of program delivery, and preferred program funding methodology.

Respondents were asked to rank order program funding options and to use a Likert-type response scale to react to a series of statements designed to determine their attitudes and opinions about the focus, delivery, and funding of programs for at-risk youth. For each statement, respondents indicated whether they "strongly agreed" (SA), "agreed" (A), "neither agreed nor disagreed" (N), "disagreed" (D), or "strongly disagreed" (SD). The following discussion includes the pattern of responses for the entire population and reports instances in which responses of a subgroup differed from the profile of the larger group.

Focus, Delivery, and Funding of At-Risk Programs

Survey respondents were asked their opinions about three at-risk program policy concerns: focus, delivery, and funding.

Preferred target group. Respondents indicated that their preferred target group for at-risk programs was preschool youth; 72% of the respondents strongly agreed that programming should be aimed toward this group. The only other preferred target group with more than 50% strongly agreeing was K-3 children (69%); this group was followed by intermediate school youth (43%) and junior high youth (36%). Fewer than 20% strongly agreed that the preferred target group should be high school youth.

The majority of the respondents disagreed with the statement that local school districts should have discretion in determining the target programming population.

Primary focus of programs. The preferred at-risk program focus for the total population was socioemotional programming (62%), followed by parent/family programs (55%), academic remedial programs (51%), and vocational education programs (19%).

Preferred form of program delivery. When respondents were asked to indicate their preferred form of at-risk program delivery, the greatest proportion preferred mainstreaming in the regular classroom (46%), followed by off-campus alternative programs (15%) and pullout programs (9%). Almost half of the total respondents (47%) disagreed with the statement that pull-out programs "best" serve the majority of at-risk students.

Focus on high-need students. All groups disagreed with the statement that at-risk programs should concentrate on a limited number of high-need students.

Program availability to all students "as needed." In response to a statement that at-risk programs should be available to all students as needed, 70% of the total sample strongly agreed.

Allocations for specific state-approved programs. A statement that state funds should be allocated for specific state-approved programs and activities for at-risk students found 26% of respondents strongly agreeing. State dropout coordinators, more than any other group, strongly agreed with this statement (31%), followed by state school finance officers (30%). Fewer national experts (18%) and legislative liaisons (21%) supported the statement.

Allocation of program funds. Respondents had different opinions concerning desired allocation procedures. Of the total population, 40% of the population strongly agreed that the preferred allocation method is to include at-risk funds in the state funding formula and to use equalization formulas to provide more funds per pupil to poorer school districts. Of the total population, 30% strongly agreed that allocations should be made to individual schools, and 8% strongly agreed that unequalized categorical grants should be used.

Distribution of limited funds. When asked about the method of distributing limited funds for at-risk programs, 46% of the respondents strongly agreed that funds should be targeted to districts with high concentrations of at-risk youth, followed by 28% who favored distribution through an equalization formula to provide more funds per pupil to poorer school districts and 16% who wanted funds to be shared among all districts on the basis of the number of at-risk youth in each district. The most favored method for distribution of limited funds was to target funds to districts with high concentrations of at-risk youth. Legislative liaisons favored this method the most; state school finance officers favored it the least. State school finance officers preferred sharing limited funds among all districts on the basis of the number of at-risk youth in the school district. National experts favored the distribution of funds through an equalization formula; this method was rejected by a majority of state dropout coordinators.

Higher per pupil payments for concentrated at-risk youth. When the "strongly agree" and "agree" responses were combined, all groups agreed that, in districts where the *percentage* of at-risk youth is higher than the state average, the per pupil payment per at-risk youth should be higher. From a different perspective, all groups supported the statement that additional state funds per youth should be allocated to districts with *significant numbers* of at-risk youth; 39% strongly agreed with the statement.

At-risk programs funding outside the state aid program. When asked to respond to a statement that, in view of the different needs of at-risk youth, the state should make special provisions for funding these programs—that is, fund them outside of general state aid—36% of the respondents strongly agreed.

Fiscal accountability. In response to a statement that school districts should be required to demonstrate that they have used state at-risk funds to support district programs for at-risk youth, 65% of the respondents strongly agreed. Individually, the groups overwhelmingly supported this statement: 64% of national experts, 59% of legislative liaisons, 80% of state dropout coordinators, and 52% of state school finance officers strongly agreed.

Cooperative agreements for program delivery. In responding to whether state-funded programs should require cooperative arrangements or programming with other school districts, public service agencies, or private social service agencies, 51% of the respondents favored cooperative arrangements with other public service agencies; 28% favored cooperative programs with private social service agencies, and 22% advocated cooperative agreements between school districts. In summary, all groups supported the development of cooperative programs with other public service agencies. State dropout coordinators and national experts also supported cooperative arrangements between school districts and with private social service agencies. In addition to cooperative programs with other public service agencies, the majority of state school finance officers also supported cooperative programs between school districts and private social service agencies. The majority of legislative liaisons did not support cooperative agreements between school districts or with private social service agencies.

Use of funds to supplement existing programs. Respondents indicated that school districts should be required to demonstrate that state funds for at-risk youth are used to supplement existing programs. The "strongly agree" responses represented 46% of the total population. More than any other group, state dropout coordinators most strongly agreed with the statement (55%); this was the group's median response.

Preferred Funding Methods

When asked to rank six methods of funding at-risk programs in order of preference from 1 (most favored) to 6 (least favored), 30% of the population selected categorical grants as their first preference, followed by weighted pupil allocation (24%) and allocation based on the predicted number of at-risk youth or index of need (22%). The least preferred funding alternative was competitive discretionary grants; 45% of the population gave it a rank of 6.

When the mean response for each funding method was calculated, weighted pupil allocation ranked first ($M = 2.730$), followed by index of need ($M = 2.875$), categorical grants ($M = 2.882$), excess cost funding ($M = 3.632$), personnel units ($M = 4.270$), and competitive discretionary grants ($M = 4.474$). The discrepancy between the mean ranks and the percentage frequency ranks was due to the number of respondents who assigned ranks of 2 and 3 to a particular funding method. For example, 72% of the respondents assigned a rank of 1, 2, or 3 to weighted pupil funding, while 64% assigned a rank of 1, 2, or 3 to categorical grants.

The only statistically significant difference in the ranked responses among the groups was in regard to competitive discretionary grants ($F = 6.205$, $p < .001$). State dropout coordinators gave competitive discretionary grants a mean rank of 3.714, compared with legislative liaisons, who assigned a mean rank of 5.000, and national experts, who gave a mean rank of 5.162.

In summary, the total population preferred pupil weights, index of need, and categorical grants as funding methods. Their least preferred method was competitive discretionary grants. Legislative liaisons preferred pupil weights and index of need as funding methods; their least preferred funding methods were competitive discretionary grants and personnel units. State dropout coordinators and state school finance officers favored categorical grants as a funding method. State dropout coordinators were the only group who gave a positive ranking for competitive discretionary grants; their least favored funding method was personnel units. National experts most favored pupil weights and index of need as funding methods; their least favored funding method was competitive discretionary grants. Competitive discretionary grants received more low ranks from national experts than from any other group.

From this survey, the major findings related to program focus, delivery, and funding are as follows:

(1) The respondents most favored targeting at-risk programs toward preschool and K-3 children.

(2) Socioemotional and parent/family programs were the most preferred program focuses of respondents.

(3) The most favored program delivery, for all respondent groups, was mainstreaming in the regular classroom. Pull-out programs as a method of program delivery were not favored by any respondent group.

(4) Respondents generally agreed that program funds should be available to all youth and that funds should be provided through the state funding formula and equalized. At the same time, respondents favored targeting funds to districts with high concentrations of at-risk youths.

(5) When limited state funds are available, respondents' most favored method of distribution was through targeting funds to districts with high concentrations of at-risk youth.

(6) Respondents agreed that state funding programs for at-risk youth should require that school districts develop cooperative programs with other public service agencies.

(7) Both groups of state-level respondents supported the idea that school districts should be required to demonstrate that state at-risk funds support state-approved at-risk programs; district-level respondents and national experts did not endorse this concept.

(8) In view of the different needs of at-risk youth, all respondent groups supported the idea that states should make special provisions to fund at-risk programs.

(9) Respondents strongly endorsed the concept that school districts should be required to demonstrate that state at-risk funds have been used to support programs for at-risk youth. They also felt that school

districts should be required to demonstrate that state at-risk funds were being used to supplement existing programs.

(10) Respondents most preferred state funding of at-risk programs through a mechanism within the general state aid formula. A pupil weight was their first choice.

Conclusions

Survey findings and the review of the related research support programs and methods to fund at-risk programs and form the basis for the following conclusions:

(1) Since early intervention to reach youth at risk is critical, program development should be focused on the early years to provide children with early and sustained success in school.

(2) If at-risk programming is targeted at preschool and K-3 children, the needs of a decade of school-aged youth that are beyond that program focus may be neglected.

(3) To address the numerous factors outside the school environment that place a youth at risk, programs should focus on socioemotional and family/parent situations.

(4) Because aspects of socioemotional and parent/family programs are largely beyond the control of schools, school districts should investigate the establishment of collaborative at-risk programming with other public service agencies.

References

Brodinsky, B. (1989). *Students at risk: Problems and solutions.* Arlington, VA: American Association of School Administrators.

Center for Research on Elementary and Middle Schools. (1987). *Research identifies effective programs for students at-risk of school failure.* Baltimore: Johns Hopkins University Press.

Coley, R. J., & Goertz, M. E. (1987). *Children at risk.* Washington, DC: Council of Chief State School Officers.

Davis, W. E., & McCaul, E. J. (1990). *At-risk children and youth: A crisis in our schools and society.* Orono: University of Maine.

Durian, G., & Butler, A. (1988). *Effective school practices and at-risk youth: What the research shows.* Portland, OR: Northwest Regional Educational Laboratory.

Grossnickle, D. R. (1986). *High school dropouts: Causes, consequences and cure.* Bloomington, IN: Phi Delta Kappa Educational Foundation.

Hodgkinson, H. (1985). *All one system: Demographics of education, kindergarten through graduate school.* Washington, DC: Institute for Educational Leadership.

Jordan, K. F., Lyons, T. S., & McDonough, J. T. (1990). *Alternative state funding allocation methods for local school district programs to serve "at-risk" students.* Tempe: Arizona State University, College of Education.

Kunisawa, B. N. (1988, January). *A nation in crisis: The dropout dilemma.* Washington, DC: National Education Association.

Levin, H. M. (1989, Spring). Financing the education of at-risk students. *Education Evaluation and Policy Analysis, 11,* 47-60.

Natriello, G., Pallas, A., & McDill, E. (1987). Taking stock: Renewing our research agenda on causes and consequences of dropping out. In G. Natriello (Ed.), *School dropouts: Patterns and policies* (2nd ed., pp. 168-178). New York: Teachers College Press.

Orr, M. T. (1987). *What to do about youth dropouts? A summary of solutions.* New York: Structured Employment/Economic Development Corporation.

Pellicano, R. R. (1987, March). At-risk: A view of social advantage. *Educational Leadership, 44,* 47-49.

Slavin, R. E., & Madden, N. A. (1989). What works for students at risk: A research synthesis. *Educational Leadership, 46,* 4-13.

Wehlage, G. C. (1983). *Effective programs for the marginal high school student: Fastback 197.* Bloomington, IN: Phi Delta Kappa Educational Foundation. (ERIC Document Reproduction Service No. ED 235 132)

SIX

State Funding Alternatives
for At-Risk Programs

TERESA S. LYONS

Nationally, the interest in improving educational opportunities for at-risk students is high. This concern has recently been reinforced by President Bush and the National Governors' Association's (1990) development of national educational goals, goals that, in part, directly target at-risk populations. For the future social well-being and economic growth of the nation, educational experts and economists have made a case that it is critical that these students be adequately educated (Committee on Economic Development, 1987; Levin, 1989). The state, as the level of government with the primary responsibility for ensuring that each child has access to an adequate education, has a special interest in identifying alternative methods for allocating funds through a state funding formula to local districts for programs and services to serve at-risk youth.

If state policymakers wish to maximize the efficiency and effectiveness of need-based supplemental aid to at-risk youth, a procedural framework for evaluating alternative methods for the allocation of this aid might be helpful. This chapter focuses on the evaluation of six funding alternatives and provides an in-depth look at the top-

AUTHOR'S NOTE: The initial research for this chapter was partially funded by Contract No. R117E90146, accorded by the Office of Educational Research and Improvement in the U.S. Department of Education. I am indebted to K. Forbis Jordan and Lloyd K. Bishop for their critical review.

ranking alternative, exploring ways that it might be developed for use in state-level allocation formulas.

Selection of Funding Alternatives

The applicability of six different funding alternatives to funding programs for at-risk youth was examined. Selection of the alternatives was based on (a) their frequency of use in other need-based funding mechanisms, and/or (b) their preference by state and national experts on at-risk programming and school finance as ascertained by McDonough (1990). The six alternatives selected for analysis are described below.

Equalized per pupil allocations. These grants are per pupil allocations within the general aid formula. Under an equalized foundation formula, the combined state and local funding per pupil from the guaranteed foundation program and the at-risk programs would be the same in all districts, but the state share would be higher in poorer districts and lower in wealthy districts (Sherman, 1987).

Index of need. This option is similar to the federal Chapter 1 model for allocating funds for the education of the disadvantaged in that calculations are based on estimated incidence. Eligibility for funds and the measure of need are based on a number of educational and socioeconomic factors associated with at-risk students. Individual students need not be identified for funding calculations. The index is a proxy for the magnitude of the problem in a given school district, rather than a count or listing of actual students (Arizona Department of Education, 1989).

Categorical (flat) grants. Funds per pupil are allocated on the basis of the programs in which the students are being served; the state prescribes program standards and per pupil funding amounts for specific programs. It differs from the first option, equalized per pupil allocations, in that all districts get the same amount per student regardless of how wealthy or poor a district is.

Excess cost reimbursements. In this option, districts are reimbursed for the costs of providing special programs and services to the target group that exceed the expenditures for regular pupils. Districts may be reimbursed for a percentage of the excess cost or for the total excess cost of the program (Guthrie, Garms, & Pierce, 1988).

Personnel (classroom) unit allocations. A fixed amount of funds is provided for each approved personnel or classroom unit. Under this option, the state has eligibility standards for units based on the type and number of pupils served, as well as standards for staffing patterns and minimum and maximum class size (Hartman, 1980).

Competitive discretionary grants. In this option, school districts compete for funds by submitting project proposals and applications supporting need and giving assurances of compliance with state laws and regulations relative to the grant (Sherman, 1987). Assurances might include documentation of the target group to be served and a statement that grant monies would be utilized to supplement and not supplant current district programs.

The relative merits of each funding option can be analyzed by using a systematic evaluation process. The design of the following analysis involved two steps. The first was a review of currently used need-based funding methods and an analysis of potential incentives and disincentives associated with these methods. The second was a review of existing evaluation criteria that could be used to evaluate funding alternatives for the allocation of fiscal resources for programs and services for at-risk youth.

Incentives and Disincentives
of Need-Based Funding Alternatives

Although states use several types and combinations of the aforementioned formulas, Hartman (1980) makes the case that the distinctions among them are more nominal than substantive. He states that any formula is simply a mechanism for transferring dollars earmarked for a targeted population from one level of government to another. Hodge (1981) supports this concept, using the special education formulas of Utah and Oregon as examples: "These 'formulas' yield approximately the same amount per pupil in spite of the fact that Utah employs a comprehensive weighting system and Oregon uses the cost reimbursement approach" (pp. 26-27). Hartman contends that each of the alternative methods of allocation can be made to yield the same amount of money.

Given that alternative methods of funding are not the critical discriminator for the overall amount of monies allocated, the issues become the way in which different funding alternatives *affect the distribution of monies* and how the inherent incentives and disincentives of each funding alternative *affect program and management issues*. Hartman (1980) analyzed those issues relevant to need-based formulas that were utilized to fund special education programs. His analysis is also useful in evaluating options for at-risk funding; decision makers can learn from the incentives and disincentives that resulted from various funding mechanisms used in allocating monies for special education.

In reviewing each of the need-based formulas, Hartman addressed several program and management issues; these are summarized in Table 6.1. He categorizes special education funding strategies into three broad types: resource-based formulas (unit allocations), child-based formulas (categorical grants and equalized per pupil weights), and cost-based formulas (percentage and excess cost reimbursements).

According to Hartman's analysis, *resource-based formulas* offer a reduced incentive to overclassify students; this occurs because funding is based on allocated teacher/classroom units rather than directly related to each child in the program. A child's disability is determined through eligibility standards, while funding is based on a range in number of eligible students used to allocate each unit of service or number of personnel. These formulas tend to discourage mainstreaming, since funding is based on the number of students used to justify a unit or teacher of a special class.

Child-based formulas are the most likely to encourage overclassification of children. They provide the greatest incentive to serve unserved populations, but also provide the strongest incentives for maximizing class size and for labeling children with disabilities. Child-based formulas provide some funding to all districts, but pose a problem for smaller districts with low numbers of qualifying children. The number of children may not generate sufficient monies to fund a complete program. Planning under these formulas is less straightforward, and there may be a tendency to base programs on available dollars rather than on student needs. One advantage of the child-based approach is that school districts can explore the possibility of innovative delivery systems. As with

Table 6.1 Summary of Incentives and Disincentives of Special Education Funding Formulas

Program and Management Issues	Type of Funding Formula		
	Resource Based	*Child Based*	*Cost Based*
Classification of disabled children	less direct incentive for over-classification	encourage more children to be served, may lead to overclassification; straight sum encourages more mildly and fewer severely disabled children	least effect on overclassification
Choice of appropriate program	personnel formula may bias toward greater use of personnel	encourage placement in higher-reimbursement or lower-cost programs	depend upon district share of costs
Change of educational program	less direct incentive for keeping children in special education	encourage keeping children in special education and in higher-reimbursement programs	depend upon district share of costs
Class size or caseload	encourage maximum class size to reduce costs; full funding can encourage minimum class sizes	encourage maximum class size	encourage maximum class size (except fully funded excess costs)
Labeling of disabled children	labeling not needed by funding formulas; can fund for program and personnel units	formulas generally require labeling in order to qualify for funding	labeling not needed by funding formulas
Support of mainstreaming costs	must include mainstreaming units or personnel as acceptable for funding	funding provided for children in mainstreaming programs	reimburse approved costs of mainstreaming programs

Ability of small districts to provide programs	full funding amount with minimum number of students, but no funding below this level	inadequate funding with minimum number of students, but some funding below this level	governed by regulations, not the funding formulas
Record-keeping and reporting requirements	little information needed beyond normal pupil, personnel, and cost records and reports	need accurate data on number of children; may require great detail to obtain time spent in different programs	require detailed cost records, submission and approval of expenditure reports, and greater involvement and control by funding agency
Program and fiscal planning	most fitted to planning sequence; based on student needs with funding an automatic calculation	less direct process; tend to be based on available dollars, not educational needs	fit planning sequence, but available dollars are an early planning factor
Control of costs	done through regulations	done through regulations	percentage formula may help hold down costs through requiring district share
Obtaining state and federal priorities	higher funding levels for certain program units or personnel can encourage these programs	differential funding amounts can encourage service to certain students	priority on higher funding for certain items/programs can encourage these programs
Tracking special education funds	relatively simple to track funding to expenditures	not as possible to trace individual child funding and expenditures; must be done on an aggregate basis	most direct connections between funding and expenditures
Incorporation of future changes	updating funding amounts is straightforward, changes apparent	updating funding amounts more difficult to explain; may become arbitrary	updating funding amounts tied to cost changes

SOURCE: Hartman (1980, pp. 152-153). Reprinted by permission.

the other formulas, funding cannot be tracked to expenditures on a specific child. Expenditures are accounted for and reported on an aggregate basis for each program or classroom unit. Changes are difficult to document or explain because they are reported in program or classroom unit cost terms, then recalculated into per pupil expenditures.

Cost-based formulas offer the least incentive for overclassification. Percentage costs require districts to pay a portion of the increased costs, and excess cost formulas are theoretically fiscally neutral if all the excess costs are reimbursed. For tracking the use of funds, cost-based formulas are most effective. Cost-based formulas require more detailed accounting records than the other types of formulas, since the expenditures themselves are reimbursed. They also accommodate future increased program costs if funded on the basis of actual costs incurred.

As illustrated by the table and previous discussion, Hartman's (1980) analysis of need-based funding formulas provides a framework for decision making. It allows policymakers to (a) select a funding approach and (b) consider rules and regulations that could mitigate the problem areas of that approach so that the resulting funding mechanism would maximize the impact of programs.

Evaluation Criteria

From the school finance research literature, Jordan (1989) has identified a set of evaluation criteria for state funding programs that could be used in evaluating alternative methods for allocating resources to programs for at-risk youth. These criteria are described below.

Stability and predictability. If programs to serve special students are to continue without adversely affecting school district tax rates, state funds should not fluctuate from one year to the next. Initial funding for a program carries an implied commitment to continue funding until sufficient evidence is available to determine if the program is a success or if the need for funding continues.

Adequacy. The level of funding should be sufficient to enable local school districts to provide needed services and programs. Unrealistic expectations and an insufficient level of funds are legitimate concerns when the state decides to provide funds for a specific program or target group of students or to require that districts provide a special program to serve a particular group of students. Local school administrators are very sensitive to the nagging issue of "unfunded" and "underfunded" mandates.

Efficiency. In this context, components in the funding formula that encourage cost containment, targeted use of funds, program selection based on maximization of resources, minimal data burden on local districts, and mainstreaming of at-risk students into the regular school program would be considered efficient.

Accountability. This is the extent to which special funding is expended for programs or services to serve the target group that generated the funds rather than diverted to programs or services for other students or diluted because of the absence of a discrete program to serve the target students.

Equity. This criterion has two dimensions—student equity and taxpayer equity. Student equity is attained when a district's entitlements under a state school finance program are based on the different levels of funding required to provide individual students with an educational program congruent with their particular needs. Taxpayer equity is attained when the state school finance program provides equal revenues (combined from state and local tax sources) for equal units of tax effort. If all funds are allocated to a few districts whose students have special characteristics but not greater need, then the student equity criterion is not satisfied. If the differences in the fiscal capacity of school districts are not considered in the allocation of state funds, then the taxpayer equity criterion is not satisfied.

Responsiveness. Districts and pupils differ from a variety of perspectives. One cannot assume that all students projected to be in a target group have the same types of needs, so a state funding program should be sufficiently flexible to accommodate different types of programs as well as students with different programmatic needs. Among localities, the extent of out-of-school services will vary among school districts, and some districts will have to provide services that are available from other agencies in other districts.

Nonmanipulability. Especially with a new program, student counts and program definitions should be sufficiently precise and objective to ensure that local school officials cannot manipulate the student counts and program data to benefit their districts unfairly.

Rather than having similar purposes, the criteria described above are designed to accomplish different policy goals. The ways in which they interact are illustrative of the various interests that often merge in the political process leading to the enactment of legislation. Criteria such as equity and adequacy can be classified as "justice-oriented" goals. They represent the desires of various public interest groups who seek fairness in the operation of the program. The desires that the program's funding level be responsive to changes and that funding levels be stable and predictable might be classified as "administrative" goals. These goals will be valued highly by local school district policymakers and administrators. Efficiency, accountability, and nonmanipulability are "state-level management or control" goals designed to promote the effective use of funds and provide funding agencies with information about accomplishments. State-level policymakers and program administrators will be advocates of these goals.

Hartman's (1980) analysis of incentives and disincentives of various funding formulas and Jordan's (1989) evaluation criteria provide a comprehensive decision model for policymakers who must weigh alternatives for at-risk programs. The two methodologies have been combined in the following analysis of the effects of the selected funding alternatives.

Evaluation of Funding Alternatives

The evaluation of the six funding alternatives utilized a 6 × 7 matrix design to analyze the options based on the seven specified criteria as outlined by Jordan (1989). The funding alternatives were located on the horizontal axis of the grid and the evaluation criteria were placed on the vertical axis. Each cell provided a +, −, or ± score.

A written analysis was prepared of how each funding alternative measured against each criterion. A content analysis of each criterion description was performed to identify subtopic areas for each criterion. In addition, the incentives and disincentives in the Hartman (1980) analysis that were applicable to Jordan's seven criteria were coded and then incorporated into the content analysis. The analysis yielded 21 subtopics:

- stability and predictability
    continuation of programming
    funding procedures
- adequacy
    sufficiency of level of funding
    type of district that might be hurt; ability of small districts to provide programs
- efficiency
    targeted use of funds
    maximization of resources—if districts contributed
    ease of program and fiscal planning
    cost containment
    incentive/disincentive to maximize class size
    incentive/disincentive to label children
- accountability
    detailed cost accounting
    tracking of funds to programs
- equity—taxpayer
    equalized/unequalized
    distributional effects; benefiting poorer districts
- equity—student
    distribution in relation to magnitude of the problem
    penalization of provision of funding in some districts—restriction of the needs of students
- responsiveness
    flexibility of programming—degree of program accommodation
    incentive for innovation
- nonmanipulability
    manipulability of student counts, cost data
    incentive/disincentive to overclassify

The results of the analysis are summarized in Table 6.2. Among the alternatives, discretionary grants scored lowest. The three top-rated alternatives were the index of need, the equalized per pupil allocation, and the per pupil categorical grant. The order of analysis discussed

Table 6.2 Summary Evaluation of Funding Alternatives

Evaluation Criteria	Competitive Discretionary Grants	Unit Allocations	Excess Cost Reimbursements	Categorical Grants	Index of Need	Equalized per Pupil Allocations
Stability and predictability	– pilot/demonstration projects specified time period may not be renewed	+ funds awarded based on qualified number of units	+ funds reimbursed for extra cost of providing special service	+ funds allocated based on number of students identified for services	+ funds allocated based on indicators of student need	+ funds allocated based on number of students identified for services
Adequacy	– funding narrowly targeted unserved and underserved target population	± adequate if funding level sufficient adequate if full reimbursement percentage reimbursement may penalize poorer districts	± adequate if funding level sufficient adequate if full reimbursement percentage reimbursement may penalize poorer districts	+ adequate if funding level sufficient	± adequate if funding level sufficient adequate if adjusted so all districts qualify	+ adequate if funding level sufficient

Efficiency	+ preplanned, specified program anticipated cost/budget	− encourages traditional delivery modes may encourage greater use of specialized personnel disincentive to mainstream can encourage minimum class size minimal data burden	− full reimbursement provides incentive to maximize costs percentage reimbursement may offer incentive for prudent use of funds detailed cost accounting required	± targeted use of funds programs may be based on available dollars rather than educational need incentive for labeling children may encourage placement in higher reimbursement programs detailed cost accounting not required	+ provides resources based on single measure incentive for mainstreaming minimal data burden	± targeted use of funds programs may be based on available dollars rather than educational need incentive for labeling children may encourage placement in higher reimbursement programs detailed cost accounting not required requires some district participation
Accountability	+ highly accountable program evaluation component prespecified budget progress updates	+ able to track targeted use of funds to units	+ high degree of accountability detailed cost accounting required direct connection between funding and expenditures	+ funds based on identified number of children not as easy to track targeted use of funds	− least ability to track monies to targeted population	+ funds based on identified number of children not as easy to track targeted use of funds

(Continued)

Table 6.2 (Continued)

Evaluation Criteria	Competitive Discretionary Grants	Unit Allocations	Excess Cost Reimbursements	Categorical Grants	Index of Need	Equalized per Pupil Allocations
Equity—taxpayer	− not equalized	± equitable if equalized	− not equalized benefits wealthier, suburban, unified districts	− not equalized	+ benefits poorer, smaller, urban, and rural districts	+ equalized
Equity—student	− limited target population may not reflect distribution of problem	± may penalize smaller districts due to lack of minimum number to qualify for unit	± equitable if total cost reimbursed; if not, may penalize smaller districts	+ provides fixed amount per identified student	+ monies targeted based on magnitude of the problem	− may penalize smaller districts may penalize high-wealth/high-need districts

Responsiveness	+ allows for program flexibility to meet student needs	+ highly flexible incentive for innovation	+ allows for program flexibility to meet student needs	+ allows program flexibility to meet student needs allows updating of funding amounts as program changes occur	− limited flexibility disincentive for innovation	− possible only partial funds awarded not responsive to total state need
Nonmanipulability	± basically nonmanipulable incentive to overclassify	+ nonmanipulable to degree that funding is based on socioeconomic factors outside district control	± basically nonmanipulable incentive to overclassify	± manipulable in terms of providing program and cost data disincentive for overclassifying	± less direct incentive to overclassify	+ highly nonmanipulable terms prespecified
Total score	+ = 4 ± = 3 − = 0	+ = 5 ± = 1 − = 1	+ = 4 ± = 3 − = 0	+ = 3 ± = 3 − = 1	+ = 2 ± = 3 − = 2	+ = 3 ± = 0 − = 4

NOTE: Funding alternatives are ordered from least to most preferred, according to McDonough's (1990) survey.

below follows the rank order reported in the McDonough (1990) survey of preferred funding methodologies for at-risk programs discussed in Chapter 5 of this volume (i.e., from least to most preferred alternative).

Discretionary grants do not contribute to stability and predictability, as districts may not be assured that funding will continue. Discretionary grants often fund demonstration or pilot projects for a specified duration. Once funding stops, districts must either look for other sources of funding or subsume the cost of the program. When neither of these is feasible, programs may be discontinued and those requiring their services are left underserved or unserved.

With regard to adequacy, discretionary grants typically are not sufficient to meet the total state needs of a targeted population. These grants are usually an initial method for funding a target population. When there are no definitive answers on what types of programs and services to provide or the costs of such programs, and when fiscal resources are scarce, discretionary grants are a means for states to gather data and determine future policy regarding the target population.

Discretionary grants are efficient in that they specify the amount and duration of the funds to be received. There is a written agreement between the grantor and the grantee as to how the funds will be utilized. Accountability is one of the advantages of discretionary grants. Most require an evaluation component to document the program's impact. Status and budget reports demonstrate that funds are being spent on the target group. Discretionary grants are not equitable for the following reasons: (a) They may be awarded based on criteria that do not reflect the distribution of the problem; (b) a district may be awarded a grant because it has the necessary personnel and/or expertise to write a proposal, rather than as a result of a high incidence of need; and (c) grants may be awarded based on limited criteria so that only some districts would be eligible to apply. Typically, with discretionary grants, only a small percentage of the population needing services receives them. Grants may or may not be responsive to local program needs, depending on the requirements of the grant. They are not responsive to the total state need since they are selective. Discretionary grants are nonmanipulable in that programming and funding are prespecified.

In summary, discretionary grants scored positively on three of the seven evaluation criteria. They are efficient and nonmanipulable, and they provide a high degree of accountability. This funding method seems most appropriate as an initial data-gathering effort to determine future policy and not as a means of meeting the needs of the state's at-risk population. In the McDonough (1990) survey, this option was the least preferred alternative among state and national experts on programming and funding for at-risk youth.

Unit allocations provide stable and predictable funds to districts, since funds are allocated based on the needed number of units and an assumption of continued funding. They fulfill the adequacy criterion as long as the overall funding level is sufficient and the full unit amount is funded. If a percentage is reimbursed, it may penalize poor school districts that could not provide the local contribution.

Unit allocations may be inefficient because they can encourage traditional delivery modes. They encourage organization in terms of teachers and classrooms rather than in terms of services. The personnel formula may include bias toward greater use of certified personnel, which would have a marked impact on program costs.

Unit allocations are accountable because funds can be tracked to expenditures. They are equitable in terms of taxpayer equity if equalized. They may penalize smaller districts because these districts may not have the minimum number of students to qualify for a unit. Responsiveness to the needs of the district may be limited because this alternative does not encourage flexibility and innovation in programming, since approved units are prespecified.

Unit allocations are primarily nonmanipulable because specified standards constitute a unit. They also offer less direct incentive to overclassify students since a unit is awarded on the basis of a minimum class size. As class size reaches the maximum, however, unit allocation may encourage identification of additional students in order to secure an additional unit.

Given the wide variation of needs and delivery strategies used in at-risk programs, the unit allocations funding option has several limitations. It may tend to encourage conventional, nonintegrated approaches to service delivery. It may also encourage the use of specialized certified personnel, since it is the teacher or unit that is funded. This would have a direct impact on the cost of providing services for at-risk students. Many successful at-risk programs utilize low-cost personnel (i.e., paraprofessionals, volunteers, peer tutors). If unit allocations were selected as a funding mechanism, policymakers would want to encourage flexible staffing patterns.

In summary, unit allocations scored positively on three of the criteria: stability and predictability, adequacy, and accountability. It ranked fifth out of the six alternatives in the McDonough (1990) survey.

Excess cost reimbursements provide stable and predictable funding and, if the overall funding level is sufficient, adequate fiscal resources if the total excess cost is reimbursed. If a percentage of the total is reimbursed, this alternative may penalize poorer districts that cannot provide the local contribution. Excess cost reimbursements do not meet the efficiency criterion on two counts: cost containment and data burden.

This option does require detailed accounting to document the cost of the program. If a percentage of the excess cost is reimbursed, this may offer an incentive to keep costs down, since districts are contributing; however, if the total excess costs are reimbursed there is no incentive inherent in this option to require the prudent use of fiscal resources.

Excess cost reimbursement allows for a high degree of accountability, because of the detailed cost accounting required. This option provides the most direct connection between funding and expenditures.

Excess cost reimbursements do not meet the equity criterion for taxpayer equity, because funds are not equalized. In a simulation study of the distributional effects across a prototype state for the various funding options, excess cost allocations tended to benefit large, moderately wealthy, suburban, and unified districts (Lyons, 1990). In terms of student equity, this option would meet educational needs if the total excess costs were reimbursed. This option meets the responsiveness criterion because it allows for the flexibility of different program options. It also allows for updating funding amounts as changes in programs occur. It can be manipulable in terms of providing student and program data. This option provides little incentive for overclassifying students.

In summary, the excess cost reimbursement alternative meets three of the seven criteria: stability and predictability, accountability, and responsiveness. It ranked fourth out of the six alternatives in the McDonough (1990) survey.

Categorical (flat) grants provide stable and predictable funding because districts are assured of a given amount per pupil for those students identified as needing services. As long as the overall funding level is sufficient, categorical grants provide adequate fiscal resources. This option is efficient in terms of specifically targeting the use of funds. However, it allows for a less direct program and fiscal planning process. Programs may be based on available dollars rather than on educational need. This option encourages the labeling of children, since funds are based on child costs. If there is a range of program services at various costs, this option may encourage placing students in higher-reimbursement programs.

Categorical grants provide for accountability in that funds are based on the identified number of pupils; however, tracking of actual individual pupil funding and expenditures is not required. Categorical grants do not meet the taxpayer equity criterion because they are not equalized. In the simulation study mentioned above, this option tended to benefit wealthy, suburban, and unified districts (Lyons, 1990). Districts receive a fixed amount per identified pupil regardless of their fiscal ability to provide the program. In terms of responsiveness, categorical grants may allow for great flexibility in programming, depending on the accompanying rules and regulations. This option is basically nonmanipulable, again depending on accompanying rules and regulations. It does, however, provide an incentive to overclassify, because allocations are based on the number of pupils.

This funding alternative has great flexibility and offers multiple options through state incentives and regulations. Its drawbacks are that it necessitates the labeling of pupils to get services, and it puts a greater burden on districts that are poorer or in urban areas—districts that may also have the greatest number of at-risk youth to serve—unless the funding level is sufficient to pay the full cost.

In summary, categorical per pupil allocations scored positively on four of the seven evaluation criteria: stability and predictability, adequacy, accountability, and responsiveness. The option also scored positively on student equity, but not on taxpayer equity. It was most favored by state school finance officers (possibly because of its flexibility and the level of state control through rules and regulations) and least preferred by the liaisons of the Council of Great City Schools (possibly because urban districts tend to benefit less).

Equalized per pupil allocations provide stable and predictable funding, and adequate resources if the overall allocation is sufficient. As with unit allocations, this option may penalize small districts if they do not have sufficient students to generate adequate monies to fund programs. This option is efficient in terms of specifically targeting the use of funds; however, it allows for a less direct program and fiscal planning process. Programs may be based on available dollars rather then on educational need. Equalized per pupil allocations encourage the labeling of pupils, since funds are based on pupil costs. The option requires accurate data on the number of pupils served and may require detailed investigation to determine the amount of time each pupil spends in a given program if full-time equivalent pupils are used in the formula. This option provides for accountability, since funding requires identifying who is to be served. However, tracing funds to program expenditures is not required as in the cost-based options.

With regard to equity, equalized per pupil allocations are the most equitable in terms of taxpayer equity, because wealthier districts pay a greater share than poorer districts. However, such allocations may not result in educational or student equity. Equalized allocations tend to penalize large urban districts with high property wealth and high at-risk needs. In the simulation study previously mentioned, this option was found to benefit large, suburban, moderately wealthy, and unified districts (Lyons, 1990). This option is responsive in that it could allow for a variety of different programs and services. However, a standard cost is required in order to assign an add-on weight for per pupil allocation. This option is basically nonmanipulable, depending on accompanying rules and regulations.

Equalized per pupil allocations do, however, provide an incentive to overclassify pupils, since allocations are based on the number of students served. They also offer an incentive to keep children in programs, given that dismissal results in loss of funding. A major weakness of this alternative is that those districts with the highest incidence of at-risk youth may not receive sufficient funds to provide the needed level of programs and services.

In summary, equalized per pupil allocations scored positively on four of the seven evaluation criteria: stability and predictability, adequacy, accountability, and responsiveness. This option also scored positively on some aspects of efficiency, equity, and nonmanipulability. It was the most preferred by state and national experts on programming and funding for at-risk youth.

The *index of need* scored highest of the six alternatives. It provides a stable and predictable funding level and an adequate level if the overall allocation is sufficient and the index is adjusted so that all districts are able to qualify for some base level of funding. It is efficient in that it provides monies based on a single measure (the index) according to need; this offers an incentive to maximize resources. The data burden depends, in part, on the complexity of the index used. However, there is no inherent requirement in this option for districts to identify students. This option maximizes mainstreaming, because funding is not based on a "special class" unit. In terms of accountability, this option offers the least ability to track monies to the target group.

The index of need alternative has the potential to maximize student equity, because the monies are allocated based on the magnitude of the problem. The characteristics that are selected to determine the index, however, will affect the student equity issue. In terms of taxpayer equity, based on the simulation study, this option tended to benefit the same districts as the equalized option (Lyons, 1990); however, the index is not equalized in the traditional sense.

With regard to responsiveness, this option is probably the most flexible in being able to accommodate different types of programmatic needs. It does not inherently stipulate the programs to be funded. It is nonmanipulable to the degree that funding is based on socioeconomic indicators outside the school district's control.

In summary, the index of need meets five of the seven criteria. The only criterion receiving a minus score is accountability. This deficiency could be addressed by including accountability measures with the rules and regulations. For the adequacy criterion, this option has the potential of providing sufficient funding if it is adjusted so that all districts are eligible to qualify for some level of funding.

Policy Implications

Taking the results of the evaluation of the efficacy of the alternatives using Jordan's (1989) and Hartman's (1980) criteria, and accepting the underlying assumption that the at-risk dilemma can best be resolved by the state's facilitating dynamic and innovative approaches to programming, several possible policy directions can be identified that would maximize local innovation and decision making. This analysis and related research reported elsewhere (Lyons, 1990) support the following observations concerning the selection of a funding alternative:

(1) Since at-risk programs are still in an evolutionary state, program evaluation data are limited, and variations in delivery and cost of programs are so great, selection of a per pupil weight, even based on a median cost, may be premature. This is particularly true in the absence of studies on the cost-effectiveness of alternative delivery systems.

(2) Waiting until there is consensus that the research base is adequate before selecting a method of funding may not be prudent. The social and economic costs to society of ignoring at-risk students are becoming too great.

(3) If the goal is that all eligible students receive adequate services, using a fiscally equalized funding approach may be counterproductive. Equalized options tend to penalize property wealthy inner-city districts that often have the highest incidence of at-risk youth. Thus the local burden to provide programs and services is disproportionate.

(4) If the public policy goals are to target resources at those districts with the greatest need and to encourage local creativity in addressing the problem, the index of need appears to be the preferred funding alternative based on the foregoing analysis as well as the simulation study mentioned above, which looked at the distributional effects across a prototype state for the various funding options (Lyons, 1990). Again, its primary disadvantage is the lack of accountability inherent in the funding mechanism. If an index of need were selected as the funding alternative, policymakers would want to build accountability measures into the rules and regulations. Process and product measures might be used to determine the effectiveness of local programs.

One of the conceptual challenges in the use of the index of need is that of identifying the variables to be used in developing it. There is probably no single best indicator or set of indicators for all states. Each state would need to determine what set of indicators best reflects the need in its unique set of circumstances. The following sections explore the development of an index for use in state allocations of resources for at-risk youth.

Development of a
Prototype Index of Need

The findings from the previous analysis served as an impetus for additional research concerning the variables that might be used in an index of need. The concept of the index of need is a relatively new approach for states to use in funding the public schools. Chambers (1981) conducted preliminary research in this area, but his efforts have focused on differences in spending patterns rather than differences in the student populations.

Early work leading to the development of a state-level at-risk index was undertaken by the Arizona Department of Education (1989). Using variables that were available at the state level, the agency developed an at-risk index for local school districts based on the sum of the Z scores for a list of variables related to at-riskness. This was done to provide a basis for prioritizing the distribution of discretionary grant monies for pilot at-risk projects. One of the criticisms of the Arizona index is that highly correlated variables were given equal weight in the calculation of the index. Arizona was unable to use a predictive regression equation in the development of the index because it did not have an actual count of at-risk students to use as a dependent variable.

In a study undertaken to address some of the criticisms of the Arizona index, data for a selected group of variables related to students' being at risk were secured from the Texas Education Agency for each of the 1,053 school districts in Texas. The advantages of using Texas data for the simulation of the index include the range of data elements available for all school districts, including socioeconomic and student performance variables, the variety of school districts in the state, and the existence of a count of at-risk youth that can be used as the dependent variable in a multiple regression model.

Evaluation Criteria

Eight variables were explored for use in this study:

- RISK: The number of students reported by the school district as being at risk of dropping out of school. The definition uses state-defined criteria as set forth in 19 TAC Chapter 75.195 as amended in July 1990. At-risk criteria differ by grade level. This was the dependent variable.
- ECON: The number of students identified as being eligible for free or reduced-price meals under the National School Lunch and Child Nutrition Program, from a family with an annual income at or below the official federal poverty line, eligible for Aid to Families with Dependent

Children or other public assistance, and recipients of a Pell Grant or comparable state program of need-based financial assistance under Title II of the Job Training Partnership Act.

- LEP: The number of students in the school district identified as limited English proficient by the Language Proficiency Assessment Committee or designated professional, according to criteria established in 19 TAC, Section 77.356.

- DOUT: The number of enrolled students who dropped out of school during the school year plus the number of students enrolled at the beginning of the previous year who failed to reenroll at the beginning of the following school year. Students are not counted as dropouts if the district records indicate that the student received approval for withdrawal or transferred to another public secondary school.

- OA1: The number of students at least 1 year overage for their grade.

- OA2: The number of students 2 or more years overage for their grade.

- PTST: The number of students failing at least one test in the state's standardized achievement test battery.

- MOB: A proxy for student mobility; the variable is the number of students taking one or more portions of the state's standardized achievement test battery who have been identified as being continuously enrolled in the district for only 1 or 2 years.

These variables were selected because (a) they were a part of the state's existing data set, and (b) they were conceptually consistent with possible indicators of at-riskness. The correlation matrix for the variables selected for this analysis is shown in Table 6.3.

As can be seen from the matrix, all of the independent variables were highly correlated with the at-risk variable. The correlation with ECON was .9490; with DOUT, .9368; and with LEP, .8978. In addition, there was high correlation among the independent variables. Thus any predictive model would have the difficulty of multicollinearity. While this does not detract from the overall model performance, it reduces the precision of the individual coefficient. As a result, any weights given to specific variables within a formula for the index would have to be viewed with caution. Since the total number of at-risk students was known for the total population, several regression models were explored. The best predictive formula when compared with the actual number of reported at-risk students was based on a model with the following independent variables: ECON, MOB, LEP, and PTST (test performance). The results of the stepwise regression are shown in Table 6.4. The variables have been ranked in their

Table 6.3 Pearson Correlation Coefficient Matrix for Socioeconomic and
School Independent Variables and the Dependent Variable:
Number of At-Risk Youth for Texas School Districts
(1,053 cases)

Variable	RISK	ECON	DOUT	MOB	LEP	OA2	PTST	OA1
RISK	1.0000							
ECON	.9490	1.0000						
DOUT	.9368	.9349	1.0000					
MOB	.7689	.7223	.6990	1.0000				
LEP	.8978	.9323	.8951	.6198	1.0000			
OA2	.7565	.7512	.7176	.7069	.6997	1.0000		
PTST	.8375	.8153	.7939	.8943	.7414	.6839	1.0000	
OA1	.9034	.9336	.9062	.7108	.8925	.5790	.8666	1.000

order of contribution; the cumulative magnitude of the contribution
of each variable is identified in the right-hand column. Beta weights
are shown in the second column.

This set of independent variables explained 92% of the variance in
the number of reported at-risk youth among the 1,053 Texas school
districts used in this sample. Using the R^2 from the uncontrolled
stepwise regression, the number of economically disadvantaged
(ECON) explained 90% of the variance in the number of at-risk youth.
The addition of MOB into the regression explained an additional 1.5%
of the variance. The number of LEP students and number of students
failing a standardized achievement test (PTST) explained an additional .44% of the variance.

Using the beta weights from the regression, a predictive equation
was developed as follows:

Predicted Number at Risk = (ECON) × .3707 + (MOB) × 1.3839
+ (LEP) × .3260 + (PTST) × .1033 + 2.2767 (constant)

Using the results of the predictive equation from this regression,
two different types of analysis were used in evaluating the efficacy of
this calculation as an index of need that might be used in a state
funding formula. In the first analysis, using standardized scores, the
results of the standardized residual indicated that 72 of the cases were
within ±.25 standard deviation; 90% of the cases were within ±1.00

Table 6.4 Socioeconomic and School Independent Variables Regressed on the Independent Variable: Number of At-Risk Youth for Texas School Districts (1,053 cases)

Variable	R^2	Beta
ECON	.9490	.3707
MOB	.0146	1.3839
LEP	.0040	.3260
PTST	.0004	.1033
Constant	2.2767	
R^2 .9196		
Adjusted R^2 .9192		

standard deviations. The second analysis, the public policy funding impact of the index, showed that, comparing the predicted number of at-risk students with the actual number of at-risk students, the predicted number would have been within ±30% of the actual number in 41.4% of the school districts with 67.2% of the reported at-risk students.

Since the ECON variable alone accounted for 90% of the variance for at-risk students in the Texas data, a case can be made for using it in a single-indicator index of need. However, there may be situations in which multiple factors may be preferred over a single measure because of (a) the range in conditions that contribute to the problem, (b) the potential inaccuracies resulting from reliance on a single measure, (c) the potential credibility concerns resulting from reliance on a single measure, (d) the importance of selecting variables that cannot be easily manipulated to benefit the recipient district, and/or (e) the stability in funding provided by multiple factors. Another issue in developing an index has to do with policymakers' decisions about an acceptable tolerance level of predictive accuracy for allocation of funds.

Given the dearth of program evaluation data and cost-effectiveness studies, the variations in the target groups and programs, and the impact analysis of various funding options, the traditional state funding options of categorical programs and per pupil weights do not seem appropriate methods for states to use in funding programs for at-risk populations.

The index of need option provides a funding method that results in funds going to the districts with the greatest incidence of at-risk youth and permits local districts to develop innovative and unique programs without having to label the target group of students. However, as stated earlier, each state should carefully select its variables for the index of need to ensure that the index is an adequate indicator of at-risk conditions and that the resulting effects on students, programs, and school districts will be consistent with accepted criteria for an allocation system.

References

Arizona Department of Education. (1989). *The "at-risk" status of Arizona school districts* (Ed. STAT Report). Phoenix: Author.

Chambers, J. G. (1981). Cost and price level adjustments to state aid for education: A theoretical and empirical review in educational need and fiscal capacity. In K. F. Jordan & N. Cambron-McCabe (Eds.), *Perspectives in state school support programs* (Second Annual Yearbook of the American Education Finance Association, pp. 39-86). Cambridge, MA: Ballinger.

Committee on Economic Development. (1987). *Investing in our children: Business and the public schools.* Washington, DC: Author.

Guthrie, J. W., Garms, W. I., & Pierce, L. C. (1988). *School finance and education policy* (2nd ed.). Englewood Cliffs, NJ: Prentice-Hall.

Hartman, W. T. (1980). Policy effects of special education funding formulas. *Journal of Education Finance, 6,* 135-159.

Hodge, M. V. (1981). Improving finance and governance of education for special populations. In K. F. Jordan & N. Cambron-McCabe (Eds.), *Perspectives in state school support programs* (Second Annual Yearbook of the American Education Finance Association, pp. 3-38). Cambridge, MA: Ballinger.

Jordan, K. F. (1989). *Introduction to school finance.* Unpublished manuscript, Arizona State University, College of Education, Tempe.

Levin, H. M. (1989, Spring). Financing the education of at-risk students. *Education Evaluation and Policy Analysis, 11,* 47-60.

Lyons, T. S. (1990). *Alternative state funding allocation methods for local school district programs to serve "at-risk" students.* Unpublished doctoral dissertation, Arizona State University, Tempe.

McDonough, J. T. (1990). *A survey of opinions and attitudes toward state at-risk program focus, delivery, and funding.* Unpublished doctoral dissertation, Arizona State University, Tempe.

National Governors' Association. (1990). *National education goals.* Washington, DC: Author.

Sherman, J. D. (1987). *Strategies for financing state dropout programs.* Washington, DC: Pelavin Associates.

SEVEN

State Models for Financing Special Education

DEBORAH A. VERSTEGEN

CYNTHIA L. COX

Over time, growing attention has focused on a number of public policy issues related to the state financing of special education (see Crowner, 1985; Gallagher, Forsythe, Ringelheim, & Weintraub, 1975; Geske & Johnston, 1985; Hallahan, Kauffman, Lloyd, & McKinney, 1988; Hartman, 1980; Kakalik, 1979; Kauffman, 1989; McCarthy & Sage, 1982; McQuain, 1984; National Association of State Boards of Education, 1983; Skrtic, 1991; Thomas, 1973). Overall, of interest is the extent to which exceptional students' programmatic needs are linked to financing arrangements and how differences in costs reflect differences in programs and services available to students within and between states (Hartman, 1980, 1988, 1990; National Association of State Boards of Education, 1983; Schorr & Schorr, 1988). Also of interest are the "excess costs," above the cost of regular education, required to educate exceptional students (Chaikind, Danielson, & Brauen, 1992; Moore, Strang, Schwartz, & Braddock, 1988; Moore, Walker, & Holland, 1982), incentives and disincentives of particular special education financing schemes, and how funding streams among education, health, and social services can be integrated on behalf of special education students (U.S. General Accounting Office, 1986).

In this chapter, we discuss these issues in the context of conceptions of equal educational opportunity by providing a brief review of federal special education finance policy; summarizing state funding mechanisms for special education programs, including incentives and disincentives related to each; and reviewing data related to excess costs associated with educating exceptional students.

Special Education Finance Policy

Equal educational opportunity for all children and youth has had a long and tumultuous past and remains an uncertain prospect for the future even at the dawn of the twenty-first century. It was not until 1954 that the U.S. Supreme Court found racially segregated schools unconstitutional. Even so, dismantling the dual system of education, especially in the South, proceeded slowly over the next two decades until given impetus by the passage of the Civil Rights Act in 1964 and the Elementary and Secondary Education Act (ESEA) in 1965. The Civil Rights Act forbade federal aid to educational institutions that discriminated on the basis of race, creed, or national origin. However, at the time the legislation was passed, federal aid to education was marginal at best; withholding it provided only limited sanctions to more recalcitrant governments. The following year, however, passage of the landmark ESEA tripled the federal investment in elementary and secondary education and made schooling for the economically disadvantaged a legitimate national concern. The ESEA and its amendments also provided targeted funds to help educate disabled children through state-maintained schools and for due-process procedures in placement, assessment, and testing.

Yet, by 1970 almost 2 million children with disabilities between the ages of 7 and 17 were not enrolled in school, many excluded by state laws that designated them ineducable or untrainable; others were consigned to institutions offering only custodial care. Often the chief barrier excluding exceptional children from equal education opportunities was the insufficiency of funds to implement special education programs and services (Kakalik, 1979; Thomas, 1973). Prompted by research that showed all children could benefit from an education, and by numerous court cases that found children with disabilities were entitled to receive free public school educations,

Congress in 1975 passed the Education for All Handicapped Children Act (recently renamed the Individuals with Disabilities Education Act, IDEA). This legislation benefited children and youth with disabilities through its requirements for (a) the availability of free, appropriate special education programming to children, ages 3-21 (inclusive); (b) fairness and appropriateness in decision making about providing special education to these children; (c) clear management and auditing requirements and procedures regarding special education at all levels of government; and (d) the use of federal funds to assist state and local government efforts financially to provide special education services. Although federal aid never reached projected levels, funding was authorized under the act based on each state's number of children with disabilities who received special education, adjusted by a percentage of the national average per pupil expenditure—5% in 1978, 10% in 1979, 20% in 1980, 30% in 1981, and 40% in 1982 and each succeeding year ("Aid to Education," 1976).

In 1986 the Education for All Handicapped Act Amendments (P.L. 99-457) established an optional state grant program for children from birth through 2 years and required services for children 3 through 5 years old who were developmentally delayed, had conditions that may result in delay, or were at risk of substantial developmental delay (see Anthony & Jones, 1990).

State Assistance
for Special Education

In addition to federal assistance for special education, substantial authority and control in this area have historically been entrusted to local governments. Yet the events of the last two decades reflect a greatly augmented state role in financing, developing, and maintaining programs for special education students. For example: (a) State governments are responsible for administering federally funded special education programs; (b) states determine education policy, operation procedures, teacher certification requirements, and classifications of special education children; and (c) states provide financial aid and implement various funding mechanisms to distribute aid to localities to support the complex educational needs of exceptional students. Although all states currently provide public school programs for special education students, the specific services, levels of aid, and funding mechanisms vary greatly across the country.

Financing of Special Education

Revenue for special education is derived from federal, state, and local sources, reflecting the multilevel education finance and policy system in the United States. In FY 1987, total special education funding from all sources was estimated at $17.4 billion and constituted 10.7% of total revenue for public elementary and secondary schools.[1] Special education finances supported supplementary programs and services for nearly 11% of the elementary and secondary student population, or 4.4 million special education students. More than half of all special education funds were derived from state sources (56%), with localities contributing more than one-third of funding (36.5%) and the federal government providing less than 10% (7.5%). This compares with the federal, state, and local shares for education spending of 6.2%, 50.1%, and 43.7%, respectively. These averages mask considerable variation among states, however. Table 7.1 compares federal, state, and local revenue for special education and total aid by state. It shows:

- In 9 states, localities provide less than 5% of special education funding.
- In 14 states, localities provide nearly 50% of special education support or more.
- In 7 states, almost 15% of special education aid comes from the federal government.
- In 4 states, the state provides almost 90% of special education aid.

The average additional cost for providing programs and services for special education students beyond the regular program cost across all states—that is, the excess cost associated with special education—was $3,982 per pupil in FY 1987, compared with $3,649 per pupil in 1985-86 (Moore et al., 1988). In addition, dollars spent on special education students derived from regular education finances were estimated at $2,686 for the 1985-86 school year, totaling $6,335 per exceptional student from regular and special education revenue. Expressed as a cost ratio, the total cost of special education was 2.3 times

Table 7.1 State Financing for Public School Special Education and Total Education, School Year 1986-87

	Financing for Special Education[a]				Financing for Elementary and Secondary Education			
	Total Aid[b]	% Federal of Total	% State of Total	% Local of Total	Total Aid[b]	% Federal of Total	% State of Total	% Local of Total
Total	*17,389,021*	*7.5*	*56.0*	*36.5*	*160,498,202*	*6.2*	*50.1*	*43.7*
Alabama	224,947	9.6	87.5	2.8	1,823,200	13.1	69.4	17.5
Alaska	106,306	9.3	68.7	22.0	907,043	5.0	77.4	17.6
Arizona	171,386	11.4	47.0	41.5	1,515,000	8.4	65.0	26.6
Arkansas	75,590	16.2	54.9	28.9	1,248,638	9.2	63.5	27.3
California	1,641,621	6.1	78.3	15.7	17,769,331	7.3	68.5	24.2
Colorado	211,134	7.2	42.4	50.4	2,544,881	4.4	39.2	56.5
Connecticut	332,347	5.2	42.6	52.3	2,647,200	4.4	40.4	55.3
Delaware	51,458	12.9	62.7	24.4	450,758	8.0	68.8	23.3
Florida	659,151	5.9	60.1	33.9	6,692,075	7.4	53.2	39.5
Georgia	314,092	9.9	68.2	21.9	3,355,100	8.0	56.5	35.5
Hawaii	77,408	5.7	94.3	0.0	706,700	8.2	91.7	0.1
Idaho	49,543	9.2	90.8	0.0	562,515	7.1	60.8	32.0
Illinois	1,390,849	7.5	42.2	50.3	7,416,204	7.4	40.3	52.3
Indiana	223,311	15.1	49.3	35.6	3,616,127	3.7	58.9	37.4
Iowa	183,350	7.3	74.2	18.5	1,767,718	5.6	43.1	54.9
Kansas	166,926	6.4	45.8	47.8	1,690,826	4.9	43.3	51.7
Kentucky	189,999	11.9	70.5	17.6	1,946,600	10.9	69.4	19.6
Louisiana	251,330	5.8	70.6	23.6	2,620,080	10.9	53.2	35.9
Maine	67,165	12.6	50.4	37.0	754,983	7.1	51.3	41.5
Maryland	327,250	7.8	41.3	50.9	3,164,400	5.3	39.3	55.4
Massachusetts	598,949	7.1	44.9	48.0	3,841,002	5.6	44.9	49.5

Michigan	524,288	9.6	22.6	67.7	6,570,139	3.5	33.9	62.6
Minnesota	272,436	7.3	58.6	34.1	3,090,600	4.1	57.5	38.4
Mississippi	103,644	15.0	79.5	5.5	1,275,000	16.5	54.9	28.6
Missouri	268,888	9.0	91.0	0.0	2,765,709	5.8	40.2	54.0
Montana	37,499	10.3	72.4	17.3	678,896	7.8	49.1	43.1
Nebraska	86,269	9.1	65.1	25.8	910,023	5.4	27.3	67.2
Nevada	73,429	5.1	57.2	37.7	566,186	4.5	42.2	53.3
New Hampshire	71,893	6.3	13.8	79.9	600,723	3.5	6.4	90.2
New Jersey	429,234	11.2	83.9	4.9	6,849,500	3.9	42.9	53.2
New Mexico	117,945	8.5	90.9	0.5	983,889	10.5	77.7	11.8
New York	3,109,400	3.1	40.8	56.1	15,102,600	4.5	43.7	51.7
North Carolina	259,635	13.0	74.9	12.2	3,557,409	6.6	63.6	29.7
North Dakota	38,444	8.3	30.8	61.0	398,274	8.0	53.6	38.4
Ohio	1,090,520	5.3	62.8	31.9	6,660,000	4.8	46.5	48.6
Oklahoma	335,726	9.2	88.1	2.7	1,665,000	5.4	66.1	28.5
Oregon	189,847	8.7	17.1	74.2	1,837,300	5.6	27.8	66.6
Pennsylvania	587,077	13.3	59.5	27.2	8,289,700	4.3	45.7	50.0
Rhode Island	93,237	6.1	93.9	0.0	575,647	4.2	38.8	57.0
South Carolina	140,427	15.8	57.6	26.6	1,936,200	9.5	58.5	32.0
South Dakota	36,062	8.0	12.0	80.0	417,000	10.8	26.9	62.4
Tennessee	152,713	16.6	68.2	15.1	2,320,107	10.4	50.4	39.2
Texas	739,411	10.7	55.1	34.2	12,479,975	6.7	45.8	47.5
Utah	78,467	14.4	83.5	2.1	1,154,327	5.7	55.5	38.8
Vermont	40,410	9.0	44.2	46.8	379,040	6.3	36.4	57.3
Virginia	316,974	8.3	17.9	73.9	3,870,134	5.5	34.0	60.6
Washington	280,929	5.7	70.2	24.1	3,128,042	5.7	74.1	20.2
West Virginia	101,249	14.7	71.4	14.0	1,210,241	8.9	64.5	26.6
Wisconsin	438,875	6.4	52.9	40.7	3,463,340	5.3	34.3	60.4
Wyoming	59,982	5.6	80.2	14.2	722,820	2.6	41.1	56.3

SOURCE: Data are from U.S. Department of Education (selected years) and National Education Association (selected years). Calculations performed by D. Verstegen.

the cost of regular education (Moore et al., 1988). Research has consistently shown that the average additional cost for providing programs and services for special education students, beyond the regular program cost—that is, the "excess cost" associated with special education—is about twice that for other students (Chaikind et al., 1992; Kakalik, Furry, Thomas, & Carney, 1981; Raphael, Singer, & Walker, 1985; Rossmiller, Hale, & Frohreich, 1970; Singer & Butler, 1987). Substantial differences exist between and within states not only in spending on special education and the size of the identified special education population as a percentage of total enrollment, but also in spending among exceptionalities and instructional arrangements. For example, states provided special education services for between 6.23% (Oregon) and 17% (Massachusetts) of their public elementary and secondary school populations in FY 1987. At one extreme, $1,568 per pupil (across all exceptionalities) was spent for the "excess costs" of special education in Arkansas; at the other, $10,613 was spent per pupil in New York.

Chaikind et al. (1992) report that the average total per pupil expenditures for special education in different instructional arrangements vary more than 10-fold: from $2,463 for students receiving services in resource rooms to $29,108 for students in residential programs. Cost differences among disabilities vary by 400%, from more than $31,000 for students with deafness/blindness to less than $800 for students with speech disabilities. Generally low-incidence disabilities result in higher costs than do high-incidence disabilities; more restrictive instructional settings with additional resource personnel and materials result in higher costs than do less restrictive settings (Chaikind et al., 1992). Table 7.2 compares special education funding and populations by state and as a percentage of total funding and enrollment.

Special Education Finance Formulas

States distribute funding for special education services through four broad approaches: pupil weighting schemes, instructional unit methods, excess cost/percentage reimbursement formulas, and other approaches, including flat grants, full state funding, and combinations of approaches (see Verstegen, 1988; see also Anthony & Jones, 1990; Burrello & Sage, 1979; Crowner, 1985; Moore et al., 1982;

Table 7.2 Comparisons: State Special Education Population and Funding
to Total Regular Education Population and Funding,
School Year 1986-87

	Financing for Special Education			Special Education Population		
	Dollars per Pupil[a]	% Special of Total[b]	State Rank	Pupils per State[a]	% Special of Total[c]	State Rank
Average	**3,982**	**10.66**	—	**4,366,524**	**10.92**	—
Alabama	2,466	12.34	9	1,321	12.43	12
Alaska	8,706	11.72	12	12,211	11.06	27
Arizona	3,220	11.31	14	53,219	8.66	48
Arkansas	1,568	6.05	48	48,222	11.02	28
California	4,196	9.24	33	391,217	9.01	44
Colorado	4,264	8.30	38	49,515	8.87	45
Connecticut	5,132	12.55	8	64,758	13.72	6
Delaware	3,369	11.42	13	15,275	16.18	2
Florida	3,629	9.85	26	181,651	11.30	22
Georgia	3,369	9.36	32	93,229	8.74	47
Hawaii	6,640	10.95	15	11,658	7.09	49
Idaho	2,658	8.81	36	18,640	8.82	46
Illinois	5,604	18.75	3	248,169	13.79	5
Indiana	2,107	6.18	47	105,978	11.00	29
Iowa	3,262	10.37	22	56,205	11.68	17
Kansas	3,939	9.87	25	42,373	10.16	35
Kentucky	2,578	9.76	27	73,711	11.47	19
Louisiana	3,403	9.59	30	73,852	9.30	41
Maine	2,502	8.90	34	26,841	12.75	9
Maryland	3,624	10.34	23	90,294	13.36	8
Massachusetts	4,170	15.59	6	143,636	17.07	1
Michigan	3,247	7.98	40	161,446	9.63	39
Minnesota	3,306	8.81	35	82,407	11.61	18
Mississippi	1,861	8.13	39	55,683	11.17	24
Missouri	1,697	9.72	28	99,962	12.45	11
Montana	2,440	5.52	50	15,369	10.04	36
Nebraska	2,859	9.48	31	30,171	11.32	20
Nevada	4,981	12.97	7	14,743	9.15	43
New Hampshire	4,404	11.97	11	16,323	12.17	14
New Jersey	2,495	6.27	46	172,018	15.53	3
New Mexico	3,956	11.99	10	29,816	11.09	26
New York	10,613	20.59	1	292,981	11.31	21

(Continued)

Table 7.2 (Continued)

	Financing for Special Education			Special Education Population		
	Dollars per Pupil[a]	% Special of Total[b]	State Rank	Pupils per State[a]	% Special of Total[c]	State Rank
North Carolina	2,377	7.30	41	109,214	10.01	37
North Dakota	3,131	9.65	29	12,279	10.38	33
Ohio	5,474	16.37	4	199,211	11.12	25
Oklahoma	5,142	20.16	2	65,285	10.82	30
Oregon	3,998	10.33	24	47,487	6.23	50
Pennsylvania	2,888	7.08	43	203,258	12.25	13
Rhode Island	4,775	16.20	5	19,527	14.56	4
South Carolina	1,916	7.25	42	73,299	12.00	15
South Dakota	2,570	8.65	37	14,034	11.26	23
Tennessee	1,584	6.58	45	96,433	11.71	16
Texas	2,455	5.92	49	301,222	9.39	40
Utah	1,833	6.80	44	42,811	10.29	34
Vermont	3,543	10.66	16	11,405	12.64	10
Virginia	3,056	8.19	17	103,727	10.64	32
Washington	3,997	8.98	18	70,282	9.23	42
West Virginia	2,129	8.37	19	47,556	13.52	7
Wisconsin	5,770	12.67	20	76,067	9.91	38
Wyoming	5,507	8.30	21	10,893	10.79	31

SOURCE: Data are from U.S. Department of Education (selected years) and National Education Association (selected years). Calculations performed by D. Verstegen.
a. Chapter 1 of ECIA (SOP), and EHA-B.
b. Total school aid, all sources.
c. K-12 school enrollment.

Thomas, 1973).[2] State finance formulas for distributing special education funding to localities are shown in Table 7.3; Table 7.4 describes these programs by state. They are summarized and discussed further below. As can be seen in the tables:

- In 18 states, some form of pupil weighting scheme is used in funding special education programs.
- In 8 states, some type of instructional unit method is used in funding special education programs.
- In 15 states, excess cost or percentage reimbursement schedules are used in funding special education programs.

• In 10 states, flat grants, full state funding schemes, or a combination of funding approaches are used in funding special education programs.

Pupil Weighting Schemes

Pupil weighting schemes provide additional funding beyond that provided for regular education programs to compensate schools/ school districts for the excess costs associated with educating exceptional students. The amount of money afforded each pupil in a regular school program determines the base funding amount, which is given a weight of 1.00. The base amount is then adjusted by an additional differential or "weight" that typically varies across special education programs according to disability, instructional service arrangements, or both. This translates into more dollars spent on the special needs student, such that a weight of 1.5 provides 50% more funding for an exceptional student than is spent on a student in the regular education program. Designated weighting units theoretically reflect the service cost ratio of furnishing a basic special education program to that of providing a basic regular education program. Kakalik (1979) defines weighting schemes as follows: "The local district is reimbursed for each handicapped child served on the basis of a multiple of regular per pupil expenditures, which may vary according to the type of educational placement or type of disability" (p. 217).

The two types of weighting schemes most utilized across the states are those based on students' disabling conditions and those based on the instructional arrangement utilized to deliver services to exceptional students. These are outlined in Table 7.5.

Pupil weighting schemes that designate allocations by disability classify students and provide funds according to specific exceptionalities (e.g., mental retardation, hearing impairment, learning disability, emotional disability). Weighting schemes that allocate funds by instructional arrangement organize special education services and distribute funds according to types or levels of classroom or program services required to meet the special needs of each student (e.g., itinerant, resource, self-contained). Generally, weights are based on permissible pupil/teacher ratios necessary to generate one classroom unit.

Text continued on page 157

Table 7.3 State Models for Financing Special Education

State	Pupil Weighting		Instructional Unit		Cost/Reimbursement		Other		
	Handicapping Condition	Instructional Arrangement	Single Unit	May Vary by Category	Excess Cost	Percentage Reimbursement	Full State	Flat Grant	Combination
Alabama				X					
Alaska				X					
Arizona	X								
Arkansas		X		X					
California				X					
Colorado					X				
Connecticut						X			
Delaware	X								
Florida	X								
Georgia	X								
Hawaii							X		
Idaho									X
Illinois									X
Indiana	X								
Iowa		X							
Kansas				X					
Kentucky				X					
Louisiana				X					
Maine						X			
Maryland					X				
Massachusetts			X						

State									
Michigan						X			
Minnesota						X			
Mississippi									
Missouri				X					
Montana									
Nebraska	X								
Nevada								X	X
New Hampshire		X							
New Jersey	X	X							
New Mexico		X							
New York								X	X
North Carolina									
North Dakota					X				
Ohio									X
Oklahoma	X								
Oregon					X				
Pennsylvania					X				
Rhode Island					X				
South Carolina	X								
South Dakota				X					
Tennessee		X							
Texas		X							
Utah		X							
Vermont								X	X
Virginia	X								
Washington									X
West Virginia									X
Wisconsin						X			
Wyoming						X			
Total	10	7	1	8	6	8	1	3	6

147

Table 7.4 Interstate Financing Arrangements for Special Education

State	Special Education
Alabama	Not available.
Alaska	The costs of services for exceptional pupils are included in basic state support.
Arizona	Nine weighted categories.
Arkansas	Seven weighted categories.
California	The Master Plan for Special Education provides funding for instructional personnel service units, support services, and (where applicable) nonpublic, nonsectarian schooling sufficient to provide special education services for approximately 10% of the total student population.
Colorado	The state reimburses for excess costs of special education programs. Maximum reimbursement is 80%. The prorated payment is about 44% of excess costs.
Connecticut	State support is based on district wealth as defined in the GTB formula. Aid ranges from 30% of reimbursable costs for wealthiest district to 70% of reimbursable costs for poorest districts.
Delaware	Units for 12 categories are provided, ranging in size from 4 pupils per unit to 15 pupils per unit.
Florida	Of the 53 weighted categories in the foundation program, 15 are for exceptional pupils.
Georgia	Four weighted categories for special education.
Hawaii	Full state funding.
Idaho	A total of 80% of ancillary salaries (special education teachers, psychologists, psychological examiners, therapists) is provided. Additional support units are provided in foundation program.
Illinois	Flat grant of $8,000 per certified special education employee and $2,800 per approved noncertified employee is provided. Excess costs for pupils with severe disabilities in district-operated programs are added up to a maximum of $2,000 greater than a district's regular pupil per capita cost.
Indiana	Thirteen weighted categories in foundation program.

(Continued)

Table 7.4 (Continued)

State	Special Education
Iowa	Three weighted categories are provided for special education pupils.
Kansas	A total of 80% of special education transportation and costs is provided; $14,069 in categorical aid per instructional unit is also provided.
Kentucky	Extra classroom units are allotted per approved teacher, not to exceed the total provided in the biennial budget. For each unit allocated, 7.2 ADA deducted from basic allocation.
Louisiana	Additional instructional units are provided for 18 program categories. This includes funding for assessment teachers, school psychologists, school social workers, and other certified personnel.
Maine	In FY 1987-1988, 106% of base year costs were allocated.
Maryland	Excess cost reimbursement for special education pupils.
Massachusetts	Three pupil weighted categories are included in the foundation program.
Michigan	Districts may be reimbursed for up to 75% of added costs for most programs, subject to a capped appropriation, and 100% for certain programs.
Minnesota	State categorical aid is provided for 66% of the salary of essential personnel, not to exceed $18,400 per FTE staff person, and for 47% of expenditures for special supplies and equipment, not to exceed $47 per disabled child.
Mississippi	Instructional unit add-on for approved class.
Missouri	Reimbursement of $13,989 per approved instructional unit of special education.
Montana	Allowable costs associated with special education programs are fully reimbursed.
Nebraska	Gifted pupils receive an additional weighting of 25% of basic needs by grade level (districts qualifying for equalization aid).

(Continued)

Table 7.4 (Continued)

State	Special Education
Nevada	For 1987-88, districts receive one unit of special education support ($24,000) for every 150 pupils enrolled in the district.
New Hampshire	Five weighted categories for special education.
New Jersey	Weighted pupils (13 categories) times the state average net current expense per pupil.
New Mexico	Four weighted categories included in the foundation program.
New York	Aid for special education pupils equals weighted resident pupils multiplied by district-approved operating expense per pupil, but not less than $2,000 or more than $4,200, multiplied by district excess cost aid ratio. Aid is in addition to aid for operating expense.
North Carolina	State allocated aid for students with disabilities on the lesser of June 1 head count or 12.5% of total prior year ADM.
North Dakota	Districts are reimbursed: the excess over 2.5 times the state average cost per pupil for students placed out-of-district for services; 60% of the excess student transportation costs; 80% of boarding care costs; and varying rates for staff and contracted services per fee schedule.
Ohio	A flat grant of $7,400 per instructional unit plus salary (115% of state minimum salary schedule) is awarded for special education and $8,650 salary for vocational education units; $1,525 per unit plus 115% salary allowance awarded for special education support personnel and programs for gifted pupils. Districts receive mileage or per pupil transportation grants. Partial cost reimbursement for home instruction, teacher training, or special instructional services for students with physical or emotional disabilities.
Oklahoma	Twelve weighted categories included in foundation program.
Oregon	Reimbursement up to 30% of excess cost or pro rata share (currently about 11%).
Pennsylvania	Reimbursement of 100% of approved excess cost of pupils in district or intermediate unit-operated special classes; 80% of tuition and maintenance cost for pupils assigned to approved private schools for students with physical, emotional, or cognitive disabilities.

(Continued)

Table 7.4 (Continued)

State	Special Education
Rhode Island	Formula for special education provides excess cost aid.
South Carolina	Disabled children are weighted according to nine specific classifications.
South Dakota	Reimbursement of 100% for students with severe and profound disabilities; 50% on other allowable costs.
Tennessee	Identified and served disabled students receive additional weighting in determining pupil counts.
Texas	For the portion of the day students are served in approved programs, the adjusted allotment is multiplied by a weight varying from 2.0 to 10.0 depending on the instructional arrangement used. Twelve weighted categories included in foundation program.
Utah	Foundation program provides weighted categories for disabled students according to five levels.
Vermont	The state funds 75% of actual salaries of an approved number of mainstream special education positions. Also, 100% forward funding is provided for designated special education programs and residential placements, with the district of legal residence reimbursing the state for actual costs or district's average per pupil costs, whichever is lower.
Virginia	Additional state funds are provided for special, vocational, and adult education programs.
Washington	A program for highly capable students is funded in an amount equal to 1% of the school district enrollment multiplied by $344.23.
West Virginia	General aid formula weights special education pupils 3.0. Additional funds are provided for teaching personnel, facilities, and transportation.
Wisconsin	State reimburses 63% of approved costs for education and 100% of room and board for intradistrict transfer pupils and 51% for school psychologists and social workers.
Wyoming	Not available.

SOURCE: Verstegen (1988).

Table 7.5 States With Pupil Weights for Special Education Programs, 1987-88[a]

State	Categories		Weight
Arizona	hearing handicapped		2.312
	multiple handicapped/resource		.762
	multiple handicapped/self-contained		2.368
	physically handicapped/resource		.603
	physically handicapped/self-contained		2.648
	trainable mentally handicapped		2.042
	visually handicapped		2.900
	multiple handicapped (severe sensory impaired)		4.000
	severely emotionally handicapped		1.500
Arkansas	itinerant		.40
	resource room		.85
	self-contained		.70
	self-contained		1.10
	special school, day		2.35
	special school, residential		3.10
	gifted/talented		.25
Connecticut	30-70% of reimbursable costs one year prior, inversely related to district wealth		
Delaware	educable mentally handicapped	15 pupils	1.27
	socially/emotionally maladjusted	10 pupils	1.90
	partially sighted	10 pupils	1.90
	intensive learning center pupil	8.6 pupils	2.21
	learning disabled	8 pupils	2.38
	blind	8 pupils	2.38
	trainable mentally handicapped	6 pupils	3.17
	severely mentally handicapped	6 pupils	3.17
	hearing impaired	6 pupils	3.17
	orthopedically handicapped	6 pupils	3.17
	autistic	4 pupils	4.75
	deaf/blind	4 pupils	4.75
Florida	educable mentally handicapped		2.188
	trainable mentally handicapped		2.982
	physically handicapped		3.821
	physical and occupational therapy (part-time)		8.003
	speech and hearing therapy (part-time)		5.966
	speech, language and hearing therapy		3.700
	visually handicapped (part-time)		13.896
	visually handicapped		4.957

(Continued)

Table 7.5 (Continued)

State	Categories	Weight
Florida	emotionally disturbed (part-time)	4.058
(Continued)	emotionally disturbed	2.931
	specific learning disability (part-time)	3.506
	specific learning disability	2.272
	gifted (part-tlme)	2.104
	hospital and homebound (part-time)	9.965
	profoundly handicapped	4.429
Georgia	resource, mildly handicapped	2.415
	resource, moderately handicapped	2.872
	self-contained, moderately handicapped	3.628
	self-contained, severely handicapped	5.735
	gifted	1.775
Idaho	all handicapped categories	1.45
	80% state aid for personnel who work with special needs students	
Indiana	multiple handicapped	2.37
	physically handicapped	2.04
	visually handicapped	2.70
	hearing impaired	2.73
	emotionally disturbed (full-time, self-contained class)	2.52
	emotionally disturbed (all others)	.94
	neurologically impaired/learning disabled (full-time, self-contained)	1.59
	neurologically impaired/learning disabled (all others)	.94
	communication handicapped	.19
	educable mentally retarded	1.20
	trainable mentally retarded	1.51
	severely and profoundly mentally retarded	2.37
	homebound (two counts: [1] as of count day, [2] from day after count day of prior year to end of prior school year)	.57
Iowa	special adaptations for regular classroom instruction/handicapped pupils in special education class receiving part of instruction in regular class	1.70
	full-time, self-contained handicapped	2.20
	severely handicapped, multiple handicapped, chronically disruptive	3.60

(Continued)

Table 7.5 (Continued)

State	Categories	Weight
Massachusetts[a]	special needs programs (including regular education programs with modifications, regular education with no more than 25% time out, regular education with no more than 60% time out, substantially separate, home and hospital, day program prototypes)	4.00
Montana	salaries and benefits of special program teachers, aides, supervisors, audiologists and speech and hearing clinicians, and support staff based on FTE in special education; total costs of teaching supplies, contracted services, transportation for personnel (calculated on the same mileage rate for other travel reimbursement), and buses, used for the special education program; if total costs of program exceed legislative appropriations, each district receives a pro rata reduction based on prioritized budget items established by the superintendent of public instruction	
Nebraska	not reported	
New Hampshire	within-district self-contained classroom	2.57
	within-district mainstreamed	2.12
	out-of-district day placement	7.08
	residential placement	8.72
	preschool day placement	3.37
New Jersey	pupil weights for following categories (weights are for the 1987-88 year; weights adjusted annually):	
	educable mentally retarded	.43
	trainable mentally retarded	.78
	visually handicapped	1.27
	auditorily handicapped	1.62
	communication handicapped	.69
	neurologically impaired	.56
	perceptually impaired	.24
	orthopedically handicapped	1.73
	chronically ill	.57
	emotionally disturbed	.78
	socially maladjusted	.42
	multiple handicapped	1.03
	preschool handicapped	.21

(Continued)

Table 7.5 (Continued)

State	Categories	Weight
New Mexico	Class A programs: specially trained teacher travels from class to class or school to school to assist teachers and students on a part-time basis[b]	20.00
	Class B programs: specially trained teacher operates a resource room[b]	20.00
	Class C programs: special classroom instruction for moderately handicapped and gifted	1.90
	Class D programs: full-time special classroom instruction for severely handicapped students and 3-4-year-old handicapped	3.50
New York	pupils with handicapping conditions in special class 60% or more of the school day in either public school or BOCES Program	1.7
	pupils with handicapping conditions in special class 20% or more of the school week	.9
	pupils with handicapping conditions in special class at least two periods per week	.13
	weightings are for resident pupils; aid under the excess cost aid formula is in addition to aid for pupil attendance being included in the district's regular operating aid	
Oklahoma	vision impaired	3.80
	learning disabilities	.40
	hearing impaired	2.90
	educable mentally handicapped	1.30
	emotionally disturbed	2.50
	multiple handicapped	2.40
	physically handicapped	1.20
	speech impaired	.05
	trainable mentally handicapped	1.30
	gifted and talented	.34
	deaf and blind	3.80
	special education summer program	1.20
	bilingual	.25

(Continued)

Table 7.5 (Continued)

State	Categories	Weight
South Carolina	educable mentally handicapped	1.74
	learning disabilities	1.74
	trainable mentally handicapped	2.04
	emotionally handicapped	2.04
	orthopedically handicapped	2.04
	visually handicapped	2.57
	hearing handicapped	2.57
	speech handicapped	1.90
	homebound	2.10
Tennessee	support services	.374
	consulting	.509
	special education teacher, regular classroom	1.069
	itinerant speech therapy	.330
	resource room	1.027
	outside services	.374
	compensatory development class	4.606
	special day program	6.352
	residential facility	18.732
	home and hospital institutions	2.736
Texas	homebound	5.0
	hospital class	5.0
	speech therapy	10.0
	resource room	2.7
	self-contained, mild and moderate, regular campus	2.3
	self-contained, severe, regular campus	3.5
	self-contained, separate campus	2.7
	multidistrict class	3.5
	nonpublic day school	3.5
	vocational adjustment class	2.3
	community class	3.5
	self-contained, pregnant	2.0
Utah	handicapped pupils assigned to one of five levels for funding purposes; levels assigned are determined by a formula that considers number of hours pupil receives special education, number of handicapped pupils in class, number of teachers and aides	

(Continued)

Table 7.5 (Continued)

State	Categories	Weight	
Utah (Continued)		*Regular Classroom*	*Self-Contained Classroom*
	Level I	.60	1.60
	Level II	1.10	2.10
	Level III	2.40	3.40
	Level IV	3.00	4.00
	Level V	5.20	6.20
Virginia	not reported		
West Virginia	handicapped additional funds provided for teaching personnel, facilities, and transportation	3.0	

SOURCE: Verstegen (1988).
NOTE: Other financing arrangements are also included for some states. Data reported are from state departments of education.
a. Pupil count is FTE. A pupil who is enrolled in multiple programs that are conducted simultaneously and are therefore consolidated into one program is counted as one FTE pupil in the program that carries the highest weight.
b. Weighted classroom units.

In addition, several states provide additional assistance for the excess cost of meeting the needs of exceptional students through weighting schemes that vary by intensity of service—in essence, providing additional assistance based on needs but without labels or prespecified service delivery schemes. In the few instances where this approach is utilized, service intensity is designated by levels— for example, 1 through 4—with need and cost increasing with each successive level.

Of the 18 states that employ some type of weighting scheme to apportion funds for special education, 10 emphasize disabling condition and 8 emphasize instructional unit arrangements. However, some of these states utilize both instructional arrangement and disability in their weighting schemes. For example, 7 states incorporate both disability and instructional arrangement components. Of the 7 states that use combination weighting schemes, 5 emphasize disability and 2 emphasize instructional arrangement. Utah combines these components into a matrix, providing consideration of both the severity of the exceptionality and the servicing arrangement; Massachusetts provides "prototypes" that base assistance on "time out" of the regular classroom setting. In essence, these states attempt to provide for student needs through designated levels of servicing requirements without prespecification. Additionally, 3 states use a single weight for all exceptional students.

Instructional Unit Schemes

Instructional unit funding methods provide state money based on personnel service units and support services required. States that utilize this funding method allocate a dollar amount per special education teacher or classroom consigned to special education instruction. Theoretically, the determining factor for state funding is the level of resources (e.g., teaching staff, support personnel, instructional supplies) necessary to sustain the desired level of special education services. States utilizing this approach usually specify the maximum number of special education students per teacher or classroom unit for different exceptionalities. Thus specific class size requirements and/or minimum teacher salary schedules affect funding per unit. Kakalik (1979) defines these funding formulas as those in which "school districts are reimbursed a fixed sum by the state for each designated unit of classroom instruction (teacher), administration, and/or transportation" (p. 217).

Eight states implement some type of instructional unit funding for special education students. In some cases, states allocate set dollar amounts per instructional unit, while others vary the allocation. For example, Missouri provides $13,989 per approved instructional unit of special education, while Mississippi provides funds on a teacher unit basis, and the amount per teacher ranges between $9,000 and $15,000, depending upon teacher qualifications and years of experience.

Excess Cost/Percentage Reimbursement Schemes

Excess cost/percentage reimbursement formulas reimburse localities with state money for all or part of the costs of educating special education students, which is usually indicated by a specific percentage. States base the reimbursement on the entire cost of special education programs or on some portion of allowable expenditures. Eight states currently use percentage reimbursement funding. Maine allocates 106% of the base year costs; Montana reimburses "allowable costs." Wyoming provides a 95% reimbursement, Wisconsin reimburses 63% of approved program costs, and South Dakota provides 100% reimbursement for the costs of educating students with severe/profound disabilities and 50% cost reimbursement for all other special education students.

When special education support is reimbursed on the increment of the additional cost of special education programs beyond the costs associated with regular education programs, the financing model is usually referred to as *excess costs*. States compute excess costs by calculating special education expenditures and deducting state-defined costs of regular program students. This is typically expressed in terms of average per pupil expenditures. Then the state reimburses the district for all or a portion of the difference, which is the "excess cost." States usually stipulate the level of approved excess cost reimbursement.

Hartman (1990, p. 450) defines excess cost models as based on two alternative conceptualizations:

(1) the total costs to educate a special education student minus the costs to educate a regular student

(2) the supplemental costs for a special education student for services outside the realm of regular education

Ten states provide state reimbursement for the excess cost of special education programs. The excess cost reimbursement ranges from 30% to 100%. Some states reimburse a set amount or the entire cost, while other states vary the ratio for different groups of exceptional students or special programs. For example, Pennsylvania provides 100% reimbursement for approved excess cost of pupils in district or special classes in intermediate units, while Connecticut provides equalization aid for between 30% and 70% of approved expenditures.

Other Approaches:
Full State Funding, Flat Grant, and Combination

Other funding approaches currently exist in the remaining 10 states. Hawaii provides "full" state funding for the cost of educating special education students. This system does not include local supplements. Washington, North Carolina, and Nevada use flat grants that allocate uniform amounts of state dollars per pupil in each special education program. Kakalik (1979) refers to these financing systems as "straight sum" systems, as the "state reimburses local districts a fixed amount of money per handicapped child" (p. 217).

Six states utilize a combination of funding approaches; in three of these states, flat grants are used in conjunction with other approaches. Illinois implements a combination of flat grant and excess cost for "severely/profoundly handicapped" students (with a cap). Minnesota uses a combination of instructional unit (66% of the salary of essential personnel) and partial percentage reimbursement. Ohio uses a combination of instructional unit and partial percentage reimbursement. Vermont employs a percentage reimbursement for some teacher salaries (for those who work with mainstreamed students) and full state funding for designated programs. New York incorporates aid ratios based on property and income wealth in its excess cost aid formulas, with various maximums set for reimbursable expenses. West Virginia provides weights for special program costs conjoined with additional excess costs.

Incentives and disincentives of special education financing arrangements. Special education finance formulas create incentives and disincentives for local program practice that significantly influence school district implementation of state policies for educating exceptional children (see Moore et al., 1982). According to Moore et al. (1982):

Finance formulas are more than a technical computation of state aid. Numerous constraints, regulations, and exceptions concerning the flow and use of state funds usually accompany the technical elements of a formula. Frequently these attachments specify the services, personnel or program arrangements eligible for funding; the class size or special teacher case loads allowed; and the ceilings for particular expenditure categories. In short, a finance formula not only technically computes financial resources available to districts from the state, but also conveys important state policy choices about how handicapped students shall be educated. (p. 77)

Weighted finance systems assume consistency of children's needs and school system costs within single disabilities or instructional arrangements by assigning an average cost per student or teacher unit (see Kakalik, 1979). School systems with high costs (above average) will not be compensated for additional expenditures, creating incentives for underservice and possible inequities of educational opportunity due to differences in local ability to pay for additional uncovered costs. Conversely, districts with low expenditures (below average) will receive more funds than are required, creating incentives for the overidentification of students. Inappropriate placement decisions can also result from variable weighting schemes that assign relatively higher financial values to specific exceptionalities, whereas the utilization of the same factor across all exceptionalities discourages placements in high-cost programs that may not be adequately compensated.

For rural and small districts, special problems associated with financing special education through pupil weighting schemes arise, as they may provide insufficient funds to mount a program or hire a special education teacher in school districts with few students, unless a fixed base cost is incorporated into the scheme. Conversely, in larger school systems, class sizes may be overextended in an effort to achieve maximum economies of scale under schemes that provide additional funds for each additional child. This effect is tempered somewhat with instructional unit financing schemes in which larger increments of students (e.g., 10, 20, 30) are needed for each additional unit of funding (Hartman, 1980).

In general, weighting schemes allow a comprehensive policy approach to special needs financing across all exceptionalities; however, to be effective they require an empirical basis for cost definitions and may encourage labeling of students if funds are based on disabling conditions rather than servicing needs. Weighted approaches, like other schemes, can be allocated through the general finance formula, enhancing intrastate equity.

Reimbursement schemes "offer the least incentive for over-classification, since the percentage formula requires the school district to pay a portion of the increased costs, while the excess cost formula is theoretically fiscally neutral if all additional costs are reimbursed." Funding also can be based on reimbursement of approved program costs, eliminating classification and labeling (Hartman, 1980, p. 149).

Reimbursement schemes (excess cost and percentage reimbursement), unlike weighting plans, allow variations in the costs of providing programs and services for specific exceptionalities across the state, but usually require localities to pay for the programs out of local funds "up front" until such a time as reimbursements occur. Localities with relatively meager ability to raise funds for education will be hampered in their ability to provide appropriate educational services for all children with disabilities under these arrangements. While excess cost formulas can encourage program placements based on a child's needs, because localities are compensated for allowable expenditures, including high-cost programs and services, without constraints—such as specification of allowable expenditures, ceilings, or the requirement that districts pay a percentage of all costs—expenditures can escalate rapidly, requiring enhanced state oversight and district reporting burdens. Overall, these systems required detailed cost accounting. Also, under reimbursement schemes, because funding is based on a percentage of regular program costs, when regular costs are reduced or fail to keep pace with inflation, special reimbursements vary accordingly. As is true with all plans when reimbursement is independent of duration of service, incentives may exist for limited service duration (Kakalik, 1979). Importantly, without attendant audit regulations, no assurances exist that special education allocations will actually reach the child.

Conclusion

While funding formulas transfer resources for special education from one level of government to another and affect local practice, they do not determine the amount of aid that is distributed. The amount of money to be transferred is a product of all of the educational and policy decisions that surround the formula rather than an inherent characteristic of the formula itself (Hartman, 1980). The number of students who will receive services, their range, ages, and prevalence of disability, the level and types of programs provided, and the setting in which services are provided constitute the chief factors that drive special education costs.

In general, the level of funding available for special education can also drive critical programmatic and policy decisions, however. For example, exceptional students may be underserved or unserved when state aid does not match the costs of programs and services (Schorr & Schorr, 1988). Also, failure to account for differences across districts in the ability to raise local funds for special education can result in disparities in the provision of appropriate supplementary educational services across the state for students with disabilities. The equity and adequacy of resources available for financing the excess costs of special education, together with regulations attendant to receipt of the aid, often define programmatic quality and quantity. Thus both the special education finance formula and the level of special education revenue guide and drive the availability of equal educational opportunities for exceptional students and thus remain critical public policy issues not only for children but also for governments. As Hubert Humphrey (1977) admonished in his last speech:

> The moral test of government is how it treats those who are in the dawn of life, the children; those who are in the twilight of life, the aged; and those who are in the shadows of life, the sick, the needy and the handicapped.

Notes

1. Fiscal 1987 is the latest year for which data are available. The source for spending and population data in FY 1987 is U.S. Department of Education (1991). Data are self-reported by states. For a discussion of data limitations and comparisons of data used in major cost studies, see Chaikind et al. (1992).

2. Data are self-reported; additional information was provided by states through written/phone communications.

References

Aid to education of handicapped approved. (1976). *Congressional Quarterly Almanac, 31*, 651-656.

Anthony, P., & Jones, P. R. (1990). Special education funding. In J. Underwood & D. Verstegen (Eds.), *The impacts of litigation and legislation on public school finance: Adequacy. equity, and excellence* (pp. 123-155). New York: Harper & Row.

Burrello, L., & Sage, D. (1979). *Leadership and change in special education.* Englewood Cliffs, NJ: Prentice-Hall.

Chaikind, S., Danielson, L. C., & Brauen, M. L. (1992). *What do we know about the costs of special education? A selected review.* Rockville, MD: Westat Corporation.

Crowner, T. T. (1985). A taxonomy of special education finance. *Exceptional Children, 51*, 503-508.

Gallagher, J. J., Forsythe, P., Ringelheim, D., & Weintraub, F. J. (1975). Funding patterns and labeling. In N. Hobbs (Ed.), *Issues in the classification of children* (Vol. 2). Sacramento: California State Department of Education.

Geske, T. G., & Johnston, M. J. (1985). A new approach to special education finance: The resource cost model. *Planning and Changing, 16*, 105-117.

Hallahan, D., Kauffman, J., Lloyd, J., & McKinney, J. (Eds.). (1988). Regular education initiative [Special issue]. *Journal of Learning Disabilities.*

Hartman, W. (1980, Fall). Policy effects of special education funding formulas. *Journal of Education Finance, 6*, 135-159.

Hartman, W. (1988, March). *Special education funding: Excess costs revisited.* Paper presented at the annual meeting of the American Education Finance Association, Tampa, FL.

Hartman, W. T. (1990). Supplemental/replacement: An alternative approach to excess costs. *Exceptional Children, 56*, 450-459.

Kakalik, J. S. (1979). Issues in the cost and finance of special education. In L. S. Shulman (Ed.), *Review of research in education* (Vol. 7, pp. 195-222). Itasca, IL: American Education Research Association.

Kakalik, J. S., Furry, W. S., Thomas, M. A., & Carney, M. J. (1981, November). *The cost of special education* (Report prepared for the U.S. Department of Education). Santa Monica, CA: RAND Corporation.

Kauffman, J. M. (1989). The regular education initiative as Reagan-Bush policy: A trickle-down theory of education of the hard-to-teach. *Journal of Special Education, 23*, 256-278.

McCarthy, E. F., & Sage, D. D. (1982). State special education fiscal policy: The quest for equity. *Exceptional Children, 48*, 414-419.

McQuain, S. (1984). *An analysis of state special education finance formulas* (Grant No. G008300038). Blacksburg: Virginia Polytechnic Institute and State University. (ERIC Document Reproduction Service No. ED 254 035)

Moore, M. T., Strang, E. W., Schwartz, M., & Braddock, M. (1988). *Patterns in special education service delivery and cost.* Washington, DC: Decision Resources Corporation.

Moore, M. T., Walker, L. J., & Holland, R. P. (1982). *Finetuning special education finance: A guide for state policymakers.* Princeton, NJ: Education Testing Service.

National Association of State Boards of Education. (1983). *Financing free and appropriate public education for handicapped students* (Research & Resources on Special Education,

Issue 3, Report No. EC 170 825). Alexandria, VA: Author. (ERIC Document Reproduction Service No. ED 249 723)

National Education Association. (various years). *Estimates of school statistics.* New Haven, CT: Author.

Raphael, E. S., Singer, J. D., & Walker, D. K. (1985). Per pupil expenditures in special education in three metropolitan school districts. *Journal of Education Finance, 11,* 60-88.

Rossmiller, R. A., Hale, J. A., & Frohreich, L. E. (1970). *Education programs for exceptional children: Resource configuration and costs* (Study No. 2). Madison, WI: National Education Finance Project.

Schorr, L. B., with Schorr, D. (1988). *Within our reach: Breaking the cycle of disadvantage.* Garden City, NY: Doubleday.

Singer, J. D., & Butler, J. A. (1987). The Education of All Handicapped Children Act: Schools as agents of social reform. *Harvard Educational Review, 57,* 125-152.

Skrtic, T. M. (1991). The special education paradox: Equity as the way to excellence. *Harvard Education Review, 61,* 148-205.

Thomas, M. A. (1973). Finance without which there is no special education. *Exceptional Children, 39,* 475-480.

U.S. Department of Education. (various years). *Annual report to Congress on the implementation of the Individuals with Disabilities Act.* Washington, DC: Government Printing Office.

U.S. General Accounting Office. (1986, July). *Special education: Financing health and education services for handicapped children.* Washington, DC: Government Printing Office.

Verstegen, D. (1988). *School finance at a glance.* Denver, CO: Education Commission of the States. (Updated 1990).

EIGHT

Cost Projections for Learning Disabilities

THOMAS GERALD FINLAN

WILLIAM T. HARTMAN

The development of the category of learning disabilities occurred as a result of the realization that a large number of children, despite average to above-average IQ scores, did not seem to profit from academic instruction. Numerous causes have been put forth to explain this "hidden disability" (Kranes, 1980), including genetic factors, prenatal causes, perinatal causes, biological or biochemical causes, environmental causes, developmental causes, and educational causes (Taylor & Sternberg, 1989). None of the suggested theories regarding learning disability (LD) has been confirmed (Coles, 1987), casting doubt on the very existence of the condition (McKnight, 1982).

Even though there is much disagreement about LD, in the seven years following the passage of the Individuals with Disabilities Education Act (IDEA, P.L. 94-142), there was a tremendous increase in the number of LD youngsters identified, while there was a decrease in other exceptionalities, in Chapter 1 educationally disadvantaged students, and in the general school population. The growth in LD can be partially explained by the fact that IDEA originally placed a cap of 2% of total school population as being LD. That cap would have allowed approximately 806,000 students to be identified as LD in 1989. But the cap was lifted in the 1980s, allowing LD to grow from 21% of all children with disabilities in 1976 to 48% in 1989.

As of 1989, there were 2 million identified LD youngsters and a burgeoning body of LD literature, yet the LD controversy continued to grow. The controversy has to do with the lack of a clear definition of LD and an inability to distinguish LD youngsters from those with other conditions, such as mild mental retardation and general underachievement.

The results of this increase in LD youngsters, evident in both national totals and individual state counts, have included substantial impact on the allocation of financial resources and demands for additional funds for students in special education. Approximately $2.1 billion was spent on special education in 1976 (American Association of School Administrators, 1983), whereas $16 billion was spent on special education and related services in 1986, a 663% increase in 10 years, with 92% of the costs borne by state and local agencies. These increases in special education expenditures cannot be accounted for solely by the effects of inflation. From the 1977-78 school year to the 1985-86 school year, in terms of average per pupil expenditures, special education showed a constant dollar increase of 10%, while regular education showed only a 4% increase (Moore, Strang, Schwartz, & Braddock, 1988). It is worth noting that the actual constant dollar expenditures for special education also increased, since the total number of special education youngsters increased during that period while the total school population decreased.

In this chapter, we present the results of a study undertaken to examine the costs of LD programming. This issue is especially important because LD researchers have shown the difficulty of distinguishing a distinct group of LD youngsters, and some even deny the existence of LD as a disability. We address the fiscal consequences of this seeming contradiction in this discussion, which takes into account the current LD system and projects costs over a 13-year period by varying assumptions about the number of future LD students.

Design and Method of the Study

The problem to be addressed is one of estimating costs for LD special education based on differing projections of LD population changes over the next 13 years. The cost projections are based on different estimates of LD prevalence rates and inflation rates. The purpose of the discussion is to arrive at conclusions about the future costs of LD education using differing assumptions regarding the variables involved.

Variables

In order to project costs for special education, several data variables were needed. Following is a description of each of the variables used and its source.

Base year. The base year chosen was the 1988-89 school year, because that was the most recent year for which national student data were available. Some expenditure data were based on the 1985-86 school year, the most recent year that those data were obtainable; those amounts were increased by 15% (5% per year) to reflect more accurately costs for the 1988-89 school year.

Projected years. Costs were projected over a 13-year period, from 1990-91 to 2002-03. This period allows an entire group of students to move from kindergarten to graduation, with changes to identification rates only for new and subsequent kindergarten classes. That permits currently identified students to remain in special education with no disruption to their education.

Student population. The student population has two components: the total number of students enrolled in kindergarten through 12th grade in any particular year, and the total LD students reported by state agencies to the federal government in any particular year. The total student population in the initial year is based on numbers from the 1988-89 school year. Estimates are made for all other years using National Center for Educational Statistics (NCES) projections. Since NCES projections go only to the year 2000-01, those numbers were used for the final 2 years as well. The LD population in the initial year is based on data reported to the U.S. Department of Education by the 50 states. For all subsequent years it is based on a projected number.

Varying prevalence rates. Here, *prevalence* is defined as the number of instances of a given condition in a given population at a given time (Last, 1983). Prevalence includes new cases plus all existing cases and should be distinguished from *incidence* rate, which refers to the number of new cases identified within a given year (Last, 1983). Most reports regarding LD use prevalence figures. The prevalence rate for LD is varied in the projections with the kindergarten class only in the first year and then for subsequent kindergarten classes. The change in rate from 1976-77 to 1988-89 was 152.16%, while the change from 1987-88 to 1988-89 was 3.03% (U.S. Department of Education, 1989a). The current study varies the prevalence rate by applying growth or cap rates to the current population.

Organizational patterns. These concern the forms of special education programs in which students spend the majority of their time. The federal government requires that data be reported on eight different organizational patterns:

    regular classes (itinerant special education teacher)
    resource room
    separate classes
    public separate facility
    private separate facility
    public residential facility
    private residential facility
    homebound/hospital environment

These are the patterns used in the current study.

Number of students per unit. The number of students per unit consists of the average number of students in one unit of an instructional program. Another way of saying this is that the number of students per unit is the student/teacher ratio obtained by dividing the number of teachers per organizational pattern into the number of students per pattern. The ratios were chosen based on research conducted in 1988 (Moore et al., 1988). In the initial projections, itinerant LD teachers were assumed to have caseloads of 25, resource room teachers caseloads of 20, and full-time teachers caseloads of 13.

Resources, quantities, and prices. The special education planning model
(SEPM) is a resource-cost model approach for estimating costs and
was developed for use in special education (Hartman, Hartman,
Bernstein, & Levine, 1978). The SEPM specifies resources, quantities,
and prices for each instructional program. The areas of resources used
in the SEPM are divided into personnel and nonpersonnel items, and
costs are established on a cost per unit basis. The estimates do not
reflect excess costs for special education; rather, they reflect the actual
costs of the services.

Noninstructional services. These are services that are not a direct part
of the instructional costs but are necessary for the education of the
students. They are composed of related services, assessment costs,
transportation, and support services. Related services are developmental, corrective, or supportive in nature and are provided to help
students with disabilities profit from instruction, but are not instructional in nature. Occupational and physical therapy are examples of
related services. Assessment costs involve personnel costs for mandated evaluation of students. Support service is for the administration
and supervision of programs. According to Moore et al. (1988), 39%
of the total costs of special education were for those noninstructional
areas.

Inflation factor. Initial projections were made using no inflation rate
(0%) and were considered to be an indication of costs expressed in
constant dollars, although the NCES salary projections from 1990 to
2000 show an average increase of 4.01% in constant dollars (U.S.
Department of Education, 1989b). An inflation factor was used in
additional projections to reflect changes in costs in future years. The
inflation rate chosen (6.41%) is an average of the inflation rates used
by NCES for middle alternative projections for elementary and secondary expenditures for the years 1990 to 1995 (U.S. Department of
Education, 1989b).

Building the Model

The LOTUS 1-2-3 microcomputer spreadsheet program was used
to build the cost models. The first step was to construct a model for
the cost of one instructional unit for each of the service delivery

programs. An instructional unit is defined as the cost of (as needed) a teacher, an aide, benefits, materials, travel expenses, and noninstructional expenses for each of the three defined organizational patterns for service delivery. For the other service delivery models, cost per pupil was used.

The specific costs per unit used are listed in Table 8.1. Teacher salary in the base year was from NCES projections (U.S. Department of Education, 1989b). Aide salary was considered to be 44% of a teacher's salary (Hartman, 1979), with 43% of teachers having aides (U.S. Department of Education, 1989a). Benefits were derived from salaries based on percentages. All other figures are from Moore et al. (1988). Noninstructional costs were estimated at 39% of total costs.

Average Per Pupil Cost

Table 8.2 shows the calculation of the average per pupil cost for special education. For the itinerant, resource room, and separate class organizational patterns, the number of students reported by the states to the federal government based on organizational pattern (U.S. Department of Education, 1988) was divided by the student/teacher ratio to obtain the classes needed. That number was multiplied by the cost per unit of the programs. The total cost of the other five programs was calculated using the cost per student figure from Table 8.1. The resulting total costs were summed to obtain an overall cost of $7,784,868,352. The total students, 1,912,522, was divided into the overall cost to obtain an average per pupil cost of $4,070.

Growth Rate Cost Projection Model

With this model, the number of LD students and subsequent costs were projected for the next 13 years using various assumptions about future growth rates of the LD population. This model is illustrated in Table 8.3, using a 3% growth rate. The top of the table displays the variables used to project the costs. The total LD population in 1989 (1,997,206) was obtained from a report by the U.S. Department of Education (1989). Graduating students (153,631) made up one thirteenth of the total LD population in 1989. The growth rate of LD was set at 3%. The figure for total enrollment in 1989 (40,323,000) was obtained

Table 8.1 Unit Costs per Program for the 1988-89 School Year

Program	Resource	Costs ($)
Itinerant	teacher	28,584
	benefits	9,433
	materials	500
	travel	1,000
	noninstructional	25,265
total		64,782
Resource room	teacher	28,584
	43% of aide	5,408
	benefits	11,217
	materials	500
	noninstructional	29,224
total		74,934
Separate class	teacher	28,584
	43% of aide	5,408
	benefits	11,217
	materials	500
	noninstructional	29,224
total		74,934
Public separate facility	pupil cost	7,029
Private separate facility	pupil cost	10,657
Public residential facility	pupil cost	32,550
Private residential facility	pupil cost	36,358
Homebound/hospital	pupil cost	4,595

from NCES projections. The per pupil cost of $4,070 was obtained from Table 8.2. The inflation rate was set at zero and was assumed to reflect costs in constant dollars. The 1989 cost of $8.1 billion was obtained by multiplying the total LD population by the per pupil cost.

Figures in the column showing total school population were obtained from NCES projections. The estimate of total LD students was determined by adjusting the prior year's number by the assumed students leaving, those entering with the new class, and any growth or decline.

Table 8.2 Total Costs per Program and Average Pupil Cost

Program	Resource	Costs
Itinerant	number of students	336,271
	student/teacher ratio	25
	classes needed	13,451
	cost per unit	$64,782
	total cost	$871,372,317
Resource room	number of students	1,130,922
	student/teacher ratio	20
	classes needed	56,546
	cost per unit	$74,934
	total cost	$4,237,225,457
Separate class	number of students	415,834
	student/teacher ratio	13
	classes needed	31,987
	cost per unit	$74,934
	total cost	$2,396,931,150
Public separate facility	number of students	17,159
	cost per student	$7,029
	total cost	$120,610,611
Private separate facility	number of students	8,293
	cost per student	$10,657
	total cost	$88,378,501
Public residential facility	number of students	801
	cost per student	$32,550
	total cost	$26,072,550
Private residential facility	number of students	925
	cost per student	$36,358
	total cost	$33,631,150
Homebound/hospital	number of students	2,317
	cost per student	$4,595
	total cost	$10,646,615
	Total students	1,912,522
	Overall cost	$7,784,868,352
	Per pupil cost	$4,070

Table 8.3 Cost Projections for LD With 3% Growth Rate and Zero Inflation Rate

Total LD population in 1989	1,997,206		Per pupil	$4,070			
Graduating students	153,631		Inflation	0%			
Growth rate of LD	3%		1989 cost	$8,128,628,420			
Total enrollment in 1989	40,323,000						
LD as a percentage of total enrollment	5%						

Year	Total School Population	LD Students				Per Pupil Cost ($)	Total Cost ($)	Percentage Change
		Current	Graduating	New	Total			
1990-91	40,772,000	1,997,206	153,631	216,732	2,060,306	4,070	8,385,446,779	3
1991-92	41,306,000	2,060,306	153,631	220,678	2,127,354	4,070	8,658,328,842	3
1992-93	41,833,000	2,127,354	153,631	224,909	2,198,631	4,070	8,948,429,637	3
1993-94	42,455,000	2,198,631	153,631	229,247	2,274,248	4,070	9,256,187,455	3
1994-95	43,023,000	2,274,248	153,631	233,701	2,354,317	4,070	9,582,069,392	3
1995-96	43,453,000	2,354,317	153,631	237,756	2,438,442	4,070	9,924,458,942	3
1996-97	43,788,000	2,438,442	153,631	241,569	2,526,379	4,070	10,282,364,216	3
1997-98	43,974,000	2,526,379	153,631	244,922	2,617,670	4,070	10,653,918,264	3
1998-99	43,997,000	2,617,670	153,631	247,749	2,711,788	4,070	11,036,978,972	3
1999-2000	43,954,000	2,711,788	153,631	250,407	2,808,565	4,070	11,430,858,386	3
2000-01	43,835,000	2,808,565	153,631	252,853	2,907,787	4,070	11,834,691,375	3
2001-02	43,835,000	2,907,787	153,631	255,830	3,009,985	4,070	12,250,639,353	3
2002-03	43,835,000	3,009,985	153,631	258,896	3,115,250	4,070	12,679,065,770	3
	Percentage of population	7.1					Total cost 134,923,437,383	
							Total percentage change	51

Total = Current − Graduating + Entering + Growth

The figure for new LD students in 1990-91 (216,732) is a combination of those entering from a new class and changes due to growth. Total students in LD was multiplied by the cost per pupil to arrive at a cost for LD. Each year the cost per pupil was increased by the inflation rate to calculate the subsequent year's cost per pupil.

Cap Rate Cost Projection Model

This model was identical to the growth rate model, except in the determination of new LD students each year. The number of new LD students was calculated by capping the entering student population; there was no growth included. This was achieved by multiplying one thirteenth of the current total school population by the cap rate. Thus, in the first year, the kindergarten class was limited to the cap rate. In subsequent years that cap rate was maintained for that class as it moved through the system and was applied to all new classes. Cap rates of 2%, 4%, and 6% were considered to be most reasonable, with an additional set of projections run with 0% cap rate for comparison purposes. A zero cap rate would eliminate all LD students by the final year. Table 8.4 illustrates a 2% cap rate. The cost projections were made by applying the average cost per pupil (with and without inflation) to the total LD population in a given year.

Controlling for Inflation

Two projections were run for each growth and cap rate—the first used no inflation factor and the second used a 6.41% inflation factor. The first set of projections can be seen as a method of controlling for the consequences of inflation and may be considered to be reported in constant dollars.

Varying Rates for Itinerant and Resource Programs

It has been claimed that the confounding of the LD population with mildly cognitively impaired and low-achieving youngsters has occurred

Table 8.4 Cost Projections for LD With 2% Cap Rate and Zero Inflation Rate

Total LD population in 1989	1,997,206	Per pupil	$4,070
Graduating students	153,631	Inflation	0%
Growth rate of LD	3%	1989 cost	$8,128,628,420
Total enrollment in 1989	40,323,000		

Year	Total School Population	LD Students				Per Pupil Cost ($)	Total Cost ($)	Percentage Change
		Current	Graduating	New	Total			
1990-91	40,772,000	1,997,206	153,631	62,726	1,906,301	4,070	7,758,644,757	−5
1991-92	41,306,000	1,906,301	153,631	63,548	1,816,217	4,070	7,392,004,755	−5
1992-93	41,833,000	1,816,217	153,631	64,435	1,727,022	4,070	7,028,977,662	−5
1993-94	42,455,000	1,727,022	153,631	65,315	1,638,706	4,070	6,669,532,168	−5
1994-95	43,023,000	1,638,706	153,631	66,189	1,551,264	4,070	6,313,643,228	−5
1995-96	43,453,000	1,551,264	153,631	66,851	1,464,483	4,070	5,960,446,749	−6
1996-97	43,788,000	1,464,483	153,631	67,366	1,378,218	4,070	5,609,347,886	−6
1997-98	43,974,000	1,378,218	153,631	67,652	1,292,239	4,070	5,259,413,669	−6
1998-99	43,997,000	1,292,239	153,631	67,688	1,206,296	4,070	4,909,623,468	−7
1999-2000	43,954,000	1,206,296	153,631	67,622	1,120,286	4,070	4,559,546,020	−7
2000-01	43,835,000	1,120,286	153,631	67,438	1,034,093	4,070	4,208,759,449	−8
2001-02	43,835,000	1,034,093	153,631	67,438	947,900	4,070	3,857,954,878	−8
2002-03	43,835,000	947,900	153,631	67,438	861,708	4,070	3,507,150,308	−9
						Total cost	73,035,062,997	
	Percentage of population	2.0				Total percentage change		−55

with the most mildly disabled of the LD population. The great majority of those students are educated in itinerant or resource room programs, and thus the greatest growth has occurred with that population. Since special education per pupil costs are significantly lower for those populations, additional sets of projections were run with growth and cap rates applied only to those two groups. Costs for students being educated in all other organizational patterns were projected using the current percentage of the population.

The separate projections were made by obtaining the percentage of LD students currently receiving service in each of the organization categories. The percentages were derived from numbers of students reported by the U.S. Department of Education (1988) to be receiving services. The percentage of LD students receiving itinerant services (17.58%) and resource room services (59.13%) amounted to approximately 77% of the LD population. Differing growth and cap rates were applied to those two organizational patterns, while the other 23% of the students remained at the same percentage of the total population.

Presentation and Analysis of the Data

A series of national projections were made, using both the growth rate model and the cap rate model. The projections, referred to as sensitivity analyses, were made by varying the prevalence rate, the inflation rate, and growth by organizational patterns.

National data were projected to indicate the number of LD students, the prevalence rate of those students, and the costs for educating those students in a 13-year period beginning in 1990-91. The estimates were based on an average per pupil cost for LD.

Projections Using an Average Pupil Cost

Growth Rates

Projections similar to those in Table 8.3 were run for varying growth rates with both zero and 6.41% inflation rates and are summarized for the year 2002-03 in Table 8.5. To illustrate, with a 5% growth rate in

Table 8.5 Total LD Costs With Differing Growth Rates With Zero and 6.41% Inflation Rates

Projection	2002-03 LD Population (in millions)	2002-03 Percentage of Population	2002-03 Yearly Costs (in billions of $) 0%	6.41%	Change from 1988-89 0%	6.41%	Total Cost (in billions of $) 0%	6.41%
1988-89	2.00	4.9	8.1	—	—	—	—	—
Growth								
0	2.13	4.9	8.7	19.7	7	127	108.9	174.6
1	2.40	5.6	9.8	22.3	21	154	117.3	188.7
3	3.12	7.1	12.7	28.4	51	219	134.9	220.5
5	3.97	9.1	16.0	36.2	89	298	155.6	258.3
7	5.04	11.5	20.3	45.9	135	396	180.0	303.1
14	11.30	25.8	45.7	103.1	395	944	303.6	535.7
-1	1.90	4.3	7.6	17.4	-4	102	102.2	161.8
-3	1.48	3.4	5.9	13.5	-24	61	89.3	139.1
-6	1.01	2.3	4.0	9.2	-46	13	73.5	111.5
-10	.61	1.4	2.5	5.5	-66	-29	57.3	84.1

LD for the next 13 years, the identified LD population would reach 3.97 million students, which would be 9.1% of the population in the year 2002-03. At a zero inflation rate, the annual cost for LD in 13 years would be $16.0 billion in constant dollars, an 89% increase over the current level. To reach the level of 25% of our school population to be labeled as LD, as suggested by former Secretary of Education Madeline Will (1986), would require a 14% growth rate. At that rate, the LD population would reach 11.3 million students in 2002-03. The annual cost would be in excess of $45.7 billion per year, which represents almost a 400% increase over the 13-year period.

Projections were made for negative growth rates and are also listed in Table 8.5. A growth rate of –1% would reduce the current LD population from 1,997,206 students to 1.9 million students, accounting for 4.3% of the total school population in the year 2002-03. Yearly costs with a zero inflation rate would be $7.6 billion, a 4% reduction in costs from the current school year. The total for the 13-year period would be $102.2 billion.

A growth rate of –6% would identify approximately 1.01 million students as LD in the year 2002-03, amounting to 2.3% of the population. That would approximate the original 2% of the population as provided for in P.L. 94-142. The costs would be roughly half of the current costs in constant dollars and would be $73.5 billion for the 13-year period.

Cap Rates

Table 8.6 presents a summary of differing cap rates with both zero and 6.41% inflation rates. A 4% cap would result in a total LD population in 2002-03 of 1.72 million students, or 3.9% of the total student population. It is slightly less than 4% of the total student population in the final year due to the rising population over the projection period. The annual cost would be approximately $7.0 billion in the last year, a 12% decrease from current levels.

A 5% cap rate, in effect, duplicates the current level of LD population. As such, it is equivalent to the 0% growth rate in Table 8.5, and the results are similar. A 0% growth rate produced an LD population of 2.13 million students with yearly costs of $8.7 billion in the year 2002-03. The 5% cap rate would produce an LD population of 2.15 million and would also cost $8.7 billion per year. Total costs for

Table 8.6 Total LD Costs With Differing Cap Rates With Zero and 6.41% Inflation Rates

Projection	2002-03 LD Population (in millions)	2002-03 Percentage of Population	2002-03 Yearly Costs (in billions of $)		Change from 1988-89		Total Cost (in billions of $)	
			0%	6.41%	0%	6.41%	0%	6.41%
1988-89	2.00	4.9	8.1	—	—	—	—	—
Cap								
0	.00	0.0	0.0	0.0	-100	-100	48.7	66.1
2	.86	2.0	3.5	7.8	-55	-5	73.0	109.3
3	1.29	2.9	5.3	11.8	-33	41	85.2	130.9
4	1.72	3.9	7.0	15.7	-12	84	97.0	152.6
5	2.15	4.9	8.7	19.6	8	127	109.1	174.2
6	2.59	5.9	10.5	23.5	27	168	121.1	195.8
8	3.45	7.9	14.0	31.4	65	247	145.4	239.0
10	4.31	9.8	17.5	39.2	100	321	169.6	282.2

the 13-year period would be approximately $109 billion for each projection.

A cap of 10% would allow the LD population to grow to 9.8% of the total population by the year 2002-03 and would cost a total of $169.6 billion in constant dollars for the 13-year period. That cap rate would be similar to a growth rate of 5%, which would identify 9.0% of the population as LD and would cost $154.5 billion over the 13-year period.

Effects of Inflation

With an inflation rate of 6.41%, costs are increased substantially. In the case of the 0% growth rate, $8.7 billion in annual costs would become $19.7 billion. With a 10% cap rate, the $17.5 billion annual costs would become $39.2 billion in inflated dollars. Total costs for the 13-year period would also be greatly increased (but not as dramatically) by the 6.41% inflation rate. The increase in total costs would not be as dramatic, because the cumulative effects of inflation are not fully realized until the final year of the projections. For example, a 14% growth rate with 6.41% inflation rate would increase costs by 944% in 13 years. Despite that tremendous yearly increase, the total costs over the 13 years would increase by about 300%, from $174.6 billion to $535.7 billion.

Itinerant and Resource Rooms

Growth Rate

Table 8.7 summarizes the growth rates applied only to itinerant and resource room programs (approximately 77% of the LD population). A 3% growth rate would identify 2.87 million youngsters as LD in the 2002-03 school year at an annual cost of $11.2 billion. The proportion of the total population that would be LD is 6.5%. A growth rate of 14% would identify 20.8% of the population as LD at an annual cost of $33.0 billion in constant dollars.

A comparison of the projections in Tables 8.5 and 8.7 suggests that the data vary little near the zero growth rate. For example, a zero

Table 8.7 Total LD Costs With Differing Growth Rates for Itinerant and Resource Room LD Students With Zero and 6.41% Inflation Rates

Projection	2002-03 LD Population (in millions)	2002-03 Percentage of Population	2002-03 Yearly Costs (in billions of $)		Change from 1988-89		Total Cost (in billions of $)	
			0%	6.41%	0%	6.41%	0%	6.41%
1988-89	2.00	4.9	8.1	—	—	—	—	—
Growth								
0	2.13	4.9	8.7	19.5	7	140	108.9	173.7
1	2.35	5.4	9.4	21.2	16	160	114.0	182.9
3	2.87	6.5	11.2	25.2	38	210	125.6	203.7
5	3.52	8.0	13.5	30.3	66	273	139.1	228.5
7	4.34	9.9	16.4	36.7	101	351	155.1	257.8
14	9.13	20.8	33.0	74.1	306	811	236.1	410.1
−1	1.94	4.4	8.0	18.0	−1	121	104.2	165.3
−3	1.62	3.7	6.9	15.5	−15	90	95.8	150.4
−6	1.26	2.9	5.7	12.7	−30	56	85.4	132.4
−10	.95	2.2	4.6	10.3	−44	26	74.8	114.5

growth rate in Table 8.5 identifies 4.9% of the population as being LD at a cost of $8.7 billion per year. A zero growth rate in Table 8.7 identifies 4.9% of the population as being LD at an annual cost of $8.7 billion.

As the projections move away from a zero growth rate in either direction, the variation increases. A 7% growth rate identifies 5.04 million students in Table 8.5, but only 4.34 million in Table 8.7. In addition, the costs are much less—$20.3 billion in Table 8.5 and $16.4 billion in Table 8.7. Part of the cost difference is caused by fewer students being identified, and part is caused by the lower per pupil costs associated with the itinerant and resource room classes. Negative growth rates have a different effect on the number of students identified. Since the number of students in all organization patterns, except itinerant and resource room programs, remained at the same percentage of the total population, the number of LD students does not drop as dramatically as when those negative growth rates are applied to all organizational patterns. Again, little variation is shown near the current LD prevalence rate of 5%, but as projections move to the extremes, marked differences occur. For example, a growth rate of –1% identifies 1.94 million students as LD in Table 8.5, but 1.9 million in Table 8.7. At a –10% growth rate, 610,000 students are identified as LD in Table 8.5—1.4% of the population—while in Table 8.7, 950,000 students are identified—2.2% of the population. That represents a 38% difference in identified LD students using the same rates but applying them only to itinerant and resource room programs in the second set of projections.

Cap Rate

Table 8.8 lists a summary of cap rates applied to itinerant and resource room programs. A 2% cap rate applied to the incoming kindergarten classes for the 13-year period would identify 1.16 million youngsters as being LD, or 2.6% of the population. The costs for educating those students would be $5.3 billion annually in constant dollars for the year 2002-03. The cost in inflated dollars would be $11.9 billion per year. A cap rate of 10% would allow the LD population to grow to 3.8 million, which translates to 8.7% of the total population. Costs would be in excess of $14.5 billion per year and would amount to a 78% increase in constant dollars over the 1989-90 school year.

Table 8.8 Total LD Costs With Differing Cap Rates for Itinerant and Resource Room LD Students With Zero and 6.41% Inflation Rates

Projection	2002-03 LD Population (in millions)	2002-03 Percentage of Population	2002-03 Yearly Costs (in billions of $)		Change from 1988-89		Total Cost (in billions of $)	
			0%	6.41%	0%	6.41%	0%	6.41%
1988-89	2.00	4.9	8.1	—	—	—	—	—
Cap								
0	.50	1.1	3.0	6.7	−63	−18	69.5	103.0
2	1.16	2.6	5.3	11.9	−35	46	85.4	131.7
3	1.49	3.4	6.4	14.4	−21	78	93.3	131.7
4	1.82	4.2	7.6	17.0	−7	109	101.3	145.9
5	2.15	4.9	8.7	19.6	8	141	106.3	160.1
6	2.48	5.7	9.9	22.9	22	173	117.2	188.6
8	3.14	7.2	12.2	27.4	50	216	133.2	217.0
10	3.80	8.7	14.5	32.5	78	300	149.1	245.5

Tables 8.6 and 8.8 produce some interesting comparisons. A 0% growth rate applied across organizational patterns would eliminate all LD students by the year 2002-03, but applying that same 0% cap rate only to itinerant and resource room programs would still allow a half million students to remain LD, most of them in separate classrooms.

A 5% cap rate, which in each table would most nearly duplicate the current prevalence rate, identifies virtually the same number of students—2.15 million, or 4.9% of the total population. Costs are also essentially the same for both sets of projections, with the cap on itinerant and resource rooms costing slightly less than the other projections.

A 10% cap rate would produce a difference of more than 510,000 students. The cost difference is more than $3 billion.

Summary of National Cost Data

Costs for serving the LD population were estimated to be approximately $8.1 billion per year for the 1989-90 school year. If the cap rate of 2% had remained in effect, costs would be only $3.5 billion for LD education, a 55% decrease.

If a 3% growth rate in LD occurred for the next 13 years, approximately 3.12 million students would be labeled as LD. The yearly costs would be $12.7 billion in constant dollars, amounting to a 51% increase in annual costs. Assuming that the 3% growth rate were to occur only with itinerant and resource class students, the LD population would be 2.87 million and the yearly costs would be $11.2 billion, a 38% increase in constant dollars. The savings of $1.3 billion is important, because it could be used to educate those underachievers who would become the responsibility of regular education.

The total costs in constant dollars for LD for the 13-year period ranged from $48.7 billion to $303.6 billion. The low figure was based on a yearly growth rate of –10%, which would identify only 610,000 students as LD. The high figure was based on a yearly growth figure of 14%, which would amount to 25% of the population being identified as LD by the year 2002-03.

A 395% increase in constant dollars associated with a 14% increase can be compared with a 135% increase associated with a 7% increase. One can see that a doubling of the growth rate leads to nearly a tripling of costs in a 13-year period because of the compounding effect of the growth rate.

There are now approximately 2 million LD youngsters, representing 5% of the total population. Nearly 78% of those 2 million students are in itinerant or resource room classes, suggesting that savings in those classes is most important. Also, most growth in LD will probably be with that same population, creating greater need among those classes.

The current study is concerned with the increase in costs over the 13-year period as well as the amounts of the actual increase. Although every attempt was made to use the most accurate figures available, concern with actual costs may not be as important as concern with percentage changes. Costs, it can be argued, are susceptible to change and are difficult to establish precisely. However, if the same method is used to determine costs in all years, the *percentage increases* projected will remain consistent. That is, regardless of costs, with a growth rate of 3% in LD students, costs will increase approximately 51% in 13 years, or will increase approximately 219% with a 6.41% inflation rate over that same period (see Table 8.6). Consequently, the projections of percentage increases should remain reliable even though actual cost data may vary.

Discussion, Conclusions, and Recommendations

In 1975, P.L. 94-142 mandated sweeping changes in the education of youngsters with disabilities and broadened the range of students who could be labeled as handicapped by funding a new category of students, the learning disabled. By 1989, that group grew from 21% to 48% of the handicapped population and became the single largest group of disabled students in the United States, numbering nearly 2 million. Approximately 60% more students than were originally thought to be LD have been identified as LD, amounting to nearly 1.2 million additional students. The additional special education cost for these students approximates $4.8 billion in the current year.

Providing special education for an additional 1.2 million students who are having difficulty in school could be considered an appropriate allocation of resources if special education programs were providing the type of support these students need. However, the results of efficacy studies suggest something different—special education programs may not be providing the additional support it was believed they would (Affleck, Madge, Adams, & Lowenbraun, 1988; Wang & Baker, 1985-1986).

The current study found that, depending upon the assumed prevalence of LD, total costs for the 13-year period could vary from $48.7 billion to $303.6 billion in constant dollars, a 623% difference. In inflated dollars, the differences are even greater—from $66.1 billion to $535.7 billion, an 810% difference. Of course, financial information is only one of the factors essential to developing an understanding of educational practice, but it is an area that is important in planning for the future needs of students, particularly when differences of such magnitude can be projected.

LD is the primary programmatic cause for the rise in special education costs. All other disabilities either have followed the trend of the reduction in overall population or are of minor significance. The growing level of identified LD youngsters has made our classification system and the costs associated with LD a major concern for policymakers. In a study of funding practices in all 50 states, the American Association of School Administrators (1983) notes that minimizing misclassification should be a major concern for policymakers, particularly if financial incentives are available for placing children in certain programs.

Since the financial incentives for identifying students with disabilities are great, and since LD is the primary condition for which disagreement regarding identification exists, the potential for misclassification and abuse exists there more than with other exceptionalities. Any attempt to reduce special education costs must ultimately deal with minimizing the misclassification of LD students.

References

Affleck, J. Q., Madge, S., Adams, A., & Lowenbraun, S. (1988). Integrated classroom versus resource model: Academic viability and effectiveness. *Exceptional Children, 54*, 339-348.

American Association of School Administrators. (1983). *Financing a free and appropriate public education for handicapped students*. Alexandria, VA: Author.

Coles, G. (1987). *The learning mystique*. New York: Pantheon.

Hartman, P. L., Hartman, W. T., Bernstein, C. D., & Levine, C. (1978). *Special education planning model: User guide.* Palo Alto, CA: Management Analysis Center.

Hartman, W. T. (1979). *Estimating the costs of educating handicapped children: A resource-cost model approach.* Unpublished doctoral dissertation, Stanford University.

Kranes, J. (1980). *The hidden handicap.* New York: Simon & Schuster.

Last, J. M. (Ed.). (1983). *A dictionary of epidemiology.* New York: Oxford University Press.

McKnight, R. T. (1982). The learning disability myth in American education. *Journal of Education, 164,* 351-359.

Moore, M. T., Strang, E. W., Schwartz, M., & Braddock, M. (1988). *Patterns in special education services delivery and cost.* Washington, DC: Decision Resources Corporation.

Taylor, R. L., & Sternberg, L. (1989). *Exceptional children: Integrating research and teaching.* New York: Springer-Verlag.

U.S. Department of Education. (1988). *10th annual report to Congress on the implementation of Public Law 94-142.* Washington, DC: Government Printing Office.

U.S. Department of Education. (1989a). *11th annual report to Congress on the implementation of Public Law 94-142.* Washington, DC: Government Printing Office.

U.S. Department of Education. (1989b). *Projections of education statistics to 2000.* Washington, DC: Government Printing Office.

Wang, M. C., & Baker, E. T. (1985-1986). Mainstreaming programs: Design features and effects. *Journal of Special Education, 19,* 503-525.

Will, M. (1986). Educating children with learning problems: A shared responsibility. *Exceptional Children, 52,* 411-416.

NINE

Special Education in Rural Areas

DAVID C. THOMPSON

ROBERT H. ZABEL

In recent years there has been tremendous growth in the numbers of children with disabilities, especially since the passage of P.L. 94-142 (the Individuals with Disabilities Education Act, IDEA). In addition, there has been an overwhelming increase in the numbers of children who have not traditionally been included in special education populations, but who are at risk of failure. Because these combined groups have consumed vast economic and human resources, and because American society has largely accepted the view that the amount and quality of education children receive can be visibly linked to success or failure on economic and personal dimensions, some have argued that most public school students of the future will have special needs requiring concerted attention to prevent a drastic decline in the social and economic well-being of the nation.

Although awareness of these problems is widespread, the dilemma of adequately serving special needs students is difficult to resolve, because these students often share disadvantages for which there seems to be little opportunity for redress in our society. Their condition has been exacerbated by an educational system that has become bureaucratically paralyzed and insensitive to the natural human condition, seeking instead to serve the most able while condoning active decline and encouraging passive indifference toward those who compete from a position of disadvantage. The result is a nation increasingly characterized by racial and class segregation brought about by economic stratification based on educational skills and frustrated by dependence on federal, state, and local governments that respond to political realities rather than to the enduring ideals of equality and justice.

These assertions provide the foundation for the three major points argued in this chapter. Inasmuch as it has been argued elsewhere that the nation's schools are about to be overwhelmed by both traditionally defined and newly emergent special populations arguably constituting nearly an entire generation at risk (Thompson, 1992), we first maintain that federal interest in special needs populations has been both narrow and inadequate, and that while states have been left to respond to unfunded mandates with very uneven results, local units of government have not generally been able or willing to fill the void due to multiple competing educational and economic crises. Second, we argue that while attention has been deservedly focused on the plight of urban schools, there is a more silent crisis facing rural schools disproportionate to their representation in the population, which may accurately be described as a crisis of indifference. Third and finally, we suggest that in a changing demographic context that is occurring simultaneously with a fundamental debate over the limits of government support for special needs populations, optimism is not possible in the foreseeable future—a future that holds little promise for a vast number of persons who will increasingly make up the economic and political base of the nation.

The Federal Interest

Federal interest in special needs populations has been sporadic and restrictively limited. Although federal aid to education can be traced to the 1700s, federal interest in special populations has generally been limited to crises at particular moments in history. The civil rights movement, national defense, and higher education occupied most of the federal government's interest until the 1960s, when the first targeting of disadvantaged elementary and secondary students occurred with the War on Poverty, which coincided with other federal interests in economic development.[1]

With enactment of the Elementary and Secondary Education Act (ESEA, P.L. 89-10) in 1965, the federal government launched its biggest effort to provide aid to economically disadvantaged children, particularly through Title I (P.L. 90-247) of the ESEA. This first large-scale federal assistance to LEAs with high concentrations of children from low-income families made funding provisions for migrant, handicapped, neglected, and delinquent children. The ESEA was also amended under Title VII to include dropout prevention in areas with high percentages of poor families. Since the findings of Congress revealed acute educational problems stemming from lack of English proficiency, Title VII (Bilingual Education Programs Section 701) was also enacted. In 1981, Congress authorized the Education Consolidation and Improvement Act (ECIA, P.L. 97-35), which consolidated 42 ESEA programs into seven block grants to states. These grants were to be distributed to states based on expenditure per pupil and the number of poor children, enlarged the population served to include Native American children, eliminated much paperwork and accountability, and reduced administrative funding in response to lowered reporting requirements.

Chapter 2 of the ECIA represented the other major federal attempt to help disadvantaged children. Subchapter A targeted basic skills in reading, math, and language arts and provided funds for creating and distributing material to parents to help their children and for conducting teacher and parent training workshops. Subchapter B, Educational Improvement and Support Services, allowed state and local agencies to carry out programs for educationally deprived children and minorities. Subchapter C, Special Projects, permitted SEAs and LEAs to carry out projects to ease the student transition from school to work and to provide academic and vocational training for delinquents as well as programs for disadvantaged students seeking medical careers. The only other notable federal programs enacted in response to growing needs of special populations were the Bilingual Education Act (P.L. 90-247 Title VII), in response to growing numbers of limited-English-proficient children; the Refugee Education Assistance Act of 1980 (P.L. 96-422), to provide impact aid for education of Cuban, Haitian, and Indochinese refugee children; and Title VI of the Emergency Immigrant Education Act of 1984 (P.L. 98-511), enacted in response to rapid increases in alien populations.

Despite these efforts to establish a federal interest, there has been no consistent and broad federal role in education, even for special populations. Although by some accounts federal expenditures for education belie the notion of limited interest, the bulk of federal education dollars has been too small to have a lasting impact. In fiscal year 1989, federal funds totaled $19.6 billion for elementary and secondary education, $11.9 billion for higher education, $11.8 billion for research, and $3.2 billion for other programs (National Center for Education Statistics, 1989). Yet of those seemingly large amounts, only $7.2 billion (42%) went directly to elementary and secondary children, representing a 3% decline in federal aid unadjusted for inflation since 1980. The shift in federal interest away from K-12 education is evident in comparison with other federal education expenditures, as federal K-12 education funds fell 12% and federal tax expenditure for education dropped 19% between 1980 and 1988, while higher education tuition aid rose 23%.

The narrow interest of the federal government has also been apparent in apportionment of money among special needs populations. Of the dollars devoted to K-12 disadvantaged children, traditional special needs populations receive the bulk of resources. From 1980 to 1989, grants for the general category of disadvantaged children increased from $3.2 billion in 1980 to almost $4.6 billion in 1989, an increase of approximately 44%. Bilingual education rose from $169.5 million in 1980 to $197.4 million in 1989, increasing about 16%. Although disadvantaged and bilingual classifications appear to have had sizable increases, total dollars were small compared with other federal aid for children with disabilities, which in contrast rose from $1.5 billion in 1980 to $4.2 billion in 1989, with the largest increases going to early childhood and rehabilitation (Thompson, 1991b). A gradual decrease in total federal responsibility for education has continued, with the federal budget for FY 1990 providing only $350 per identified child under the IDEA. In a total scheme of educational funding that sees the federal government supplying an average of only 7.6% of education dollars to local districts, resources appear to have been largely captured by programs for traditional special populations rather than redirected toward a more global view of at-risk children.2 In a political climate of budget reductions and turning control back to the states, the federal government has chosen to set largely unfunded policies and to leave the states to decide whether and how they will address the needs of growing numbers of disadvantaged children—policies obviously too little, patently too narrow, and perhaps too late.

The State Interest

Leaving states to their own initiative has not produced a strong base for educating at-risk populations and has resulted in a patchwork of dissimilar and awkward systems that are ill equipped to deal with the simultaneous demands for increased services and reduced taxes so prevalent among the individual states. State legislation affecting special populations yields a mixed picture that preempts optimism about success or concerted efforts to redress these needs. While all states have been forced by federal mandates, courts, and popular sentiment to provide some assistance to students with disabilities, a search for legislation providing compensatory education reveals a highly uneven voluntary commitment on the part of individual states (Thompson, 1992). While the most populous states have faced the greatest fury of demographic change, rural states are also affected (Thompson, 1990). In many ways, urban and rural distinctions have begun to fade as demographic change is pressing the nation without regard to location. For example, few states can legitimately claim that there are no bilingual children in need of services, even fewer where conditions such as poverty, low income, family disintegration, and drug abuse do not exist, and there is no state that can claim a utopian finance formula that fully redresses all child-based needs regardless of urban, suburban, or rural locale. Because all states contain significant numbers of disadvantaged students, it is an inevitable conclusion that as long as such problems exist without aggressive redress, efforts may be too little, and, for some children, too late. While these problems are endemic to the nation, there is evidence to suggest that for rural states the crisis may become unmanageable because the same level of concern for disadvantage that has been exhibited in urban states is conspicuously absent in rural settings. In many ways, the rural crisis can be called a case of indifference.

Focus on Rural Versus Urban: A Case of Indifference

The enormity of the educational needs of at-risk populations is having a powerful impact on traditionally rural states, which, in many instances, find themselves unable to decide whether they are in fact more urban than rural, or more rural than urban. Except in a very few instances, the sharp lines dividing rural from urban have become blurred in recent years, with the result that traditionally rural states are also coping with clusters of disadvantaged populations. For some such states, awareness that the disadvantage normally attributed to urban centers is growing so rapidly that the complacency of ruralness is being challenged by pressure on state and local governments to recognize and redress such needs. The resulting choice is not pleasant, as increased resources are difficult to garner, both from a perspective of economic vigor and resistance to wealth sharing and because of the extraordinary difficulty in shaking people loose from centuries of traditional thought.

The Case of Kansas

The increasingly blurred line between traditional urban disadvantage and ruralness is exemplified by recent court action in Kansas. Traditionally viewed as a highly rural state, Kansas nonetheless has distinctive urban populations located in Wichita and Kansas City. Currently, four separate lawsuits challenging the system for funding education are working their way through the state's court system (*Hancock v. Stephan*, 1990; *Mock v. State of Kansas*, 1990; *Newton USD 373 v. State of Kansas*, 1990; *USD 259 v. State of Kansas*, 1991). In separate actions attacking various parts of the state's scheme for financing schools, the lawsuit brought by the Wichita school district can be characterized as seeking redress for urban populations, while a coalition of approximately 40 rural schools led by the Baxter Springs school district claiming disadvantage in a special needs context challenges assumptions about agrarian serenity. The data supporting these lawsuits both confirm growing urban disadvantage and destroy the myth of rural self-sufficiency.

At issue in the Wichita lawsuit is the constitutionality of the 1991 Kansas Legislature's amendments to the Kansas School District Equalization Act (SDEA, 1973) (Thompson, 1991a, 1991b). In a series of complicated events stemming from state revenue shortfalls, the net sum of the 1991 Legislature's actions was to reinstate the SDEA (inactive in 1990) through passage of H.B. 2428 and to concurrently enact an appropriations bill, H.B. 2122, which was intended to introduce $55 million in new state monies to the SDEA. Because the legislature correctly anticipated dramatic realignments in state aid due to wealth shifts and reappraisal of property, H.B. 2428 included language to protect districts against state aid losses by guaranteeing that districts would be held harmless to at least 87.5% of any loss between the prior year's aid entitlement and anticipated aid for 1991-92. In May 1991, the governor signed H.B. 2428, but vetoed the appropriation increase contained in H.B. 2122. With subsequent failure of the legislature to override the veto, the SDEA was reinstated as amended to include both hold-harmless and a $700,000 cap, but without the revenue necessary to prevent either dramatic shifts in state aid among the 304 Kansas school districts or the loss by some districts of amounts well in excess of the cap and in excess of the intended percentage limit. As a result, approximately 22 Kansas school districts were held harmless at a rate far less than the 87.5% guarantee. Upon enactment, the Wichita school district filed a lawsuit charging that the legislature abdicated its constitutional obligation to provide adequate and equitable financial support for schools by instituting an arbitrary and capricious cap on hold-harmless aid because, as a primary consequence of size, large districts stood to lose the greatest amount of state aid. Given other factors, including potential line-item cuts from the governor's office, the Wichita district was permitted to receive only approximately 6% of its prior year's state aid entitlement.

The impact of losing 94% of state aid under the worst scenario was the instant loss of nearly $11 million or 6.6% of the district's total budget. While the loss would be large by any standard, its impact on the district, due to the district's urban nature, exacerbated the effects. While many of the 45,900 children the district serves in 1991-92 come from traditional families, many others do not. The district has a high incidence of poverty, with 35% of students considered poor according to national standards.

The problem of at-risk children is so significant that 11 of the 14 middle schools in Wichita have a student support teacher program for at-risk students, with as many as 50% of students in some schools defined as being at risk. The district currently serves approximately 2,900 low-income students with Chapter 1 reading services, and another 1,600 students are served by Chapter 1 math. Chapter 1 services are also provided for kindergarten children, and prekindergarten provides half-day school for 3- and 4-year-olds. Although the budget for Chapter 1 services was $4,883,569 in 1990-91, an additional 7,650 students qualified for Chapter 1 services but were not served because of a lack of funds. Approximately 12% of all Wichita students receive special education services at a very high cost. For 1990-91, per pupil costs attributable to special education categories were as follows: autistic, $11,988; behavior disorder, $7,812; educable mentally handicapped, $6,968; gifted, $3,558; hearing impaired, $13,297; learning disabled, $5,184; physically impaired, $12,197; severely multiple handicapped, $16,374; trainable mentally handicapped, $9,703; and visually impaired ($13,814). In addition, the district calculates an additional cost of $1,100 to support each middle school at-risk student. Direct costs from the general fund to support social service expenditures were $16,795,778 for 1990-91, or a directly attributable percentage allocation of 10.13%, up from 9.21% a year before.

At the same time the district must serve these children, the state is facing an economic crisis coupled with a bitter quarrel over state aid. While the district recognizes special populations through the described programs, state aid to general education in the district is being cut nearly $11 million through the operation of hold-harmless, the $700,000 cap, and state budget cuts, and other aid to special education was also reduced from $125,560,963 in 1990 to $119,437,500 for 1991. At the same time, statewide special education expenditures are expected to go up from $244,172,725 to $267,792,303 in order not to reduce services and to serve increasing numbers of children with disabilities. In addition to cuts in aid entitlement to regular education in the district, special education is funded at only 73% of excess cost in 1991-92, making it necessary to transfer revenues from the general fund in order to cover the cost of mandated special education programs. Other direct state cuts to transportation and special education increase the district's losses by about another $2 million. Concurrently, the district is anticipating the costs of salaries, utilities, and increased enrollments to require an additional $8 million over prior year expenditures. The district's cash reserve has dropped over the last several years as a result of holding tax increases down, requiring an additional $5.5 million for 1991-92. Finally, the district's tax delinquency rate has increased in recent years; it is expected to reach 7% for 1991-92.

These factors require that the Wichita Board of Education institute drastic cuts or dramatically increase taxes in the district to provide educational services. A report delivered on July 21, 1991, included cutting 200 teachers and 24 administrators, reducing 141 other nonteaching staff, cutting $192,000 from sports, slashing $190,000 from transportation, permitting a $2.9 million shortfall in special education, a $1.5 million shortfall in vocational education, and a $300,000 shortfall in teacher training budgets. The cuts eliminated 19 of 32 directors in areas including finance, food service, transportation, elementary and secondary education, and athletics; cut 10 of 33 coordinators supervising learning disabled, gifted, and social services; and eliminated 2 (17%) high school principals, 20 (71%) assistant high school principals, all 21 assistant middle school principals, 13 (21%) elementary principals, and all 18 elementary assistant principals.

On July 29, the board finally approved a stark budget for 1991-92 adjusting for anticipated losses in state aid. The budget represented dramatic change from prior years. Table 9.1 illustrates the forced choices made in balancing the budget against expected losses in state aid. Although the district increased its general fund budget, vocational education support dropped significantly (–3.37%), as did funding for capital improvements (–20.7%), bilingual programs (–4.41%), food service (–1.26%), and teacher in-service (–50.0%). At the same time, expenditures increased for special education (+6.43%), transportation (+1.25%), adult education (+14.2%), and adult supplementary education (+6.45%). In addition, state aid losses through the equalization formula had to be offset by local tax effort in order to permit a general fund increase (+4.65%). While increases and decreases represent a larger budget than for 1990-91, they come at considerably greater tax effort, as the mill rate rose by 16 mills (+23.26%).

While these efforts balanced the budget as required by law, the rest of the story is lodged in the true drama of losses to at-risk populations. As seen in Table 9.1, the district had to fund salary increases under state law in the amount of $1,716,100, as well as benefits and extra duty pay of $2,061,204. Major increases for urban characteristics emerged, as increases were required for indigent texts (+$152,500), Cities in Schools (+$35,000), North High Language Project (+$19,200), bilingual transfer (+$152,500), and transfers to mandated special education programs (+$3,933,500). These increases were especially significant in light of cuts the district was forced to make. Under the proposed budget, the district would lose the services of 7 administrators (–$285,700), 158 teachers (–$3,466,450), 86 other personnel (–$1,324,479), and a series of student-centered purchases including computer program products (–$66,200); supplies and textbooks ($426,300); furniture, equipment, and computer purchases (–$28,500);

Table 9.1 Wichita 1991-92 Budget, Major Increases and Decreases

Total 1990-91 budget		$165,072,200
Increases ($)		
administrative merit	300,000	
benefits/extra duty pay	2,061,204	
built-in salary costs	1,716,100	
science kits	500,000	
indigent texts/teachers editions	152,500	
Cities in Schools	35,000	
gasoline	53,500	
utilities	121,500	
toxic waste/landfill	75,000	
North High Language Project	19,600	
transfer to vocational	1,069,000	
transfer to in-service	100,000	
transfer to bilingual	152,500	
transfer to transportation	220,000	
transfer to special education	3,933,500	
transfer to Parents as Teachers	150,000	
attorneys' fees	50,000	
maintenance agreements	87,700	
repairs/buildings/grounds	60,700	
tuition GYOT	27,000	
postage	20,000	
total		10,904,804
Decreases ($)		
7 administrators	−285,700	
158 teachers	−3,466,450	
86 classified personnel	−1,324,479	
PRIDE	−24,000	
employee recognition	−9,500	
physicals	−25,000	
in-service/travel	−360,500	
personnel recruitment	−79,850	
banking fees	−5,900	
building rentals	−16,500	
equipment rental	−39,000	
computer program products	−66,200	
supplies/books	−426,300	
furniture, equipment, computers	−28,500	
insurance	−55,200	
election	−39,000	
minigrants	−25,000	
athletics support	−192,800	
discretionary funds	−551,000	
custodial support	−45,000	
consultants, professional services	−103,650	
student projects	−16,000	
miscellaneous	−51,475	
total		−7,237,004
1991-92 published budget		$172,748,900

SOURCE: Thompson (1991b).

athletics (–$192,800); and student project support (–$16,000). While $10,094,804 was added to the budget to fund programs generally relating to high-cost populations, $7,237,004 would be cut from the budget, generally in areas that have negative impact on instructional quality for regular education students, including significant losses of personnel. To fund the proposed budget, the district would reduce program offerings and supplies and equipment to thousands of regular education children by transferring already reduced general fund revenues to special programs and transportation—a process requiring unprecedented local property tax increases and reduction of cash reserves—a most unwise act when any other choice exists. Under conditions demonstrating that the general picture of the Wichita district is one of urban disadvantage, declining cash carryover, increasing special population costs, declining state aid, increasing local property tax effort, increased tax delinquency, and severe budget cuts, it is clear that this increasingly urban district faces formidable obstacles in providing quality educational services, particularly to those students whose fundamental demographic features demand increased, rather than diminished, resources.

A more expected crisis is facing rural schools in the state of Kansas. In a state comprising 304 school districts scattered over 82,000 square miles ranging in student population from an estimated low 79 FTE to more than 45,000 students, and in which the median FTE enrollment is fewer than 600 students, it is not surprising that ruralness is a predominant characteristic of most of the state's school districts. Neither is it surprising that the historic funding scheme in Kansas has favored the most rural schools by permitting fiscally inefficient districts to continue to operate at a very high cost, so that in 1991-92 the budget per pupil ranged from an approximate low $2,800 to nearly $11,500 for regular education, principally because of diseconomy of scale inherent in extremely small districts. What is surprising, however, is that many rural schools believe they are generally mistreated under the state's equalization formula, and with significant implications for funding high-risk special populations. The perceived lack of state support for rural schools led to a lawsuit filed by approximately 40 mostly rural districts in *Hancock v. Stephan* (1990) and yet another lawsuit by 6 semirural districts in *Newton USD 373 v. State of Kansas* (1990).

These lawsuits portray highly uneven treatment of rural districts in Kansas. At issue in *Hancock* are the vast unadjusted differences among school districts in Kansas in tax base equality. Although differing tax bases are expected because of natural income inequality among communities, there is a basic expectation that an equalization formula will offset those differences in order to provide equality of revenues across districts. That this has not occurred is evident in the data on the state's most rural school districts. For example, to fund a 1990-91 budget per pupil of $4,507 the Baxter Springs school district would have received approximately $2.76 million in state aid while levying 57.9 mills to fund the local share, while the Burlington school district would receive about $252,000 but would be required to levy only 8.24 mills to spend its budgeted $4,605 per pupil. Similarly, the Lebo-Waverly school district adjacent to Burlington was slated to receive approximately $1.59 million in state aid while levying 52.5 mills, a ratio of 6:1, compared with its wealthy neighbor's tax rate of only 8.24 mills. Near the extremes of wealth variation, the state aid formula has provided the Augusta school district with only approximately $3.14 million in aid while requiring an exorbitant 99.13 mills to fund a budget per pupil of $3,134, compared with Burlington, which funds a budget per pupil of $4,604 on 8.29 mills—a ratio of 12:1.

While the issue of financing rural schools is complex for many states, the dilemma in Kansas is exacerbated by vast extremes of wealth and poverty among the state's most rural districts. Several plaintiff districts in *Hancock* are among the poorest in the state, with school buildings, curriculum, and teacher salaries lagging behind the rest of the state. The Galena district, for example, has been historically the poorest in the state, with an assessed valuation of only about $8.4 million to support approximately 700 students. Baxter Springs also numbers among the poorer districts, with a wealth base of $18 million for about 900 students, and the Troy district has historically vied for last place in wealth among the districts in the state, with only $10.9 million in assessed value for its 400 students. In sharp contrast, other rural districts hold vast amounts of wealth for small populations. Burlington's nuclear power plant produces a wealth base of more than $500 million for fewer than 900 students—a scenario similar to some other sparsely populated areas of the state that contain power plants or vast energy reserves. At the same time, there are other rural pockets of economic depression where despite higher levels of state aid, budgets, facilities, salaries, and educational productivity do not begin to approximate those found in wealthier areas of the state. Understandably, these areas also often contain higher levels of special needs populations, especially in a broader definitional context that embraces the chronic effects of intergenerational disadvantage. Although these lawsuits are provocative in representing the extremes of the urban/rural dilemma, they still do not embrace the limits of disadvantaged populations because in many states, including Kansas, distinguishing between rural and urban school districts is increasingly difficult. The issue is nonetheless critical to serving the new demographics of the nation because the educational needs of all children can be served only by delimiting the definition of disadvantage. For districts that are neither exclusively urban nor exclusively rural, a significant disadvantage has long existed unrecognized in states such as Kansas, which contains many communities in transition (Thompson, 1990). This concept is strikingly illustrated by *Newton USD 373 v. State of Kansas*. While none of the six plaintiff districts in the *Newton* lawsuit would be considered especially rural because district populations are above the median enrollment for the state and because a fundamental element in the districts' complaint draws favorable analogy between their individual and collective demographic profiles and the most highly urbanized areas of the state, many of their basic characteristics are highly rural. As such, the circumstance in *Newton* blurs the line between rural and urban, while these districts suffer the most negative consequences of both extremes without the redress offered by the state aid formula to highly urban and rural special populations.[3]

The data in Table 9.2 provide a profile of plaintiff districts, a profile of the entire state, and a composite profile of all districts immediately contiguous to plaintiffs using mean and median values on the variables of wealth and budget per pupil, amounts of income tax payments rebated under state law to schools, enrollment, tax rate, and selected demographic variables related to socioeconomic status. Such an analysis suggests that there are three kinds of districts in Kansas—very large, very small, and all others—an analysis that then breaks the current lawsuits into haves and have-nots by virtue of urban plight, generally small wealthy districts, and the plaintiffs who are caught between being neither very large nor very small by Kansas standards. This scheme permits the observation, based on Table 9.2, that legislative redress of disadvantage is still highly incomplete because these plaintiff districts are significantly disadvantaged in virtually every category that could result in increased costs and especially so in disadvantaged student population. For example, mean plaintiff

Table 9.2 Selected Mean and Median Measures of School Districts' Fiscal Comparability in Kansas, 1990-91

| | Plaintiff Districts | | Statewide | | | | All Contiguous Districts | | | |
	Mean	Median	Mean	% Difference	Median	% Difference	Mean	% Difference	Median	% Difference
Wealth/pupil ($)	69,075.07	68,044.14	94,071.78	36.19	77,941.67	14.55	87,279.08	26.35	84,732.89	24.53
Income rebate ($)	389.06	386.58	329.53	-15.30	315.73	-18.33	310.93	-20.08	298.12	-22.88
Unused budget ($)	54,171.00	30,047.50	110,632.69	104.23	42,514.00	41.49	119,287.52	120.21	42,564.00	41.66
General fund BPP ($)	3,314.22	3,269.47	4,834.33	45.87	4,783.97	46.32	4,979.08	-50.23	4,855.45	48.51
FTE enrollment	3,154.45	3,102.9	1,368.29	-56.62	555	-82.11	477.46	-84.86	395	-87.27
Total mills	75.19	73.36	59.59	-20.75	60.73	-17.22	56.84	-24.40	56.38	-23.15
% minority	12.93	12.82	5.52	-57.31	2.63	-79.49	2.19	-83.06	1.86	-85.49
% free/reduced-price lunch	29.17	28.00	36.53	25.23	27.00	-3.57	28.17	-3.43	26.00	-7.14

wealth per pupil ($69,075) is 36% below mean state wealth ($94,072), mean budget per pupil ($3,314) is 46% below the statewide mean ($4,834), and mean unused budget authority per pupil ($54,171) is 104% below the statewide mean ($110,833). In contrast, mean plaintiff FTE (3,154) is 57% above mean statewide FTE (1,368), while mean tax rate (75.19) is 21% greater than the mean for the state (59.59). Importantly, significant differences in high-cost populations are also observed, as plaintiff districts contain 79% more minority populations and 28% free/reduced-price lunch recipients. The classic template of formula disadvantage is seen in the Dodge City district, which has 48% less wealth than the mean wealth of its neighbors, 92% more students, a mill rate higher by 35%, and 94% more minority students, while budgeting 52% less per pupil. At the same time, the Dodge City school district has only $47 in unused budget leeway, compared with its wealthier neighbors, which hold a mean of $124,389—a striking differential in local ability to improve educational service delivery to needy populations (Thompson, Honeyman, & Wood, 1990, 1991). These data are generally descriptive of the differences present throughout the state even when the extremes are removed, making it obvious that school districts in Kansas reflect a needs and tax profile that does not affirm equal treatment or adequate concern for disadvantaged students through the aid formula.

That these plaintiff districts are caught in a formula trap that ignores special population disadvantage (except nominal recognition in the very largest districts) is further borne out by data confirming inability of plaintiffs to cope with growing stagnation and socioeconomic problems. Most communities in Kansas have large aging populations, and socioeconomically disadvantaged populations are also significantly represented. The profile of plaintiff districts includes a significant proportion of persons who are unwilling or unable to support higher school taxes. Per capita income in several plaintiff districts is nearly $2,000 below state average, and the picture of low-income/poor families is striking. Repeatedly, plaintiffs report difficulties in obtaining sufficient monies for adequate staffing, teaching materials and supplies, and programs, including those associated with early childhood and socioeconomically disadvantaged children. For example, plaintiffs report inability to provide enough elementary counselors and librarians, failing to fill vacant teaching positions, reducing in-service budgets, using outdated textbooks, averaging only $122 per teacher for instructional budgets, using old buses in excess of 150,000

Table 9.3 Rural, Urban, and Suburban Special Education Students
in Kansas, 1991

Type	Percentage
Rural	52.1
Suburban	27.1
Urban	20.8

SOURCE: Zabel and Costello (1991).

miles, and taking money from regular education to recover a 20% state reduction in special expenditures (Thompson et al., 1991).

The data suggest that needs of special populations are high. The plight of urban schools nationally is genuinely desperate, but there is also a vast need among rural school special populations. A particular danger for rural schools is a fundamental belief that rural schools are untouched by the tidal wave of demographic change. Failure to focus on the full continuum of district size is to assure that a large number of children in this nation will never receive their full entitlement. In the highly rural state of Kansas, differences permitted under the state aid formula are startling—a condition undoubtedly repeated across the nation as rural and urban districts struggle over meager resources while other districts fall between the cracks. To such districts, the state aid scheme seems highly indifferent to their needs.

Rural Special Education Shortages

If the future is not bright for the masses in urban areas, the future for rural special needs populations appears equally dim. The outlook is particularly disheartening as districts not only struggle to cope with the changing nature of their clientele, but are also faced with public indifference demonstrated by an increasing lack of commitment to community service through teaching. Special education personnel supply, already tragically thin across many states' urban school districts, is shrinking at alarmingly faster rates than in regular education, with shortages most severe in rural areas. In a nation where the majority of states can still be characterized as rural and in which traditional and newly defined special needs populations are increasing rapidly, there is

Table 9.4 Unfilled and Unbudgeted Positions in Kansas: All Teachers and Related Service Personnel, 1991

Area	Rural		Suburban		Urban		Total	
	N	%	N	%	N	%	N	%
Unfilled	172	43.7	54	13.7	42	10.7	268	68
Unbudgeted	77	19.5	22	5.6	27	6.9	126	32
Totals	249	63.2	76	19.3	69	17.5	394	100

SOURCE: Zabel and Costello (1991).

reason to believe that a growing segment of the nation's socioeconomically disadvantaged children will be increasingly underserved. The danger is most pronounced in rural areas, as demand for personnel to serve these children is rapidly outstripping supply. For example, Table 9.3 illustrates that in Kansas slightly more than half (52%) of all special education students are located in rural districts, while 64% of personnel shortages are occurring in rural districts (see Table 9.4). Discrepancies in related services personnel shortages in rural areas are even greater, with rural districts holding the same 52% of special populations but with 67% of personnel needed (Zabel & Costello, 1991).

These data are not surprising when the realities of attracting qualified personnel to rural areas are considered, but they are especially disturbing because the ultimate impact is disproportionate on rural children and because the data reflect a rapidly shrinking personnel pool. As seen in Table 9.5, attrition in Kansas is far outpacing new endorsements, and districts across the state report both unfilled positions and the need to budget for additional personnel without legal authority and resources to satisfy their needs. As damaging as the evidence appears, the effect is still not complete until it is recognized that the shortfall in staff applies only to special needs populations traditionally defined—a condition that still does not embrace a broader definition of either program or personnel needs of newly emerging special populations. Although these data are bad enough, they are indicative of a deeper problem: when the declining number of persons preparing to serve traditional special populations is combined with staff attrition and the lack of budget authority to hire staff, even if such persons were available, the obvious conclusion is that too few persons

Table 9.5 Number of Teachers Needed, Newly Endorsed, and Lost
to Attrition in Kansas

Area[a]	Unfilled 1989-90	New Endorse-ments	Attrition 1988-89	Attrition as Percentage of New Endorsements
Learning disabled	35	189	112	59
Behavior disorder	36	92	67	73
Learning/behavior disorder	20	7	20	286
Educable mentally retarded	7	24	48	200
Trainable mentally retarded	5	12	19	158
Educable/trainable mentally retarded	3	62	10	16
Mentally retarded, learning disabled	1	9	16	178
Mentally retarded, behavior disorder	2	1	0	0
Mentally retarded, learnng/ behavior disorder	9	1	46	4600
Gifted	26	65	52	80
Early childhood	24	92	20	22
Severely multiple handicapped	11	31	19[b]	61
Visually impaired	5	0[c]	5	—
Hearing impaired	6	11	16	146
Homebound	4	0	1	25

SOURCE: Zabel and Costello (1991).
a. No special preparation exists for categories other than the areas shown here. Districts choosing to implement at-risk programs must do so at their own expense and without certification requirements beyond those of normal staff at the level in which instruction will occur.
b. Includes severely multiply handicapped and trainable mentally retarded/severely multiply handicapped.
c. There is no preparation program in Kansas for teachers of the visually impaired.

are preparing to teach special populations, that states are failing to recognize the new demographics, and that funding for at-risk students may be too little, too narrow, and perhaps too late.

Conclusions

If the nation is indifferent to problems of urban and rural distress related to the vast demographic changes under way, real crises are only delayed. Special needs students must be served by all levels of government. The federal government must redefine its role in education to encompass an understanding that the economic fortune of the country and preservation of democracy are endangered more by failing to redress such problems than by their attendant costs. States must take a vital interest in bringing at-risk children to the forefront, because without such attention states will continue to deal with their problems in isolation or, worse, remain oblivious. Government at all levels must convince the private sector of its stake in developing students' skills to participate in the economy.

Massive infusion of financial resources over several decades may not have produced notable signs of improvement, but it may be assumed to have mitigated a worse fate. There is no doubt that America is changing. Whether it will change for the better depends on our will to overcome indifference to our tremendous social needs. In urban and rural America alike, the future of democracy hangs in a balance imperiled by unredressed disadvantage.

Notes

1. For example, in 1963 the federal government implemented the Vocational Education Act of 1963 (P.L. 88-210) in recognition of the need for research, training, and demonstrations in vocational education, and the following year Congress enacted the Economic Opportunity Act of 1964 (P.L. 88-452), which established the Job Corps to increase employment options of young persons and authorized the first support for disadvantaged youth programs such as Head Start, Follow Through, and Upward Bound. Additionally, Part C of P.L. 83-452, known as the Voluntary Assistance Program for Needy Children, allowed the Office of Economic Opportunity to coordinate volunteer services to needy children.

2. When viewed in the context of expanding special needs populations, federal interest can be seen as severely inadequate benevolence, because increased funding has not followed observable outcomes. A prime example lies in the impact of Head Start and Chapter 1 programs. Comparative data have shown a return of $8:1 on investment in Head Start (Berrueta-Clement, Schweinhart, Barnett, Epstein, & Weikart, 1984), finding that participating children were more likely to be employed (60% versus 32%), more likely to graduate (64% versus 50%), more likely to enroll in college (40% versus 23%), more likely to be functionally competent (60% versus 50%), less likely to be arrested (30% versus 60%), and less likely to be on welfare (20% versus 40%). Yet Head Start has never had sufficient funding, serving only about 20% of eligible children. Legislation beyond Head Start has been introduced but not passed in Congress at least six different times since 1970 (Administration for Children, Youth, and Families, 1987). Similarly, despite the findings of the House Subcommittee on Elementary, Secondary, and Vocational Education that Chapter 1 appears to be the legislation providing both the broadest sweep and greatest effect for economically and educationally disadvan-

taged students (U.S. Congress, 1986), the ECIA (1981) returned responsibility and control to the states, reduced funding even though eligibility under poverty guidelines increased, authorized paperwork reduction whereby efficacy of the program can no longer be determined, reduced parent interaction, increased pupil/teacher ratios nearly 13%, and increased incidence of beginning teachers being assigned to Chapter 1 (Dougherty, 1985). There appears to be little sentiment to change as the Reagan 1989-1990 federal budget provided no increase for Title XX income support for the fourth straight year and deleted funds for independent living and juvenile justice. The Bush administration has proposed elimination of the Administration for Children, Youth, and Families administered by the U.S. Department of Health and Human Services and has reduced aid for the Office of Adolescent Pregnancy Programs. Additionally, the Act for Better Child Care (S. 1885/H.R. 3660), which would have provided $2.5 billion in child care for working families, died in the Senate. For further development of this concept, see Ward and Anthony (1992) and Thompson (1992).

3. The SDEA offers special consideration to highly rural districts through a sparsity factor incorporated into enrollment categories recognizing economies of scale. The most urban districts have also received special legislative treatment by the creation of a separate enrollment category that provides a higher budget per pupil authorization due to their special population characteristics. Although the smallest districts fiercely protest attacks against their extremely high budgets per pupil and although the largest districts argue that their special recognition is woefully inadequate to redress their disadvantage, the third group of districts, of which the Newton plaintiffs are members, is held to the lowest budget per pupil authority because the state argues their historical revenue patterns profile them as needing less revenue—a theory of efficiency. These plaintiffs and others similarly situated thereby claim discrimination because they do not receive the legislative protection offered to the unarguably rural and urban districts. See Thompson et al. (1991).

References

Administration for Children, Youth, and Families. (1987, January). *Head Start fact sheet*. Washington, DC: Author.

Berrueta-Clement, J. R., Schweinhart, L. J., Barnett, W. S., Epstein, A. S., & Weikart, D. P. (1984). *Changed lives: The effects of the Perry Preschool program through age 19* (Monograph No. 8). Ypsilanti, MI: High Scope Educational Research Foundation.

Dougherty, J. (1985). A matter of interpretation: Changes under Chapter 1 of the Education Consolidation and Improvement Act. In *Report on changes under Chapter 1 of the Education and Improvement Act* (Serial No. 99-B; GPO Publication No. 1985 50-5240). Washington, DC: U.S. Congress, House of Representatives, Committee on Education and Labor.

Hancock v. Stephan, Shawnee County District Court, Case No. 90-CV-1795 (1990).

Hodgkinson, H. (1985). *All one system: Demographics of education, kindergarten through graduate school*. Washington, DC: Institute for Educational Leadership.

Mock v. State of Kansas, Shawnee County District Court, Case No. 90-CV-0918 (1990).

National Center for Education Statistics. (1989). *Digest of education statistics*. Washington, DC: U.S. Department of Education, Office of Educational Research and Improvement.

Newton USD 373 v. State of Kansas, Shawnee County District Court, Case No. 90-CV-2406 (1990).

Thompson, D. (1990). Consolidation of rural schools: Reform or relapse? *Journal of Education Finance, 16*(2).

Thompson, D. C. (1991a). *Affidavit on behalf of plaintiffs in USD 259 v. State of Kansas*. Manhattan, KS: UCEA Center for Education Finance.

Thompson, D. C. (1991b). *Report to USD 259 on the impacts of hold-harmless aid on select school districts in Kansas*. Manhattan, KS: UCEA Center for Education Finance.

Thompson, D. C. (1992). Special needs students: A generation at risk. In J. G. Ward & P. Anthony (Eds.), *Who pays for student diversity? Population changes and educational policy* (pp. 97-124). Newbury Park, CA: Corwin.

Thompson, D. C., Honeyman, D., & Wood, R. C. (1990). *Fiscal equity in Kansas under the school district equalization act: Consultants' analysis on behalf of Turner USD 202 in Mock v. State of Kansas*. Manhattan, KS: UCEA Center for Education Finance.

Thompson, D. C., Honeyman, D., & Wood, R. C. (1991). *Educational fiscal equality in Kansas under the School District Equalization Act: Consultants' analysis on behalf of plaintiffs in Newton USD 373 et al. v. State of Kansas*. Manhattan, KS: UCEA Center for Education Finance.

U.S. Congress, House of Representatives, Subcommittee on Elementary, Secondary, and Vocational Education. (1986). *Targeting students for Chapter 1 services: Are the students in greatest need being served?* Washington, DC: Government Printing Office.

USD 259 v. State of Kansas, Shawnee County District Court, Case No. 91-CV-1009 (1991).

Ward, J. G., & Anthony, P. (Eds.). (1992). *Who pays for student diversity? Population changes and educational policy*. Newbury Park, CA: Corwin.

Zabel, R., & Costello, J. (1991). *Needed and recently endorsed special education personnel in Kansas (1989-90): Data collected and analyzed for the Comprehensive System of Personnel Development (CSPD)*. Unpublished manuscript.

TEN

State Policy for
Integrating All Students

GRETCHEN B. ROSSMAN

A major restructuring effort is taking hold in many of our nation's schools, one calling for the inclusion of special needs students in regular classrooms. An expression of increasing concern about the equity and finance of special education, this integration initiative was first articulated as federal policy in the 1980s (the Regular Education Initiative). As states and local districts have assumed a larger role in both policy considerations and the funding of education, however, the locus of the integration initiative has shifted. In its current form, integration is often fostered by the state through a complex mix of policy strategies, in conjunction with local initiatives.

The purpose of this chapter is to present alternatives for states to consider should they move toward integration policy. This is accomplished through a discussion of the current debate on the integration initiative in the context of educational reform, the local conditions necessary to support integration, and the policy instruments available to states to help create those conditions. The chapter ends with a description of two state initiatives: Vermont's mandated inclusion model and Massachusetts's experimental integration strategy.

AUTHOR'S NOTE: The preparation of this chapter has been supported in part by the Massachusetts Department of Education (Grant 267-001-1-3321-7). No official endorsement should be inferred.

The Context of Reform

The decade of the 1980s was a period of intense state involvement in education. Growing concern over the quality of American education found expression in the National Commission on Excellence in Education's *A Nation at Risk* (1983), which described schools as infected with a "rising tide of mediocrity." Spurred by such evocative rhetoric, state policymakers initiated a series of reforms that both reflected and encouraged a reappraisal of the status of American education. Prodded sharply by an increasing awareness that the U.S. economy was no longer preeminent in world markets, the early reform initiatives targeted student outcomes, curriculum and testing, and standards for teacher training and certification. Taken together, this first wave of reform included efforts to "forcefully repair the sinking vessel" (Hawley, 1988, p. 418) of American education.

To the surprise of some, the movement has not withered away, as have so many previous reform efforts. Instead, responsibility seems to be shifting from the state house, with its necessarily regulatory emphasis, to a shared responsibility between state departments of education and local school districts. Many states have enacted legislation, funded experimental grant programs, or provided training and technical assistance to districts to implement school-based management, build structures promoting greater community involvement in schools, disseminate exemplary and often collaborative teaching practices, develop interdisciplinary and experiential curricula, and identify authentic assessment procedures. In some cases, while enacting legislation or funding discretionary programs supporting local reform, states have not closely constrained the particulars of those experiments (see Shanker, 1990). Although restructuring initially focused on governance structures—elements outside of the classroom—recent reform efforts have placed the locus of change directly in the classroom, with efforts to alter profoundly how children are organized for learning and to create environments conducive to the growth of all children together. Taken together, these restructuring initiatives have become the hallmark of the third wave of reform efforts.

The Policy Debate

Growing out of this third wave is the current debate in special education about inclusion, or integration. This debate centers on finance and equity concerns and on the relationship of special education to regular education. On the one hand are the proponents of integration, who argue that current patterns of financing both regular and special education systematically exclude certain categories of children from full participation in available educational resources and are, therefore, inherently inequitable. On the other hand are those who assert that the hard-won battles of the 1970s for handicapped children will be lost if full inclusion is implemented.

Background of the Debate[1]

In 1975, P.L. 94-142, the Education for All Handicapped Children Act (EAHCA), was passed by Congress, guaranteeing to disabled children the right to a free appropriate public education. EAHCA's original mission was to provide disabled students with access to an education and the delivery of special education services within as normal an educational environment as possible. Guided by *Brown v. Board of Education* and its concept of equal educational opportunity for all children, Congress mandated that states initiate the identification of all children requiring special services, that parents be apprised of their legal rights in receiving educational services for their handicapped children, and that the dual philosophies of "mainstreaming" and educating handicapped children in the "least restrictive environment" be paramount in the educational placement of such children. Since the passage of EAHCA, the number of children identified as requiring special education services has increased substantially: Currently, 12.5% of all U.S. students are enrolled in special education programs (Massachusetts Department of Education, 1990).

As the numbers of special education students have increased, so also have the costs. This has been a source of growing concern in many states. While the federal appropriation for special education approaches $4 billion (*Education of the Handicapped*, 1989), the heaviest burden for financing special education programs rests squarely on the shoulders of states and local school districts. Sluggish state economic trends in recent years, resulting in inadequate state revenues, have provided a basis for claims that special education is too expensive, is not cost-effective, and utilizes an inordinate amount of tax dollars for one population of students to provide services not available to all the rest. Coinciding with the increasing concern over cost issues, a debate focusing on the effectiveness of current state special education programs developed during the 1980s. Studies conducted by Gartner and Lipsky (1987) acknowledged the accomplishment of P.L. 94-142 in providing services to many more students, but also highlighted trouble spots, particularly in the areas of referral and assessment procedures, placement options, benefit of educational programs, least restrictive environment issues, and parental involvement. Advocates of integration proposed that rather than operating two systems of education—one for "regular" students and another for disabled students—states should offer a unitary system of education. The Regular Education Initiative was subsequently advanced by federal officials who urged states to reconsider their methods of organizing and administering special education programs, arguing that children with mild handicaps and learning disabilities would particularly benefit from being educated in the regular classroom (Will, 1986).

Other researchers dispute Gartner and Lipsky's findings, and urge that integration be viewed with caution. Of utmost concern is the future placement of mildly disabled and behavior-disordered students. Braaten, Kauffman, Braaten, Polsgrove, and Nelson (1988) argue that although the regular classroom is appropriate for *many* of these students, it is by no means appropriate for all. In another study, Kauffman, Gerber, and Semmel (1988) raise the issue of integration being utilized as a cost savings mechanism rather than as a method for improving programs and enhancing the education of children with special needs. With many states facing deficits in their budgets, such concerns are not unwarranted.

The Equity Issues

Inherent in both these issues—the growing fiscal crisis surrounding the delivery of services to children in need of special education, and the relationship of special education to regular education—is a larger question concerning educational equity. On the one hand, there are those who contend that special education students receive an inordinately large portion of the available education dollars; that these dollars fund an inefficient, segregated, and non-cost-effective system of education; and that the continuance of this system is detrimental to the quality of both special and regular students' educational programs. Proponents of this line of thought argue that education dollars should be utilized more efficiently for the equal educational opportunity of all students.

In the wake of EAHCA, related concerns about equity arose as the education system responded to differences by "creating new and separate programs" for gifted, disadvantaged, and at-risk students (Kane, 1991, p. 2). Increasingly, students were removed from regular education services and taught by specialists governed by "their own rules, certifications, curriculums and bureaucracies" (p. 2). Programs serving special populations have come under attack as being separatist.

These arguments are buttressed by the growing sociological literature identifying the stratification effects of schools. According to this research, one important function of schools may be to confer a particular status on the students (Metz, 1978; Oakes, 1985). In sorting their "clients" into groups and labeling those groups, schools are seen as mechanisms of social control that have profound influence over students' life chances (Ogbu, 1985).

When segregated into substantially separate classrooms or treated as "different" through pullout programs or resource room services, special needs children are denied, it is argued, the full experiences of the classroom. These inequities also extend to children with disabilities who are served in the regular classroom, but often with children deemed "slower" or "remedial." These children are then doubly at risk, because the instructional resources and teaching strategies available to students placed in "lower tracks" have been found to be impoverished (Metz, 1978; Page, 1984): The pace and complexity of instructional tasks is simplified and fragmented in lower-ability classes (Page, 1984), and more experienced and more effective teachers are found disproportionately to be teaching higher-ability groups and tracks (Gamoran & Behrends, 1987). From this perspective, the notion of integration without simultaneous heterogeneous grouping becomes insupportable.

In the other camp are those who, while acknowledging that there are problems with the current status of special education programs, maintain that to adopt integration and place disabled students back into the regular classroom would be a return to a "pre-P.L. 94-143" era. These individuals view integration chiefly as a cost-cutting mechanism developed to assist states in grappling with the expenditures engendered in delivering required special education services to handicapped children. They contend that the resources allocated to special education students will be subsumed into the larger regular education system, resulting in a loss of educational equity for special education students. In summary, the debate centers on the following questions. If a state utilizes integration as the model for delivering special education services to disabled children, how will this affect these children's access to educational opportunities? Second, as the method chosen by a state to deliver special education services, is integration more cost-effective and does it offer a qualitatively better education for children with special needs?

Several states have responded to these questions with sweeping reform of their special education delivery systems intended to promote adoption of inclusion models at the local level. Arguing that continued segregation of special needs children obviates democratic principles of equal opportunity for both special needs and regular children, and buttressed by growing fiscal pressures and increasing demands for schools that are responsive to diversity, states have enacted legislation, funded experimental programs, and promoted reform of teacher education, all in support of integration efforts.

Educational Conditions Supporting Integration

The educational conditions necessary to support integration have district- and school-level elements, each with governance, organizational, instructional, and staffing elements. Many are characteristic of successful schools, with specific consideration given to special needs children. In general, successful schools are characterized by a shared vision for education among a dedicated, enthusiastic, and stable staff; caring teachers who have mastered a variety of instructional strategies and have thorough knowledge of subject matter; a challenging curriculum that is integrated across grades and interdisciplinary in nature; and opportunities for parents to participate in educational decision making (Purkey & Smith, 1985; Smith & O'Day, 1990). Each is an element of integrated schools, with additional consideration given to responsiveness to learners' diverse needs, and can be clustered into governance and administrative responsibility, organizational structures, instructional practices and the curriculum, and teacher roles.

Governance and Administrative Responsibility

To support integration fully, district and building administrators should impart a vision of inclusive schools—schools that are responsive to individual learners and sensitive to diversity. This vision is enacted through formal policy statements and attention to the overall climate of the district and school in ways that promote and implement the conditions outlined below. In addition, for integration initiatives to succeed, it is crucial that administrators foster teacher, parent, and community participation in decision-making bodies; promote teacher and administrator growth and renewal, and curriculum reform; strictly monitor the placement of special needs children across and within district schools; and support building-level coordination of all categorical services as well as increased flexibility in their provision.

These conditions suggest that one feature of a state strategy supporting integration is the policy to vest greater authority and responsibility in the local school and its community than has historically been the case. School-based management, with increased involvement of teachers, community members, and parents in programmatic, curricular, staffing, and fiscal decisions that affect daily operations, is a feature of many state and local reform efforts.

Organizational Structures

Organizational structures are often driven by bureaucratic considerations rather than educational ones. Which children are placed together in both schools and classrooms, how they are organized to learn within those classrooms, and the flexibility of the services they receive are critical elements shaping a child's educational experience. Thus placement decisions and grouping practices should be examined to ensure that those structures are responsive to diverse needs within the school and classroom.

At the district level, the placement of special needs children within district school structures constrains or enhances their opportunities for interactions with their nondisabled peers. Children with special needs are best served if they attend their home schools, defined as the schools they would attend if they were not disabled. Although the clustering of those requiring services in one location is widespread (based on the argument that it is more cost-effective), this practice often means that children spend larger amounts of time being transported than do their nondisabled peers, places them in segregated settings, and thus excludes them from the benefits associated with the neighborhood school. Friendships with nondisabled peers become less likely as children attend different schools. In similar manner, the placement of children with similar disabilities in one school creates unnatural conditions that are not reflective of the larger school population. As a result, both regular and special needs children develop perceptions of the distribution of disabilities in the population that are inaccurate. Finally, ensuring that all disabilities are represented in each school (to the extent possible) promotes greater sensitivity to diverse needs for the total school population.

The organization of children for learning *within* schools also has a profound effect on their participation in the available educational resources. Initiatives that support heterogeneous grouping should extend to children with special needs so that they are able to interact with and learn from their peers. Furthermore, special needs children should be placed in age- and grade-appropriate classrooms rather than those consistent with cognitive functioning level. Such placements within the school foster friendships with age-mates and encourage social interaction.

At the building level, the administrative elements necessary for full inclusion of special needs children include the assumption of authority and responsibility for categorical programs. Typically, special programs are administered centrally, while regular education programs are managed at the school level. This has resulted in a "parallel 'second system' " of education (Sailor, Gerry, & Wilson, 1991, p. 177). Principals often find themselves unable to manage effectively school personnel who report to district officials. Excessive restrictions in the delivery of services, moreover, constrain administrators and teachers in creatively supporting children who are at risk of failure or referral to special education. With building-level authority for and increased flexibility in the provision of categorical programs, services are more responsive to the specific needs of the children served by the school. These organizational elements suggest features of integration policy that restructures schools to bring disabled students into greater contact with their nondisabled peers and provides them needed services, unconstrained by excessive regulation. A sustained critical look at the ways in which students are brought together to learn (placements across and within schools, age/grade groupings, ability grouping and tracking) and relaxation of the restrictions surrounding categorical services are necessary to promote integration.

Instructional Practices and the Curriculum

District- and building-level administrative support coupled with appropriate and sensitive organizational structures are insufficient to foster integration, because the classroom is where daily educational experiences occur. In the final analysis, the resources made available to children through the curriculum and instructional practices become the litmus test of true integration. In addition to more flexible school structures, varied instructional practices that are sensitive to the needs of diverse learners are required. These include project-based, experiential, and both individual- and group-oriented strategies. The curriculum, moreover, should reflect constructivist notions about knowledge, higher-order thinking skills, and problem solving rather than the mastery of discrete facts.

Teachers' Roles

To support an integration initiative, teachers must come to construe their roles more broadly. Increasingly, regular educators have come to think of special needs programs as those that serve students who do not perform at expected achievement or behavioral levels, resulting in increasing referrals to special education for all learning or behavior problems (Massachusetts Department of Education, 1990). Teachers must be supported to reconceptualize their roles as more inclusive. Both preservice and in-service development is necessary. This in turn suggests that state policy revamp teacher training programs at institutions of higher education and provide extensive and sustained staff development opportunities.

Moreover, the deployment of teachers to work in integrated settings works best when those individuals are open to the changes that come with working with another adult in the classroom, are respectful of their specialist colleagues and willing to learn from them, and have been encouraged to experiment with integration with a supportive peer. We call this the "friendship model of coteaching," where teachers seek one another out to create integrated classrooms. Top-down mandates pairing teachers often create avoidably difficult situations for all involved.

In summary, the educational conditions supportive of integration include a vision for integrated schools articulated at the district and school levels; shared governance among educators, parents, and community members; vigilant monitoring of district and school placements of special needs children; coordination of services at the building level and increased flexibility in their provision; and sustained professional development designed to expand teachers' roles. The challenge for states is to formulate comprehensive policies that will promote these conditions.

State Policy for Integration: Dimensions and Instruments

In order to mount an integration initiative, states must determine the complex mix of strategies that will encourage or mandate the educational conditions necessary for integration to succeed. Such an initiative cannot proceed on a piecemeal basis; systemic change is needed. Far-reaching change will be necessary in organizational, administrative, and governance structures, and in curriculum, instructional practices, and professional knowledge and skills. Site-based decision making, flexible structures, collaborative problem solving, integration of services, and supple instructional practices are all required for comprehensive restructuring to support integration. The challenge to states is to devise policy strategies that support such systemic change.

Dimensions of Systemic Change

One perspective on systemic change looks at the technical, political, and cultural dimensions of any policy initiative (House, 1981; Oakes, 1992; Tichy, 1983). This view argues that attention must be paid to all three for change to proceed successfully. Large-scale change and innovation in education have a mixed record of success (Firestone & Corbett, 1988). Over the decades, however, we have learned that successful change requires, for example, providing teachers with the new skills demanded and risk-free opportunities to practice them (attention to the technical; see Little, 1982); building communication sensitivities in school and district administrators, to help them be more humanistic leaders (attention to the technical and political; see Crandall, Eiseman, & Louis, 1986); sufficient time to create a supportive network of key people (attention to the political; see Corbett, Firestone, & Rossman, 1989); and reshaping and creating a shared vision of the school that captures the new ideas and ideals (attention to the cultural; see Rossman, Corbett, & Firestone, 1988). Examining proposed policies through each dimension may well enhance the chances for facilitating ethical, substantive change.

The systemic change demanded by restructuring for integration cannot proceed on a fragmented basis. Sufficient attention must be paid to building the technical knowledge and skills needed by all affected people, from children in classrooms who need sensitivities and skills in dealing with more diverse classmates, to superintendents and school board members who need the knowledge and skills to share power and authority, to shape a vision, and to give people room to experiment in risk-free ways. Attention to the political is also crucial in building support across various constituent groups (at both district and school levels) to support the initiative. This will require sustained attention, openness of communication, provision of information, and opportunities to discuss fears and doubts.

Finally, attention to the deeply held and widely shared beliefs of those involved—the culture of the school or district—is also crucial. Integrating all children more fully into all classrooms entails a rethinking of schooling. It implies a move from individualistic, competitive models in which instruction is teacher centered to group-oriented, cooperative models where children construct knowledge and the teacher is a facilitator, an architect of the environment, and a resource. This suggests a change in our basic beliefs about education.

Policy Instruments

McDonnell and Elmore (1987) have identified four generic instruments available to policymakers to enact reform in the public sector: mandates, inducements, capacity building, and system changing. Each is embedded in a set of assumptions about reform, and can be fruitfully viewed as having technical, political, and/or cultural implications. States can adopt one instrument as the primary mechanism for enacting the public will, or some mix of instruments. Of the four, capacity building and system changing are the most complex and multifaceted. Each is considered in turn below as an option for states to consider in implementing integration policy. The following discussion draws largely on the work of McDonnell and Elmore (1987).

Mandates

Rules and regulations governing "the actions of individuals and agencies" (McDonnell & Elmore, 1987, p. 138) are mandates. The expected result is compliance and, typically, no transfer of money is made as an incentive. Mandates attempt to ensure uniformity in actions and tend to set up adversarial relations between the policymaking body and the targeted individuals or agencies (p. 141).

Mandates have been criticized because they often foster pro forma compliance and do not take into account the differing political and cultural contexts of schools (McDonnell, 1988). While seen as exclusively focused on the technical dimensions of change, mandates also carry the threat of sanction. Although little state scrutiny typically follows mandated change (McDonnell, 1988), laws and regulations can be powerful enforcement strategies.

Inducements

Inducements involve the transfer of money from the policy body to individuals or agencies to effect changes in their actions. These "conditional grants of money" (McDonnell & Elmore, 1987, p. 138) are expected to produce something of value, as in the case of the California incentive programs or the Carnegie Schools grants for school reform, where money is awarded in anticipation of comprehensive restructuring. Unlike mandates, inducements assume that the agency has some capacity to effect change and that money will mobilize those resources.

Inducements take into account the technical and cultural dimensions of change by acknowledging differences in local capacity and will to restructure. While they may foster change in the funded populations, statewide reform is unlikely through this approach. Furthermore, inducements may be criticized from a political perspective as being inherently inequitable.

McDonnell and Elmore (1987) outline the differences between mandates and inducements as follows:

> First, mandates use coercion to affect performance, while inducements transfer money as a condition of performance. Second, mandates exact compliance as an outcome, while inducements are designed to elicit the production of value as an outcome. Third, ... mandates assume that the required action is something all individuals and agencies should be expected to do, regardless of their differing capacities, while inducements assume that individuals and agencies vary in their ability to produce things of value and that the transfer of money is one way to elicit performance. (p. 139)

Capacity Building

Capacity building is a longer-term policy instrument than either mandates or inducements. It is intended to produce some future benefit, but the return on that investment is more "uncertain, intangible, immeasurable, and distant" (McDonnell & Elmore, 1987, p. 139). The costs of capacity building rest with the policy body that invests in the future.

In a manner similar to inducements, capacity building primarily addresses the technical and cultural dimensions of change. Through funding to meet public needs more efficiently, capacity building encourages the targeted agencies to build technical capacity that is reflective of their local cultural contexts.

System Changing

The most far-reaching of the four instruments is system changing, which entails the altering of "official authority among individuals and agencies" (McDonnell & Elmore, 1987, p. 139). Reasoning that current institutional arrangements will not (or cannot) produce the desired results, policies that alter the relations among institutions and individuals seek new outcomes. These new arrangements, however, may well create a new set of problems. As McDonnell and Elmore note, "System-changing policies, then, have a tendency to devolve or degrade into incremental modifications of existing institutions and into more traditional mandates and inducements" (p. 144).

Of the four instruments, only system changing addresses the political changes necessary for a full transformation in the identified policy domain. Through its demands for alterations in governance structures, system changing may well promote the kind of systemic change called for in current restructuring proposals.

Each of these instruments, or some complex mix, is available for states to consider in crafting the reform of special and regular education necessary for integration to be successful. The Commonwealth of Massachusetts's experimental grants program, Restructuring for the Integration of All Students, provides an example of an inducements policy strategy. In contrast is Vermont's Special Education Reform Act, which contains elements of all four strategies. The two different approaches are discussed below.

The Massachusetts Experiment: Inducements for Change

Late in 1990, the Massachusetts Department of Education announced a 5-year competitive grants program to support districts in experimenting with restructuring. Intended to promote the integration of primarily special needs children into the regular classroom, successful grant proposals would also focus on those children identified as needing Chapter 1 and bilingual services. Using federal special education discretionary funds, this inducements program is intended (a) to increase the coordination of all school programs (special education, Chapter 1, bilingual education, remedial reading, school counseling and psychological services, and occupational education); (b) to increase the number of special needs students, including the most challenged, receiving their education within the regular classroom; (c) to expand and adapt assessment techniques, the curriculum, and support services to ensure that the individual academic, physical, and emotional needs of all students are met; (d) to reduce pullout programs by integrating all services into the regular classroom; and (e) to reduce the number of children referred to special education (Massachusetts Department of Education, 1990). These five goals are to be accomplished through comprehensive restructuring of the districts and schools, defined as

> the reorganization of district or school-wide structures, governance mechanisms, policies, programs and/or services to raise academic achievement, improve students' social-emotional development, enhance the school climate, and expand roles of staff, while providing individual and group support to those students who are at risk of academic failure or referral to special education. (p. 1)

Seven districts have been awarded grants for 5 years. The districts are broadly representative of Massachusetts school districts, including three urban city districts, an urban/suburban district, two wealthy suburban districts, and a quite rural union district in western Massachusetts. The districts evidence substantial variation in local capacity (fiscal and human resources), history of support for integration efforts, and commitment to the new service model.

Grants to the districts range from approximately $25,000 in the smaller districts to more than $125,000 for the largest. Use of the monies is not stipulated by the DOE, based on the assumption that local context should shape the exact form of the initiatives. In the first 20 months of implementation (January 1991 through August 1992), the bulk of the monies have been used for staff development. Other uses include funding minigrants for teachers; compensating consultants, district planning team members (including parents, in some cases), and substitute teachers; purchasing materials and other supplies; and funding travel to conferences and other schools where integration is taking place. The level of effort supported by the grants varies considerably. In the case of most districts, integration efforts had already been initiated at the time of the grant award; thus the DOE was funding the expansion of efforts rather than the start-up of dramatically new practice.

For several reasons, the discretionary grant program funded by the Massachusetts Department of Education will provide useful information to other states. First, of the 50 states, Massachusetts has the highest number of children enrolled in special education: 16.8% of all Massachusetts pupils; in some districts, the rate is as high as 25%. Pullout programs have remained the chosen method for delivering special education remediation services, despite research evidence regarding the ineffectiveness of these programs. Since 1986, there has been an increase of 3,000 special education students who are being educated in substantially separate programs (Massachusetts Department of Education, 1990). Moreover, Massachusetts is currently in a state of fiscal crisis, with a state budget deficit of $1 billion. The state public education system is directly affected by this crisis, as seen in massive teacher layoffs, termination of programs, and unmet maintenance needs.

In addition to the above conditions, the Massachusetts state special education law, Chapter 766, is unique in that it is broader than most state statutes in its criteria for identification of handicapped students. And it incorporates a higher standard than the federal law for what is appropriate placement, mandating that the individual educational program maximize the child's potential.

The Vermont Reform: A Comprehensive Policy Strategy

In May 1990, Vermont's Governor Madeline E. Kunin signed into law Act 230, a comprehensive and sweeping reform of special education services within the state. The act is based on the premise that all schools must design comprehensive systems of educational services that will support the success of all students in the regular classroom (Special Education Reform, Act 230). The act contains all four policy instruments: mandates with which districts must comply, inducements through the provision of discretionary funds, capacity building in the form of training and technical assistance, and system changing through alterations in governance structures.

The act calls for the state department of education (a) to provide training for all teachers and administrators to enable them to work more effectively with students who are at risk or have learning difficulties, (b) to tighten the state's eligibility standards for special education, (c) to provide districts with support in establishing instructional support teams and training for those teams, (d) to permit more flexible use of a portion of districts' special education funds, (e) to require all districts to offer special education services to children ages 3 through 5, (f) to require districts to justify excessive special education child counts, (g) to bring students back from out-of-district residential placements, and (h) to establish maximum allowable costs for private residential schools.

The act further calls for all districts (a) to follow the stricter eligibility standards for special education, (b) to provide services to all eligible children from age 3, (c) to develop early identification and intervention strategies so that children with disabilities will be served in the early grades before more serious difficulties develop, (d) to train regular education teachers to serve students with a wide range of learning styles and different strengths and weaknesses, and (e) to make greater use of local resources for teaching all students in the regular classroom.

Act 230 followed close on the heels of Act 235 (1988), which provided a new special education funding formula designed to contain the costs of special education and would grant more predictability for local districts, greater equity in the distribution of funds across districts, and a 50/50 sharing of costs between the state and local districts by 1992 (Hull, 1990). These changes addressed many of the most pressing funding issues but did little to contain rising costs, increasing residential placements, and high referral rates to special education. As a result, comprehensive reform of the entire Vermont education system was proposed, with the intent of radically altering the state's strategies for dealing with diversity in the classroom. Act 230 was a direct result of that reform proposal (Kane, 1991).

Conclusions

The challenge to states considering policies that foster the integration of special needs children in the regular classroom is to devise a comprehensive strategy that will promote desired changes. Clearly, Vermont's integration initiative is more multifaceted than is that of Massachusetts and is linked to the comprehensive restructuring of both regular and special education services. Vermont's strategy assumes that children should not have to be labeled as disabled for their learning needs to be met. It also derives from the premise that state efforts should build the capacity of the regular education system to deal with diverse learning needs rather than create multiple layers of specialized services (Kane, 1991). As such, Vermont's reform strategy may well serve as a model for policy development. The challenge of reforming education to meet the needs of learners who will come of age in the next millennium is formidable. Creating systems of empowered and caring people who work through flexible and democratic structures that are responsive to diversity should be the guiding vision of state policy for the integration of all students.

Note

1. This section is taken from the original proposal of a MDOE-funded grant, "An Evaluation of Restructuring Schools for the Integration of All Students," authored by Patricia Anthony and Gretchen Rossman.

References

Braaten, S., Kauffman, J. M., Braaten, B., Polsgrove, L., & Nelson, C. M. (1988). The regular education initiative: Potent medicine for behavioral disorders. *Exceptional Children, 55,* 21-27.

Corbett, H. D., Firestone, W. A., & Rossman, G. B. (1989). Resistance to planned change and the "sacred" in school cultures. *Educational Administration Quarterly, 23*(4), 36-59.

Crandall, D. P., Eiseman, J. W., & Louis, K. S., (1986). Strategic planning issues that bear on the success of school improvement efforts. *Educational Administration Quarterly, 22*(3), 21-53.

Education of the Handicapped. (1989). Vol. 15, No. 2, 9-10.

Firestone, W. A., & Corbett, H. D. (1988). Planned organizational change. In N. J. Boyan (Ed.), *Handbook of research on educational administration* (pp. 321-340). New York: Longman.

Gamoran, A., & Behrends, M. (1987). The effects of stratification in secondary schools: Synthesis of survey and ethnographic research. *Review of Educational Research, 57,* 415-435.

Gartner, A., & Lipsky, D. K. (1987). Beyond special education: Toward a quality system for all students. *Harvard Educational Review, 57,* 367-395.

Hawley, W. D. (1988). Missing pieces in the educational reform agenda: Or, why the first and second waves may miss the boat. *Educational Administration Quarterly, 24,* 416-437.

House, E. R. (1981). Three perspectives on innovation: Technological, political, and cultural. In R. Lehming & M. Kane (Eds.), *Improving schools: Using what we know* (pp. 17-41). Beverly Hills, CA: Sage.

Hull, M. E. (1990). Synopsis of Act 230, reforms in special education. *Newsletter of the Vermont Department of Education.*

Kane, D. (1991, Spring). Act 230: Regulation or revolution? *Vermont Education.*

Kauffman, J. M., Gerber, M. M., & Semmel, M. I. (1988). Arguable assumptions under-lying the regular education initiative. *Journal of Learning Disabilities, 21,*(1), 6-11.

Little, J. W. (1982). Norms of collegiality and experimentation: Workplace conditions of school success. *American Educational Research Journal, 19,* 325-340.

Massachusetts Department of Education. (1990). *Request for proposals for the evaluation of "Restructuring for the integration of all students."* Quincy: Author.

McDonnell, L. M. (1988). *Coursework policy in five states and its implications for indicator development* (Working Paper). New Brunswick, NJ: Center for Policy Research in Education.

McDonnell, L. M., & Elmore, R. A. (1987). Getting the job done: Alternative policy instruments. *Educational Evaluation and Policy Analysis, 9,* 133-152.

Metz, M. H. (1978). *Classrooms and corridors: The crisis of authority in desegregated secondary schools.* Berkeley: University of California Press.

National Commission on Excellence in Education. (1983). *A nation at risk: The imperative for educational reform.* Washington, DC: Government Printing Office.

Oakes, J. H. (1985). *Keeping track: How schools structure inequality.* New Haven, CT: Yale University Press.

Oakes, J. (1992). Can tracking research inform practice? Technical, normative, and political considerations. *Educational Researcher, 21,* 4, 12-21.

Ogbu, J. (1985). *The next generation: An ethnography of education in an urban neighborhood.* New York: Academic Press.

Page, R. N. (1984). *The social construction of the curriculum in lower-track high school classrooms.* Paper presented at the annual meetings of the American Educational Research Association, San Francisco.

Purkey, S. T., & Smith, M. S. (1985). Effective schools: A review. *Elementary School Journal, 83,* 427-452.

Rossman, G. B., Corbett, H. D., & Firestone, W. A. (1988). *Change and effectiveness in schools: A cultural perspective.* Albany: State University of New York Press.

Sailor, W., Gerry, M., & Wilson, W. C. (1991). Policy implications of emergent full inclusion models for the education of children with severe disabilities. In M. Wang, H. Walberg, & M. Reynolds (Eds.), *Handbook of special education* (Vol. 4). Oxford: Pergamon.

Shanker, A. (1990). A proposal for using incentives to restructure our public schools. *Phi Delta Kappan, 71,* 344-357.

Smith, M. S., & O'Day, J. (1990). Systemic school reform. In S. Fuhrman & B. Malen (Eds.), *The politics of curriculum and testing* (pp. 233-267). London: Falmer.

Tichy, N. M. (1983). *Managing strategic change: Technical, political and cultural.* New York: John Wiley.

Will, M. (1986). *Educating students with learning problems: A shared responsibility* (Policy paper for U.S. Department of Education, Office of Rehabilitative Services). Wash-ington, DC: Government Printing Office.

ELEVEN

Impact of Personnel Policies
on Students With Disabilities

STEPHANIE BROWN

MARSHA CRAFT-TRIPP

SUSAN GURGANUS

CATHY CROSSLAND

BETTYE MacPHAIL-WILCOX

Personnel policies and personnel administration practices affect a school's capacity to educate at-risk populations in many ways. They have direct and indirect impact on the efficiency and equity of education afforded all students, but their impacts are particularly salient for at-risk students. Because of their unique and often extensive educational needs, students with disabilities may be considered an at-risk population within the public schools.

The direct and indirect effects of personnel policies and administration concern the availability, adequacy, and distribution of qualified personnel. These conditions then influence the efficient and equitable education received by students. For example, personnel policies alter the demand for special education services, thereby influencing the supply of personnel. Policies and practices that prescribe training and certification affect the quality of the special education teacher labor

229

force. Similar effects occur through the specific administrative practices of personnel selection, evaluation, and in-service training. Clearly, personnel policies and personnel administration practices have important implications for the quality of education received by special populations of students.

The long-range effects of such policies on schools and students result in a set of economic and social costs or benefits. Studies computing these costs and benefits to society have only recently been initiated, so findings are limited. But the logic of the argument is clear. Failure to educate at-risk populations results in a substantial loss of human capital and a host of protracted costs associated with providing a variety of highly specialized services over the life of the individual. Some projections indicate that the direct costs of special education will increase steadily as the numbers of students needing services continues to rise. The escalating size of this at-risk population seems to stem from expanded drug abuse, birth trauma and defects, and the continuing decline of other stable social institutions, particularly the traditional family.

Producing an adequate supply of special education personnel is just a starting point of a plan that will provide for the educational needs of this at-risk population. Policies and practices that affect the quality of work life and the ability of teachers to be successful with special education students can threaten both the retention and the productivity of these teachers. Consequently, personnel policies have multiple important implications for the efficient and equitable education of at-risk populations of students.

In this chapter, we examine the demand and supply of special educators relative to the student populations served currently and those anticipated for the immediate future. We explore personnel practices such as appraisal and staff development relative to the goal of improving the educational attainments of at-risk youth, herein defined as students needing special education services. We close the chapter with a set of research questions relative to the field of special education that have important implications for policymakers and administrators who wish to improve educational outcomes for at-risk youth.

Demand for Special Educators

The number of special education teachers needed is a function of many related factors. Among these are medical and technological advances, demographic changes, shifting cultural values, and the means by which these needs are addressed in educational institutions. As the demand for special education services changes in terms of student load, types of services required, and the availability of specialized labor, obvious fiscal issues emerge.

Efficiency requires that the greatest student gains be obtained with the least costly resource configuration. *Equity* can be defined and assessed in any number of ways. Equity analyses may focus on school inputs, such as fiscal and human resources, or access to particular school processes, such as unique educational treatments and program structures, or the distribution of specific outcomes attained by students. The current emphasis on accountability suggests that vertical equity, equity concerned with the distribution of resources relative to need and the attainment of an equitable distribution of outcomes, is a critically important performance criterion for at-risk populations. This conceptual definition of equity is used throughout the chapter.

Medical, Technological, Professional, and Cultural Factors Affecting Demand

Medical advances often reveal the causes, limitations, and proper treatments of special needs among students. Consider the discovery that the blindness accompanying retrolental fibroplasia was caused by the overadministration of oxygen to infants. Once this was understood, there was a reduction in the incidence of the condition, thereby reducing the demand for selected specialized services placed on public schools.

Technological and professional advances provide an ever-expanding and sophisticated set of treatments for disabilities. These effects are evidenced, for example, in the development of electrical amplification devices for the hard of hearing and the very recent cochlear implants used with the deaf and hearing impaired. Such inventions alter the level of unique programs and services needed by special education students while simultaneously enhancing some students' capacities to learn (Mullins, 1986).

Advances such as these interact with demographic conditions, particularly birth and mortality rates, to define a need for special education services among youth. However, cultural changes and values also affect the number of students with disabilities. They do so by their influence on individuals, families, and other social institutions. The increased incidence of drug abuse and emotional problems stemming from dysfunctional families are two readily obvious instances. In addition, cultural values, as reflected in the policy-making process, determine whether, how much, and what kinds of services will be provided to students with disabilities through public schools (National Association for Perinatal Addiction Research and Education, 1988; National Easter Seal Society, 1988).

The complex effects of these interactions on the demand for special education personnel are evident in a chronological analysis of special education services. Such an analysis evidences a meteoric rise in the number and complexity of educational options made available to the special needs population over the last 30 years (Wooden, 1980). As awareness of the existence of special education populations increased and technological advances enhanced the ability to teach these students, fiscal resources for the education of special populations were increased. Public values were expressed through legislation that mandated and increased services provided to children with disabilities in the public schools.

The increasing demand for various types of special education personnel is evident in three national surveys conducted by the Council of Exceptional Children. Reported data demonstrate that increasing numbers of students are being served and that educators are required to increase their levels of specialization in order to provide these services (see Table 11.1).

The number of students between 0 and 21 years of age served in federally supported special education programs increased 23% between 1976-77 and 1988-89. Changes in student classifications are also apparent. For example, the population of learning disabled students increased from 21.6% to 43.6%, while the population of mentally retarded students served declined from 26% to 12.7%. The numbers of students classified as multihandicapped and seriously emotionally disturbed also increased significantly, while the proportion of students with all other disabilities seemed to decline. Changes such as

Table 11.1 Children 0 to 21 Years Old Served in Federally Supported Special Education Programs, by Type of Handicap: 1976-77 to 1988-89

Type of Handicap	1976-77	1978-79	1980-81	1982-83	1984-85	1986-87	1988-89
				Number Served (in thousands)			
All conditions	3,692	3,889	4,142	4,255	4,315	4,374	4,544
Learning disabled	796	1,130	1,462	1,741	1,832	1,914	1,987
Speech impaired	1,302	1,214	1,168	1,131	1,126	1,136	967
Mentally retarded	959	901	829	757	694	643	564
Seriously emotionally disturbed	283	300	346	352	372	383	376
Hard of hearing and deaf	87	85	79	73	69	65	56
Orthopedically handicapped	87	70	58	57	56	57	47
Other health impaired	141	105	98	50	68	52	43
Visually impaired	38	32	31	28	28	26	23
Multihandicapped	—	50	68	63	69	97	85
Deaf-blind	—[c]	2	3	2	2	2	2
Preschool handicapped[b]	—[c]	—[c]	—[c]	—[c]	—[c]	—[c]	394

SOURCE: Adapted from U.S. Department of Education (various years, Table 47) and the Common Core of Data Survey of the National Center for Educational Statistics.

a. Includes students served under Chapter 1 and Education of the Handicapped Act (EHA).
b. Includes preschool children 3-5 years served under the EHA and 0-5 year served under Chapter 1.
c. Prior to 1987-88, these students were included in the counts by handicapping condition. As of 1987-88, states are no longer required to report preschool handicapped students (0-5 years) by handicapping condition.

these may result from medical advances, improved technologies of identification, goal displacement mechanisms in funding schemes, or shortages of particular forms of specialized labor among teachers. Fiscal goal displacement and specialized labor shortages make it difficult to estimate the actual demand for special education services. When governments use categorical and head-count funding to provide resources for special education, one form of education or one type of student is emphasized and not another. School units may then seek to take advantage of available resources by reclassifying students to match the funding guidelines. Thus the need for specific services may appear to rise or fall more than it does in actuality. In the past, governments responded to this form of goal displacement by capping the number or proportion of a population that might be identified as needing special services. To the degree that these are inappropriate caps, the adequacy, efficiency, and equity of programs may be compromised.

Other regulations may lead to irregularities that obstruct efficiency and equity. For example, schools are mandated to provide services even though they may not be able to hire appropriate personnel. They may hire persons who are not properly trained or credentialed in order to "place someone in charge" of the classroom or service, or they may adopt least-cost program structures that are less than optimal for the particular students served. The effects of such practices on programs and students have not been investigated adequately.

For reasons such as the foregoing, data describing the type and scope of special education services provided or received are not necessarily reliable indicators of actual population need. Just as it is difficult to discern whether necessity is the mother of technology or vice versa, extant data make it difficult to know precisely the scope and quality of special education services needed.

Other population data can be used to supplement an estimate of need for special education services. For example, it seems clear that the number of drug-exposed preschoolers is increasing. Approximately 375,000 newborns per year are at risk for health and education problems resulting from drug use by their mothers while the babies were in utero. Cocaine abuse among pregnant women has increased 3,000% during the last 10 years (Marilee, 1990). Similarly, dramatic changes in family structures and economic conditions are affecting students' capacities to profit from the traditional educational treatments offered in public schools. These changes increase the number of students who require special education services. Table 11.2 summarizes the number of special education teachers employed and the number needed to serve students between the ages of 6 and 21 in 1988-89. Despite the appeal of such data, their reliability are suspect because extant information and knowledge of the future are imperfect. It is not possible to predict accurately the impact of current or future social, medical, and technological advances on the number of children whose need for special education services will change. External data, particular those derived from medical and sociological sources, suggest that many students who are most severely damaged from the conditions described are likely to need special education programs and services. It seems clear that present medical, technological, and cultural trends point toward an increased demand for special education services, which is consistent with the directionality implied in Table 11.2.

An increased demand for special education personnel has obvious fiscal implications for schools and institutions of higher education that train special education personnel. The increased demand for services and training will be satisfied either by new resources or by the reallocation of existing resources from programs serving non-special education students. While the former is a severely constrained decision economically, the latter is both economically and politically constrained.

Effects of Program Structure
and Professional Technologies
on the Demand for Personnel

The ways in which special education services are organized and delivered are referred to here as *program structure*. This is a broad term that includes the distribution of students and teaching labor, as well as the use of alternative technologies and resource configurations. Residential schools, separate class settings, mainstreaming, resource classrooms, and so on represent different kinds of program structures.

Implementation of each program structure requires different kinds and levels of resources that, of course, generate the need for fiscal

Table 11.2 Number of Special Education Teachers Employed and Needed
to Serve Children With Disabilities Ages 6-21 for School Year
1988-89 (data as of October 1, 1990)

State	Employed	Needed	State	Employed	Needed
Alabama	4,655	376	New Hampshire	1,427	283
Alaska	547	50	New Jersey	13,511	538
Arizona	3,926	347	New Mexico	2,508	151
Arkansas	2,719	232	New York	28,264	6,254
California	21,318	899	North Carolina	6,172	1,472
Colorado	3,508	87	North Dakota	826	119
Connecticut	4,039	52	Ohio	11,571	360
Delaware	1,215	72	Oklahoma	3,580	4,145
District of Columbia	666	38	Oregon	2,373	104
Florida	11,644	2,681	Pennsylvania	12,404	766
Georgia	6,546	327	Puerto Rico	2,633	0
Hawaii	1,065	173	Rhode Island	1,195	25
Idaho	993	52	South Carolina	4,062	303
Illinois	16,594	458	South Dakota	958	80
Indiana	5,247	715	Tennessee	4,423	347
Iowa	4,125	604	Texas	17,076	1,369
Kansas	2,864	84	Utah	2,402	306
Kentucky	4,288	897	Vermont	816	48
Louisiana	6,072	1,322	Virginia	7,138	372
Maine	1,700	211	Washington	3,963	94
Maryland	5,905	130	West Virginia	3,055	458
Massachusetts	7,726	417	Wisconsin	6,085	501
Michigan	10,974	599	Wyoming	735	319
Minnesota	6,558	198	American Samoa	30	16
Mississippi	3,436	241	Guam	135	54
Missouri	6,596	1,521	Northern Marianas	27	23
Montana	860	241	Trust Territories	—	—
Nebraska	1,726	25	Virgin Islands	121	6
Nevada	1,034	97	Bureau of Indian Affairs	511	52

SOURCE: Excerpted from U.S. Department of Education (1991, Table AC1).

resources. Table 11.3 summarizes the latest available data on program structures or educational environments for special populations between the ages of 3 and 21.

Resource room settings continue to be the most prevalent program structure. Regular class and separate class settings are second and third in numbers of children served. These structures are followed by

Table 11.3 Number of Children Ages 3-21 Served in Different Educational Environments During School Year 1988-89, All Disabilities (data as of October 1, 1990)

State	Regular Class	Resource Room	Separate Class	Public Separate Facility	Private Separate Facility	Public Residential Facility	Private Residential Facility	Correctional Facility	Homebound/Hospital Environment
Alabama	—	67,514	24,791	1,429	58	—	151	446	354
Alaska	7,445	3,690	1,874	31	1	25	0	37	66
Arizona	4,282	27,128	9,865	747	489	278	328	101	57
Arkansas	20,056	18,874	5,954	225	1,297	458	187	53	78
California	121,542	171,374	114,765	13,976	5,632	0	—	557	—
Colorado	13,108	26,807	9,710	1,259	391	233	387	171	338
Connecticut	30,621	11,625	14,105	2,537	1,766	195	985	296	387
Delaware	3,967	5,200	2,227	1,676	11	19	55	112	184
District of Columbia	1,420	1,852	2,409	791	434	10	280	76	67
Florida	64,182	69,361	58,142	10,178	1,081	762	351	173	2,462
Georgia	1,015	65,004	24,144	1,646	100	1,081	69	85	50
Hawaii	4,665	4,661	3,297	149	28	50	39	27	52
Idaho	9,857	4,708	2,619	193	0	136	111	0	0
Illinois	65,772	75,073	75,244	10,288	5,414	2,682	1,182	1,060	1,097
Indiana	41,632	31,634	29,406	4,554	6	824	121	37	61
Iowa	13,034	32,825	8,835	1,120	0	549	87	143	295
Kansas	16,969	12,892	9,362	830	503	814	478	332	456
Kentucky	22,696	36,407	11,426	1,014	160	429	53	24	437
Louisiana	25,795	13,380	25,085	2,999	95	1,136	159	134	717
Maine	14,331	8,396	3,449	402	493	99	213	107	512

(Continued)

Table 11.3 (Continued)

State	Regular Class	Resource Room	Separate Class	Public Separate Facility	Private Separate Facility	Public Residential Facility	Private Residential Facility	Correctional Facility	Homebound/Hospital Environment
Maryland	37,620	16,395	24,107	6,088	1,475	711	377	81	245
Massachusetts	83,514	20,968	25,679	2,710	4,223	732	845	83	764
Michigan	63,620	43,732	40,707	10,039	—	646	411	690	1,350
Minnesota	12,890	47,750	17,205	2,119	0	965	0	30	186
Mississippi	21,643	22,263	14,086	646	55	8	30	13	223
Missouri	45,372	41,428	23,396	5,110	2,020	390	286	1,364	410
Montana	8,624	3,850	2,539	140	10	195	88	16	88
Nebraska	19,105	6,606	4,550	521	83	200	46	100	278
Nevada	3,924	8,579	2,403	730	2	1	10	105	170
New Hampshire	9,118	3,557	3,737	377	570	43	260	30	95
New Jersey	66,385	35,375	50,785	9,714	8,933	632	119	561	716
New Mexico	15,431	9,117	5,456	51	82	298	0	36	86
New York	21,752	98,174	122,168	23,094	19,228	1,900	1,772	621	1,541
North Carolina	55,975	33,398	18,815	2,868	392	1,229	430	222	542
North Dakota	8,827	1,213	1,794	342	22	122	86	9	94
Ohio	71,800	48,187	55,115	13,773	11,497	1,048	0	660	2,130
Oklahoma	32,196	18,945	11,175	847	101	638	117	23	224
Oregon	28,273	12,285	5,831	195	603	383	115	128	277
Pennsylvania	72,185	53,431	57,000	5,049	721	315	167	766	1,423
Puerto Rico	3,852	16,054	11,040	2,088	1,075	160	149	53	1,937
Rhode Island	10,099	2,892	5,479	202	584	0	220	101	174

South Carolina	26,121	31,149	15,747	1,776	6	734	56	212	400
South Dakota	1,235	10,813	1,564	55	49	256	335	0	89
Tennessee	45,382	33,321	16,787	1,966	519	916	159	155	1,050
Texas	11,969	244,852	36,753	7,381	415	641	154	512	14,677
Utah	16,260	16,384	5,957	1,787	0	204	0	4	196
Vermont	9,431	953	1,307	112	203	4	190	3	328
Virginia	42,863	28,478	29,245	1,893	514	821	492	296	963
Washington	29,211	24,256	14,419	964	377	259	8	122	855
West Virginia	20,322	13,608	8,913	464	32	45	7	55	83
Wisconsin	24,345	30,050	21,882	1,459	26	504	9	205	115
Wyoming	2,681	3,416	1,181	42	3	90	45	0	29
American Samoa	201	35	16	81	0	0	0	0	1
Guam	616	588	419	62	0	0	1	1	0
Northern Marianas	65	73	139	0	0	0	0	0	0
Trust Territories	—	—	—	—	—	—	—	—	—
Virgin Islands	150	230	853	33	1	0	24	0	21
Bureau of Indian Affairs	800	4,384	535	18	90	—	—	—	27

SOURCE: Excerpted from U.S. Department of Education (1991, Table AB1).
NOTE: The number of students served in correctional facilities is a duplicate count. These students are also reported as being served in one of the eight educational environments.

public separate facilities, private separate facilities, homebound/hospital environments, public residential facilities, and private residential and correctional facilities. It is important to note that judgments about the adequacy of program structure are not grounded in empirical research findings.

Unfortunately, the professional knowledge base in special education does not reveal underlying relations among student learning outcomes, alternative program structures, and different teaching technologies. Not surprisingly, this professional knowledge lags behind the development of a similar knowledge base in regular education. It is, of course, possible to calculate the resource costs for alternative program structures and teaching technologies. However, this information must be combined with valid learning outcome data if is to be used to determine the effects of alternative program structures and teaching technologies on different types of students. Such information is essential for improving program efficiency and ensuring vertical equity in resource decisions. Without it, educators and policymakers are not empowered to predict accurately the specialized labor needs for educating special education populations efficiently and equitably.

Despite the absence of a strong professional knowledge base, political recognition of the need for special facilities and services has led to a simultaneous concern about the qualifications of personnel who provide these services. Thus the supply of special educators is also an issue in the efficient and equitable education of at-risk populations.

The Supply of
Special Education Personnel

The supply of special education personnel is a function of demand, the efficiency of programming in preparatory programs, and incentives for individuals to specialize in the field of special education, to seek employment as special educators, and to remain in this labor force. The quantity and quality of the supply of special education personnel would seem to have important influences on the learning outcomes achieved by students. This, however, is an assumption, rather than an established empirical fact.

Available information suggests that special educator shortages are a serious problem, second only to supply shortages in bilingual education (Akin, 1988). Demographic projections, reported teacher shortages, and an escalating rate of emergency certification among special educators are limited evidence of the problem. The potential for educational inefficiencies and inequities resulting from short supplies of special education personnel are manifest indirectly by the uneven incidence of teacher shortages in different types of school districts (Darling-Hammond & Green, 1988, p. 148; Wendling & Woodbury, 1984).

Preparatory Programs

College preparatory programs in special education have their roots in the work of European physicians and psychologists who attempted to educate "insane" and "idiotic" children in the 1800s. From these beginnings the field of special education evolved to encompass a multidisciplinary knowledge base derived from medicine, psychology, sociology, linguistics, social work, and related health fields (Hallahan & Kauffman, 1986).

Because "educating" the disabled was, for many years, a matter of how to maintain them in residential institutions, formal preparation of teachers to work specifically with these students was not undertaken by most preparatory colleges until the middle of this century. Thus the first generation of persons who served as educators for special education students acquired their knowledge on a trial-and-error basis, through on-the-job experience.

In 1922 there were teachers at the Summer School of Teacher's College of Columbia University who worked in the field of special education and wanted to upgrade the quality of educational services delivered to disabled children. In 1923, the first set of standards for teachers in the field of special education were formulated by a small group that included many of these teachers. But decades passed before a uniform set of standards for special education teachers was upheld by teacher preparation institutions, states, and local school districts.

During 1966, the Council for Exceptional Children (CEC) released a document addressing the issue of professional standards for special education teachers (Heller, 1982). The rapid changes in the field rendered it irrelevant quickly. The effort continued, however, through the joint efforts of the CEC and the National Council for Accreditation of Teacher Education (NCATE).

As of 1991, teacher education institutions were required to meet CEC approval as part of the NCATE process for accreditation, but the impact of these standards was diluted by the absence of a mandate for colleges and universities to prepare teachers to be members of NCATE. Consequently, there is still wide variation among programs in special education and state accreditation requirements. In addition, provisional and emergency certification as well as lateral entry programs are used to offset labor shortages in the special education field (National Clearinghouse for Professions in Special Education, 1990; Patton & Braithwaite, 1979, 1990). These conditions would seem to increase variation in the quality of labor available for special education assignments.

Without uniform standards, issues pertaining to the quantity and quality of labor available for special education assignments have been exacerbated further by an elaborate categorical structure of teacher certification. This categorical scheme resulted from theoretical and empirical knowledge advances about the exceptional patterns of learning and behavior among children. Increasing categories of exceptionality led professionals to formulate distinct forms of classroom settings and educational curricula appropriate to the needs and capacities of different special education students. The goal was to ensure that special education students would experience the "least restrictive" environment possible, given their handicapping condition. The emergence of state laws and regulations regarding programs and personnel followed quickly on the heels of these developments.

Perhaps owing to the age of the field and the increasing demand for special educators, 24 states continue to report that their certification programs in special education are noncategorical (Berkley, 1990; Geiger, Whiteside, & Rock, 1982). However, 20 of these states do offer special categorical certificates in the areas of hearing and vision impairment, giftedness, and emotional handicaps or emotional disturbance. Thus, while professional preparation lags behind the classification of students, it seems clear that specialized training and certification within the field of special education are on the rise.

Currently, special education in early childhood education is coming of age. This development will include the detection of learning-related disabilities in infants and preschool children, triage, and referral to the appropriate sources of assistance, and planning for these children's school-entry service needs from the time they have been identified. Early childhood special education certification is already a separate category of professional certification in nearly half the states, and in some of these, prekindergarten and kindergarten certification are offered within several separate disability categories.

Clearly, certification and credentialing programs are reactive to social and political pressures for change. Each program development subsequently influences the quantity and supply of special education personnel available to the public school labor market. In fact, the limits of specialized training programs are often constrained by the crossfire between a short labor supply and evolving demands for specialized services. Many regulatory education agencies favor cross-categorical training and certification programs where there are labor shortages or a high degree of overlap between specializations. Preparation for addressing mental retardation, learning disabilities, and emotional or behavioral problems is an example of such overlap. Nonetheless, as disabilities become more tightly specified and the professional knowledge base expands, there will likely be greater differentiation in the ways personnel are trained and certified.

Program structures used to deliver special education services also influence the preparation of teachers who are not special educators. Teachers in classrooms where exceptional learners have been mainstreamed must be equipped through their training to deal with the special learning problems that these students present. The increasing need for some overlap in preparation is evident in the fact that 71% of all states did not require relevant course work for regular classroom teachers in 1979, but most did by 1990.

Valid national data reflecting the numbers of teachers certified in special education do not appear to exist. This makes it impossible to examine the supply of appropriately trained personnel relative to demand for them. Given the absence of such data and the apparent short supply of personnel in special education, it is important to examine incentives to specialize in the field.

Incentives to Specialize in Special Education

Studies investigating why teachers enter special education reveal that the motivation is primarily intrinsic. The driving forces include a desire to help exceptional children, a personal encounter with a special education student, the anticipated benefits of working with small groups of children, professional interest in the special education curriculum, and the expectation that working with gifted students might require less planning and direct instruction. Relatively few teachers report pursuing this specialized training in order to take advantage of wider employment opportunities (Chapman & Hutcheson, 1982; Gentry & Wen, 1988).

Current data do not illuminate how school districts might improve their efficiency in the recruitment of special education personnel. No studies offer comprehensive descriptions of theoretically important attributes of those who enter special education relative to other populations. Neither are there sufficient data to illuminate the effectiveness with which selected categories of special educators deliver programs and services. The Office of Special Education and Rehabilitative Services of the U.S. Department of Education (1982) asserts that the person who will work effectively as a special education teacher will have good interpersonal skills, aspire to continual professional growth, and be able to work in very difficult situations, freely altering procedures so that instruction accommodates the special abilities of students. Clearly such individuals will be, for a variety of reasons, personally committed to the education of children with exceptionalities.

Impact of Work Conditions on Supply

Retention of special education teachers is also a challenging problem with educational efficiency and equity implications. Low salaries, low status, lack of recognition for their work, poor working conditions in schools, and the absence of help or advice from others on the job are reasons cited by teachers for their decisions to leave the field. Professional isolation appears to be an even more significant contributor to teacher decisions to leave the field in rural school districts. On the other hand, special education teachers report that they are attracted to difficult and interesting assignments and opportunities to work with people they enjoy (Gentry & Wen, 1988; Lortie, 1975).

Some studies indicate that stress and burnout contribute to decisions to leave the profession and also promote less effective job performance. Teachers report that lack of administrative support, lack of support from other teachers and parents, little job recognition, little opportunity for involvement in decision making, unclear job responsibilities, inadequate time to perform duties, excessive paperwork, large caseloads, poor student attitudes and behavior, lack of student progress, feelings of professional isolation, difficult first-year experiences, poorly trained teachers' assistants, and inadequate facilities and resources contribute to their job dissatisfaction (Aloia, 1983; Correa, 1990; Cosden, 1990; Evans, 1981).

Other studies provide information that administrators can use to design and target interventions to reduce turnover among special education teachers. These studies indicate that burnout and attrition are higher among teachers of emotionally disturbed students, resource teachers with a wide range of students, teachers of severely or profoundly handicapped students, teachers with less than 5 years of experience, and secondary special education teachers. Findings such as these suggest that special school structures, resource allocation plans, and administrative support are critical in ameliorating stress and preventing eventual burnout symptoms (Aloia, 1983; Correa, 1990; Cosden, 1990; Evans, 1981; Gentry & Wen, 1988; Lortie, 1975).

Other unique work expectations and conditions experienced by special education teachers have a strong impact on their retention. In addition to instructional responsibilities, teachers must participate in formal and informal assessment, the development of individualized educational plans (IEPs), and implementation and monitoring of the same. Implementation of an IEP requires that special education teachers work closely with regular education teachers, either as resource teachers bridging regular and special education or serving multiple categories of students with disabilities. As legislation has provided more and more unique services and programs to special education students, the duties of special education teachers have expanded, without concomitant substantial adjustments in special education teachers' job expectations.

These expanded work expectations and responsibilities are often apparent in special education teachers' ambiguous job descriptions, problems of prioritizing activities given limited time and large caseloads, and lack of understanding of their expanded responsibilities by principals and regular education teachers. An examination of the job demands and job characteristics of special education teachers, with the intent of redesigning the job through school restructuring efforts, might be one means of reducing the tendency for teachers to burn out in these assignments.

Personnel Appraisal

Another important work condition affecting retention and the effectiveness of special education teachers is personnel appraisal. Special education teachers most often are subjected to performance appraisal criteria and processes that, because of their narrowness and rigidity, seem particularly unsuited for persons working with special populations of students. The use of undifferentiated evaluation instruments is widespread. Survey data indicate that only 17% of 24 states employ different procedures or evaluation instruments with special education teachers. In this decade many states and localities have adopted evaluation instruments based on the "effective teaching" research, and most special education teachers believe these criteria are not entirely applicable to or flexible enough for their unique assignments (Friend & McNutt, 1987; Gurganus, 1990; Johnson, 1987; Shank & Hooser, 1988).

Usually, teacher evaluation instruments do not encompass all of the special education teacher's major job responsibilities, nor do they take into consideration the particular context of the evaluation (Gurganus, 1990; McKenna, 1981). In other words, the student, classroom, and school variables that may influence what the teacher does with the students are not significant elements in planning for, conducting, or reporting performance evaluations for special education teachers. Not surprisingly, special education teachers report a preference for clinical rather than checklist approaches to evaluation (Ashendon-Johnson, 1986).

Special educators report also that evaluator qualifications and credibility of evaluators pose unique problems for them. In some instances, teachers indicate that they are not observed or supervised at all. Others assert that evaluators do not have the qualifications to provide expert assistance (Breton & Donaldson, 1991; Weinstein, 1989). To the degree that they do not receive useful assistance to improve instruction through the evaluation process, efficiency is not promoted.

The absence of administrative understanding of the special educator's job responsibilities, program characteristics, and unique student populations, along with the use of inappropriate or undifferentiated appraisal criteria and processes, seems to undermine the satisfaction and effectiveness of special education teachers. To the degree that these conditions exist, they impair teachers' abilities to meet the unique instructional needs of their students. The resulting stress and burnout appear to be related to withdrawal from teaching, decline in work effort, higher absenteeism, and the use of other strategies for distancing teachers from their work (Billingsley & Cross, 1991; Byrne, 1991; Dworkin, 1987; Schwab, Jackson, & Schuler, 1986).

Unsatisfactory work conditions and evaluation processes appear to contribute to a reduced supply of appropriately qualified special education teachers. Similarly, they appear to lend little to the process of improving instruction. Improving both would be an avenue for affecting the efficiency and equity of education provided to and attained by special education students.

Staff Development

The field of special education and the policy issues that support it continue to evolve rapidly. Consequently, teachers with new specializations and updated knowledge of content and processes associated with special education are needed. This need is addressed through policies guiding preparatory programs and in-service education. Veteran teachers are afforded opportunities to engage in staff development activities that focus specifically on special education. Both avenues for acquiring knowledge and skill have important implications for the efficient and equitable education of special education students.

Early literature reviews indicate that in-service training for special educators focused on governance and compliance relative to special education mandates. Training emphasized how to implement legislative mandates, particularly advisory processes and writing the IEP, and this training was incorporated in endorsement and certification programs. This in-service training did not address job-specific skills that would help teachers directly to enhance the learning of students (Showers, 1990; Smith-Davis, Burke, & Noel, 1984).

The emphasis on compliance training appears to be a natural response to the national thrust to place more and more children with disabilities in regular classrooms. With the gradual acceptance of P.L. 94-142 (recently renamed the Individuals with Disabilities Education Act), the emphasis of teacher in-service has begun to shift to strategies for providing least restrictive environments and improving skills in the actual implementation of the IEP.

In-service activities for special educators are delivered predominantly through small local and regional workshops. Some school units report that they rely on higher education and various telecommunications media for training. Regardless of the training delivery mechanism, there is little evidence substantiating the impact of the training (Joyce & Showers, 1980, 1982, 1988; Showers, 1990). Like other areas of staff development and in-service for educators, evaluations have focused on teacher attitudes at the end of the training experience and a presumption of implementation. More to the point, several studies report that teachers rarely transfer the new knowledge and skills obtained in workshops to new classroom behaviors (Joyce & Showers, 1980, 1982, 1988; Showers, 1990). Thus the status of the present knowledge base makes it impossible to estimate or impute the benefits of special education training to either teachers or students. Knowledge of impact combined with cost data could be used to enhance the efficiency of training as well as the efficiency and equity of education for students.

Some direction for improving the efficiency of in-service training can be deduced from a few studies in the more general literature of staff development. Apparently, theoretical training results in considerable knowledge, but little skill development and subsequent transfer to the classroom. From this observation, several propositions to guide in-service training have been developed. One is that training that includes theory, demonstration, practice, and coaching will result in changes in classroom practices. Post-training observational studies have demonstrated that this model of in-service results in important changes for teachers and students. Teachers made greater use of new instructional strategies, better matched instructional strategies and objectives, and evidenced higher levels of demonstrated skill with particular instructional strategies. Students showed reduced disciplinary referrals and obtained increased scores on basic skills tests, and increased proportions of them met district graduation requirements (Showers, 1990).

Collegial activity by teachers also appears to enhance the effects of in-service training. Cooperative professional development models are advocated as part of this strategy (Glatthorn, 1990). Such models are characterized by small teams of experienced teachers working collaboratively to obtain their own professional growth goals. Using strategies such as peer supervision, coaching, curriculum development, and action research, teachers work as colleagues to influence their own practices and to improve the learning of their students.

Research and Policy Implications

There are many needs and opportunities for sustained programs of research regarding the impact of personnel policies on the efficiency and equity of education for students with disabilities. The knowledge needed to inform professional practices is equally important for rationally responsive policy-making.

With respect to the demand for special education personnel, reliable and valid means of identifying current and projected needs for programs and specialized services are essential. Such data will enable policymakers to undertake more efficient human resource planning. These data would provide an accurate basis for increasing or reducing the supply of specialized labor directly through preparatory programs. Also, they would facilitate the retraining and reallocation of labor necessary to meet the changing demands for particular types of special education services.

A comprehensive data base is needed that will make possible an accurate assessment of the supply of special education personnel. It is extremely important for policymakers to know the numbers of special education personnel, by specialization and certification status, who are graduated from institutions of higher education, the numbers needed by schools, and the numbers employed by schools. This data base must be coupled with accurate data describing persons employed in special education programs, taking care to indicate attributes denoting the quality of training for each individual. Without comprehensive supply data, efficient human resource planning is impossible. To the degree that the supply is inadequate, both the efficiency and the equity of services offered to students are compromised.

A number of studies have computed the costs of selected special education program structures. However, little is known about the educational benefits or student outcomes associated with different program structures in special education. Thus conditional knowledge of program effects for students with different handicapping conditions is unavailable. Knowing the differential effects of alternative program structures on selected special education populations and cost data would provide the basis for more efficient programming as well as improved estimates of the demand for specialized labor in special education.

More comprehensive knowledge about the effects of specific personnel practices and school conditions on the supply of special education personnel is needed. How do recruitment, assignment, appraisal, and staff development practices influence teacher turnover and morale? How do they affect teachers' capacity to provide an efficient and equitable education for the students with whom they work?

Bernstein, Hartman, Kirst, and Marshall (1976, pp. 34-38) developed nine criteria for evaluating the funding system for special education. Their criteria, however, are insufficient for ensuring the proper education of at-risk populations because they do not consider student outcomes. Issues and questions raised in this chapter could lead to the development of a similar set of criteria linked to specific student outcomes. These two sets of criteria used in tandem would enable policymakers and administrators to improve the educational attainments of all special education populations, by simultaneously improving the efficient and equitable allocation of fiscal and human resources and the efficient and equitable attainment of important educational outcomes.

References

Akin, J. N. (1988). *1988 teacher supply/demand report*. Addison, IL: Association for School, College, and University Staffing.

Aloia, G. (1983). Special educators' perceptions of their roles as consultants. *Teacher Education and Special Education, 6*, 83-87.

Ashendon-Johnson, B. (1986). Differences in special education and regular education teachers' attitude toward evaluation as related to prior special education training of the evaluator, type of evaluation process used, or role type of teacher. *Dissertation Abstracts International, 47*, 2380-A. (University Microfilms No. 86-23,080).

Berkley, T. R. (1990). *Special education survey of the states* (Report of the National Clearinghouse for Professions in Special Education). Washington, DC: National Association of State Directors of Special Education.

Bernstein, C., Hartman, W., Kirst, M., & Marshall, R. (1976). *Financing educational services for the handicapped: An analysis of current research and practices*. Reston, VA: Council for Exceptional Children.

Billingsley, B., & Cross, L. (1991). Teachers' decisions to transfer from special to general education. *Journal of Special Education, 24,* 496-511.

Breton, W., & Donaldson, G. (1991). Too little, too late? The supervision of Maine resource room teachers. *Journal of Special Education, 25,* 114-125.

Byrne, B. (1991). Burnout: Investigating the impact of background variables for elementary, intermediate, secondary, and university educators. *Teaching and Teacher Education, 7,* 197-209.

Chapman, D., & Hutcheson, S. (1982). Attrition from teaching careers: A discriminant analysis. *Educational Research Journal, 19,* 93-105.

Correa, V. (1990). Advocacy for teachers. *Teaching Exceptional Children, 22,* 7-9.

Cosden, M. (1990). Expanding the role of special education. *Teaching Exceptional Children, 22,* 4-7.

Darling-Hammond, L., & Green, J. (1988). Teacher quality and educational equality. *College Board Review, 148.*

Dworkin, A. (1987). *Teacher burnout in public schools.* Albany: State University of New York Press.

Evans, S. (1981). Perceptions of classroom teachers, principals and resource room teachers of the actual and desired roles of the resource teacher. *Journal of Learning Disabilities, 14,* 600-603.

Friend, M., & McNutt, G. (1987). A comparative study of resource teacher job descriptions and administrators' perceptions of resource teacher responsibilities. *Journal of Learning Disabilities, 20,* 224-228.

Geiger, W., Whiteside, L., & Rock, S. (1982). *The status of personnel preparation in special education: A report on the results of a national survey conducted by the Teacher Education Division of the Council for Exceptional Children.* Washington, DC: National Clearinghouse for Professions in Special Education.

Gentry, R., & Wen, S. (1988). *What attracts and keeps outstanding black special education teachers in the profession?* Dallas, TX. (ERIC Document Reproduction Service No. ED 298 712)

Glatthorn, A. (1990). Cooperative professional development: Facilitating the growth of the special education teacher and the classroom teacher. *Remedial and Special Education, 11,* 29-34.

Gurganus, S. (1990). *A comparison of special education and regular education teachers' views on performance appraisal as measured by national performance evaluation standards.* Unpublished doctoral dissertation, North Carolina State University.

Hallahan, D., & Kauffman, J. (1986). *Exceptional children: Introduction to special education.* Washington, DC: National Association of State Directors of Special Education.

Heller, H. W. (1982). Professional standards for preparing special educators: Status and prospects. *Exceptional Education Quarterly, 2,* 77-86.

Johnson, E. (1987). Supervision and evaluation of special education teachers and staff: The role of secondary principals. *Dissertation Abstracts International, 48,* 1413-A.

Joyce, B., & Showers, B. (1980). Training ourselves to teach: The messages of research. *Educational Leadership, 37,* 379-385.

Joyce, B., & Showers, B. (1982). The coaching of teaching. *Educational Leadership, 40,* 4-10.

Joyce, B., & Showers, B. (1988). *Student achievement through staff development.* New York: Longman.

Lortie, D. (1975). *Schoolteacher: A sociological study.* Chicago: University of Chicago Press.

Marilee, C. (1990). The shadow children. *American School Board Journal, 177*, 18-24.

McKenna, B. (1981). Context/environment effects in teacher evaluation. In J. Millman (Ed.), *Handbook of teacher evaluation* (pp. 23-38). Beverly Hills, CA: Sage.

Mullins, J. (1986). Events influencing physically handicapped and health impaired people in the United States. *Department of Public Health Journal, 9*(1).

National Association for Perinatal Addiction Research and Education. (1988). Innocent addicts: High rate of prenatal drug abuse found. *ADAMHA News.*

National Center for Educational Statistics. (1991). Common core of data survey. Washington, DC: U.S. Department of Educaton.

National Clearinghouse for Professions in Special Education. (1990). *Personnel supply and demand: A context for special education* (Information Bulletin No. 1). Washington, DC: National Association of State Directors of Special Education.

National Easter Seal Society. (1988). *Growing crisis in supply of rehabilitation professionals noted in recent Easter Seal report* [Press release]. Chicago: Author.

Patton, J., & Braithwaite, R. (1979). *Public Law 94-142 and the changing status of teacher certification/recertification: A survey of state education agencies.* Unpublished manuscript.

Patton, J., & Braithwaite, R. (1990). Special education certification/recertification for regular educators. *Journal of Special Education, 24*, 117-124.

Schwab, R., Jackson, S., & Schuler, R. (1986). Educator burnout: Sources and consequences. *Educational Research Quarterly, 19*, 14-30.

Shank, D., & Hooser, C. (1988). *Special educators' effectiveness: Perceptions of teachers versus administrators.* Paper presented at the meeting of the International Council on Exceptional Children, Washington, DC.

Showers, B. (1990). Aiming for superior classroom instruction for all children. *Remedial and Special Education, 11*, 35-39.

Smith-Davis, J., Burke, P., & Noel, M. (1984). *Personnel to educate the handicapped in America: Supply and demand from a programmatic viewpoint.* College Park, MD: U.S. Department of Education.

U.S. Department of Education, Office of Special Education and Rehabilitative Services. (1982). *Recruitment of special education personnel.* Washington, DC: Government Printing Office. (ERIC Document Reproduction Service No. 240 819)

U.S. Department of Education, Office of Special Education and Rehabilitative Services. (1991). *Thirteenth annual report to Congress on the implementation of the Individuals with Disabilities Education Act.* Washington, DC: Government Printing Office.

U.S. Department of Education, Office of Special Education and Rehabilitative Services. (various years). *Annual report to Congress on the implementation of the Education of the Handicapped Act.* Washington, DC: Government Printing Office.

Weinstein, D. (1989). The school administrator and special education programs: Quality control of placement and instruction. *ERS Spectrum, 7*, 35-40.

Wendling, W. R., & Woodbury, S. A. (1984). *The future labor market for teachers: Quantities, aptitudes, and retention of students choosing teaching careers.* Kalamazoo, MI: W. E. Upjohn Institute for Employment Research.

Wooden, H. (1980, September). Growth of a social concept: An overview. *Exceptional Children.*

TWELVE

Native American Students
REEMERGENCE OF
TRIBAL INFLUENCE ON
EDUCATIONAL PROCESSES

SIDNEY R. CASTLE

The recently released final report of the Indian Nations at Risk Task Force states that American Indian tribes and Alaska Native communities, as the indigenous peoples of the United States, are at a critical stage; the report provides ample evidence that they are, indeed, nations at risk (U.S. Department of Education, 1991). Native American communities face the challenge of attempting to retain their distinct cultural identity while at the same time preparing their youth to exist successfully in a multicultural environment with rapidly changing technology. In the midst of the struggle to prepare tribal youth to compete successfully in the mainstream, without loss of their historic tribal culture, schools located on tribal lands are often viewed as both the answer to and a contributory cause of the problem. As a result, friction all too often characterizes the relationship between tribal governments and the educational systems located on tribal lands.

This friction stems from the basic issue of who will control the educational enterprise on tribal lands; that is, where the final authority will reside for the determination of the direction and content of educational programs presented. At a time when tribal resolve to retain and continue the development of original languages and cultures in all aspects of activity on tribal lands is seen as weakening, the

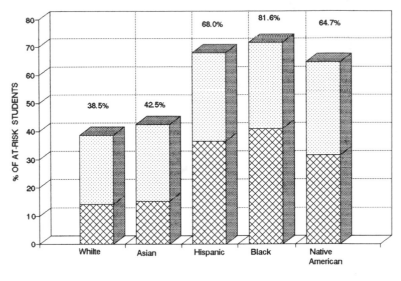

Figure 12.1. Percentages of Eighth-Grade Students With At-Risk Factors
SOURCE: U.S. Department of Education (1991).

educational systems located on tribal lands are often perceived as accelerating the process by their insistence on the use of English rather than native languages in the classroom. Tribal attempts to influence the curriculum and classroom instructional methodology are seen as unwarranted intrusions by the schools, especially since tribal funding of the schools is either minimal or nonexistent.

One area of concurrence between tribal governments and the schools is that the intellectual and academic skills of Native American children are not being adequately developed. The U.S. Department of Education (1991) report shows that eighth-grade Native American children are considered to be educationally at risk at levels nationally comparable to those of black and Hispanic students (see Figure 12.1).

From the perspective of tribal governments, one of the major barriers to better education for tribal youth is the multilayered educational system. Usually there is a combination of public, Bureau of Indian Affairs (BIA), contract, and church-affiliated school systems operating on tribal lands. Each of the educational systems differs from the others with respect to administrative infrastructure, accountability, academic standards, curriculum, and the means by which academic progress is measured. Tribal governments attempting to reach an agreement with one school system relating to administrative practices, teacher certification, educational programs, or attendance boundary issues find that the terms of the agreement are neither recognized by nor binding upon other school systems operating on tribal lands (V. Arviso, executive assistant to the president, the Navajo Nation, personal communication, August 15, 1991).

Tribal governments recognize that they need some basis of empowerment to have a more active and effective voice in the education of Native American students. This empowerment has two dimensions: statutory or legal authority to intervene in the administration of educational systems on tribal lands, and the financial capacity to fund adequately any educational programs espoused by tribal governments. The current situation is viewed by tribal governments and parental groups as a watershed period that may determine whether or not Native Americans will be able to preserve their unique cultural identities while at the same time preparing their children for productive lives in an American society that is increasingly diverse and technology oriented.

Questions such as who currently has, and who in the future should have, locus of control over educational systems on tribal lands, and what operational partnerships need to be developed among tribal, federal, and state governments to maximize the education of Native American students are salient but not easily answered. This chapter examines these questions from several standpoints. The next section addresses the high incidence of at-risk students on southwestern tribal lands, while the following describes the efforts of tribal governments in the state of Arizona to define and implement some form of control over educational programs on their tribal lands. The final section presents a possible solution to the issue of tribal government financial empowerment to support and control educational programs.

At-Risk Native American Students in Arizona

There are 21 federally recognized tribal groups whose lands lie either totally or partially within the state of Arizona. Included in this total are 6 of the largest tribal groups within the United States (U.S. Census Bureau, 1980). Most of the 21 tribal groups within Arizona are attempting to deal with issues such as high incidence of at-risk students and conflicts among tribal governments, local school districts, state education agencies, and federal educational programs (J. Jose, education program specialist, Indian Education Unity, Arizona Department of Education, personal communication, August 7, 1991). An examination of the manner in which these issues have surfaced, and the attempts made by the parties involved to resolve them, may provide direction for other tribal groups.

A 1989 study examined the performance of Native American students in Arizona public schools on the Iowa Test of Basic Skills (ITBS) (Castle & Yazzie, 1989). The report includes data on Arizona's 224 operational public school districts, including the 22 districts that are located either totally or substantially on Indian lands.

Overall, Arizona public school districts located either *totally* or *substantially* on Indian lands were found to have significantly lower normal curve equivalency (NCE) scores than other Arizona public school districts. Additionally, public school districts located *totally* on Indian lands (14 districts) were found to have significantly lower NCE scores than the 8 public school districts located substantially on Indian lands, with exception of high school mathematics scores and a few individual grade variations (Castle & Yazzie, 1989).

The most compelling finding was that in only a single instance—on one third-grade language subtest—did any Arizona public school district located totally on Indian lands attain a grade-level average NCE score of 50 points. Overall, students in the Arizona public school districts located totally on Indian lands averaged 7 to 15 NCE points below grade level on the language subtest (see Figure 12.2). National statistics for Chapter 1 students report an average annual gain score of 4 to 5 NCE points. Based upon the national statistics for Chapter 1 students, the language subtest NCE scores mean that students in Arizona public schools located totally on Indian lands average 1½ to 3 years below grade level in language skills, as measured by the ITBS (Castle & Yazzie, 1989).

Both the above-noted U.S. Department of Education (1991) report and the 1989 Arizona study (Castle & Yazzie, 1989) give a clear indication of the educationally at-risk status of Native American students. As noted in the Indian Nations at Risk Task Force report, there has been some progress over the last 20 years in addressing the

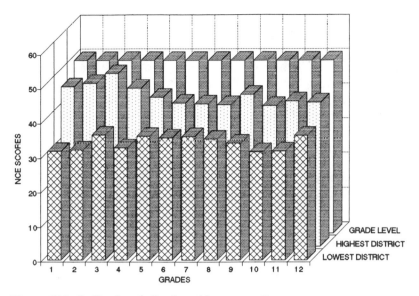

Figure 12.2. Indian Lands Students' Language Scores
SOURCE: Castle and Yazzie (1989).

educational problems facing Native American students. Increasingly, parents on Indian lands have become more involved with the development of parent-based early childhood education models and with the planning, development, and implementation of school-based programs that affect their children. School systems have developed a variety of programs addressing the linguistic, cultural, academic, health, and social needs of Native American children. Curriculum in schools on Indian lands has begun to present history, music, and visual arts from a Native American perspective in an attempt to develop positive attitudes about being Native American. Recently, tribal governments have undertaken efforts to facilitate planning among different types of school systems operating on Indian lands in an attempt to standardize educational programs.

Dynamics of Educational Programs for the Navajo Nation

The Navajo Nation is located in the Four Corners Region of the United States, where the state lines of Arizona, Colorado, New

Mexico, and Utah all connect. With an area of 16,710,194 acres, or 26,110 square miles, the Navajo Nation is larger than many northeastern states (Commission for Accelerating Navajo Development Opportunities [CANDO], 1988). The U.S. Bureau of the Census reports that there are approximately 225,000 Navajos, almost 80% of whom live on Navajo Nation lands; this produces a population density of slightly fewer than 7 Navajos per every square mile of land.

The major portion of the Navajo Nation is located within the state of Arizona, with parts extending into New Mexico and Utah. Central administration of the Navajo Nation consists of a democratically elected president, vice president, and Navajo Nation Council, which has committee assignments for such areas as education and labor. Political subdivisions of the Navajo Nation are called chapters, and their interaction with the Navajo Nation Council is analogous to that of states with the U.S. federal government. Categorical funding for programs administered by Navajo chapter governments represent approximately 66% of Navajo Nation annual revenues (Navajo Nation, Division of Community Development, 1990). Chapter governments wield considerable authority over local matters, and they represent the level at which schools obtain land-use permits for construction and operations.

The original treaty between the U.S. government and the Navajo tribe was ratified in 1850. After several years of warfare between the Navajo tribe and the U.S. government, a second treaty was negotiated and ratified in 1868 (15 Stat. 667). This second treaty, amended six times since its original ratification, remains the basis of agreement between the U.S. government and the Navajo Nation. Article VI of the Treaty of 1868 stipulates the U.S. government's obligation to provide education for Navajo children.

The Navajo population residing on the Navajo Nation has increased dramatically since the Treaty of 1868, from 9,000 Navajos in 1868 to approximately 170,000 Navajos today. The total population of Navajos was estimated to be approximately 219,000 in 1989. Age demographics of the Navajo population currently residing on Navajo Nation lands reveal the median age of youth to be 18.7 years (see Figure 12.3). The large percentage of the population that is of school age underscores the importance of the educational systems on the Navajo Nation. This also adds to the determination of the Navajo tribal government to gain an active role in the administration of

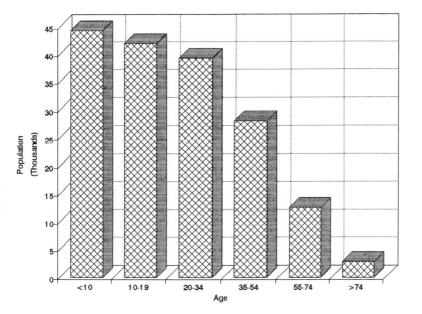

Figure 12.3. Navajo Nation Age Demographics
SOURCE: Data from Navajo Nation, Division of Community Development (1990).

educational systems on the Navajo Nation (V. Arviso, personal communication, August 15, 1991).

The major difficulty facing the Navajo tribal government in its attempt to play an active role in the administration of educational programs is the diversity of educational systems. There are three major educational systems (BIA, contract, and public) and one minor educational system (church affiliated) currently operating on the Navajo Nation. Problems associated with this arrangement were highlighted in a recent front-page story in *The Navajo Nation Today* (June 5-11, 1991) that asked the question, "How many schools does it take to educate the 90,000 plus students on the Navajo Nation?" The answer was, "[There are] too many."

Navajo Nation Public Schools

In terms of enrollments and the number of school buildings, the largest education system on the Navajo Nation is the public school system, with approximately 75% of all Navajo students. The public school system began operating on the Navajo Nation during the early 1920s, primarily to educate the dependents of non-Native American federal employees. The first major effort to construct and operate public schools serving Navajo children on a large scale began in the 1950s.

During the early 1970s, Navajo parents and tribal authorities began to push for the phase-out of BIA boarding schools in favor of local schools. The twin goals of the local school movement were the development of educational facilities in local communities, enabling Navajo children to live at home with their parents, and greater input by parents and community (chapter) governments in curriculum and administrative decisions. Passage of the federal Indian Self-Determination and Education Assistance Act of 1975 (P.L. 93-638) empowered tribal groups to exercise a greater degree of self-government over programs and services conducted by the federal government for Native Americans. Sections 2.(b)(2) and 2.(b)(3) of the act gave further impetus to the local school movement on the Navajo Nation, resulting in the conversion of some existing BIA-administered schools into contract schools with limited oversight by the Education Division of the Navajo Nation Council.

Both the newly created federal contract schools and the existing public schools empowered Navajo parents and communities through their use of locally elected governing boards. However, the public schools, relying primarily on state funds, received a higher level of financial support per student than did either the BIA or newly created contract schools, and their enrollment continued to increase as Navajo parents moved their children from BIA to local public schools. Since the mid-1980s, increased student enrollments and the acquisition of school construction funds under provisions of P.L. 81-815 (Federal Impact Aid) have resulted in a second wave of public school construction on the Navajo Nation. This second wave replaced older existing schools with larger modern facilities equipped with new electronic educational technology, further widening the gap between the quality of school facilities of public and BIA and contract school systems.

However, the public school system really is not a single system. Rather, it functions as two separate systems serving the Arizona and New Mexico portions of the Navajo Nation. The public schools located in the Arizona portion are funded by, and must meet administrative standards established by, the Arizona Department of Education, and the public schools located in the New Mexico portion of the Navajo Nation are funded by, and held administratively accountable to, the New Mexico Department of Education. The state education agencies in Arizona and New Mexico have adopted different education standards, teacher certification standards, and student attendance and graduation standards.

Comparisons of student achievement in Arizona and New Mexico public schools on the Navajo Nation are made more difficult by the use of different test instruments. Arizona uses the ITBS annually to measure student achievement in grades 1 through 8 (C. Wiley, testing programs director, Arizona Department of Education, personal communication, August 9, 1991), while New Mexico has developed its own Comprehensive Test of Basic Skills for grades 1 through 8 (New Mexico State Department of Education, 1991). New Mexico has also developed its own New Mexico High School Competency Examination, and Arizona uses the Test of Achievement Proficiency for high school students. In addition, both Arizona and New Mexico have adopted a guaranteed foundation plan to fund public education; however, differences in formula weights, categorically funded programs, basic support levels, property taxation rates, and budgetary exemptions result in significantly different rates of expenditure per student.

Navajo Nation BIA Schools

The BIA schools represent the second largest number of schools (including the only two schools in the Utah portion of the Navajo Nation) and is the oldest educational system operating on the Navajo Nation. But, because BIA facilities are older and smaller in size, and federal funding for BIA educational programs is the lowest per pupil of the three major educational systems on the Navajo Nation, BIA enrollments represent only approximately 15% of all Navajo students (see Figure 12.4). To enhance the consistency of teacher quality, teachers in the BIA system recently have been required to meet the certification standards of the states in which their schools are located (A. Barney-Nez, executive director, Navajo Area School Board Association, personal communication, August 6, 1991).

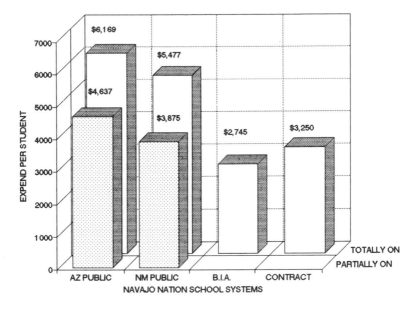

Figure 12.4. M&O Expenditures per Student
SOURCE: Data from Arizona Department of Education (1990), New Mexico State Department of Education (1990), A. Barney-Nez (personal communication, August 6, 1991), and L. Bahe (personal communication, August 8, 1991).

Since the 1950s, with the expansion of the public school system on the Navajo Nation, and accelerated by the conversion of some BIA schools to contract schools beginning in 1975, BIA student enrollment has continued to decline. Policy positions adopted by the Education Committee of the Navajo Nation Council and the Navajo Division of Education appear to advocate the total phase-out of BIA schools in favor of either contract or public schools. This position may in large measure be due to the greater extent to which contract and public schools offer Navajo parents and Navajo government entities a voice in the development and administration of their educational programs.

Navajo Nation Contract Schools

The federal Indian Self-Determination and Education Assistance Act of 1975 empowered Navajo parents and Navajo tribal authorities to exercise a greater degree of control over federal education programs and resulted in the conversion of some BIA schools into contract schools. Contract schools are similar to public schools in that locally elected governing boards have oversight authority. However, unlike public schools, they have greater local autonomy in such areas as defining teacher employment qualifications, adoption of curriculum, graduation standards, and development of school budgets (L. Bahe, executive director, Association of Navajo Community Controlled School Boards, personal communication, August 8, 1991).

The Navajo tribal government has gained a degree of authority over contract schools with the adoption by the BIA, in 1987-88, of a grant school concept of funding. The grant school concept provides that budgets proposed by contract schools must be submitted to, and receive the approval of, the Navajo Division of Education prior to funding by the BIA. This provides for a lively negotiation process, with significant impact upon contract school curriculum and administrative decisions. Currently, there are 13 contract schools operating on the Navajo Nation; their enrollment represents approximately 7% of all Navajo students (CANDO, 1988).

Navajo Nation Church-Affiliated Schools

The smallest system of schools operating on the Navajo Nation is composed of church-affiliated schools, the student enrollments of which collectively represent the remaining 3% of Navajo students (CANDO, 1988). The church-affiliated schools are not represented by a single religious affiliation, but by several different affiliations, each of which establishes its own administrative guidelines and funding levels. Because of their individual nature and small size, church-affiliated schools usually interact with chapter governments rather than with the Navajo Nation Council or the Navajo Division of Education.

Emerging Role of Navajo Tribal
Government in Educational Processes

In the early 1970s, the Navajo Division of Education proposed that a single system, similar in structure and operation to that of a state public education agency, be established on the Navajo Nation (Roessel, 1991). Dillon Platero, then director of the Navajo Division of Education, contacted all administrative groups responsible for the educational systems on the Navajo Nation in an attempt to establish a forum for discussions leading to the planning and development of a single major education system. At the time, only the New Mexico Department of Education expressed an interest in participating.

Several unresolved concerns precluded serious discussion of the establishment of a single educational system for the Navajo Nation. The single largest problem involves the financing of such a system. If the system is to be under administrative control of the Navajo Nation, then it is unlikely that state legislatures would be willing to continue to allocate the large sums of money used to support the former public schools. In general, public schools on the Navajo Nation have some of the lowest levels of assessed valuation per student in state public school systems. Without an adequate local resource base from which to fund educational programs, the public schools are heavily reliant on state funding. The Federal Impact Aid program provides some federal funding under provisions of P.L. 81-874; however, since this program was intended to compensate state public schools for the loss of local revenues due to the impact of federal activity within their district boundaries, schools under tribal control would lose that funding.

The Emergence of Self-Determination

Passage of the Indian Self-Determination and Education Assistance Act of 1975 provided the Navajo tribal government the legal basis of empowerment to exert control over educational programs, while at the same time requiring the other government entities to continue to meet their financial responsibility for the education of Navajo children.

Each of the three major educational systems on the Navajo Nation has developed its own professional association, which is used to disseminate information among member schools, to facilitate planning, and to provide a unified voice to lobby Navajo, federal, and state governments on behalf of member schools. The Navajo Nation Council has established annual budget line items to support the administrative costs of the three educational associations (V. Arviso, personal communication, August 15, 1991).

The public schools operating on the Navajo Nation were the last to formalize a professional association, due in large part to differences in state funding, administrative regulations, and simple geographic considerations; the Chuska mountain range lies along the Arizona-New Mexico state line and effectively limits daily interaction. The Navajo Nation Public School Boards Association (NNPSBA) formally incorporated in 1988 and selected as founding executive director an individual who previously had held an administrative consultant position with the Navajo Division of Education. Shortly thereafter, the chairman of the Education Committee of the Navajo Nation Council and the executive director of the Navajo Division of Education submitted a written request to NNPSBA asking that the NNPSBA executive director be allowed to assist in the development of a planning model for Navajo education. This demonstrates how, with a minimal amount of funds and lacking a clearly defined legal authority, the Navajo tribal government has been able both to gain a degree of administrative authority over the public school system and to secure its role in the development of planning for Navajo education.

A Navajo Educational Summit was convened in March 1989 to address the issue of establishing a Navajo Department of Education with state agency empowerment by the year 2000. All of the educational systems operating on the Navajo Nation were invited to submit position papers addressing issues surrounding the Navajo Nation Council's proposed implementation of the Navajo Department of Education and to participate in a series of discussion and planning sessions during a two-day conference. The Association of Navajo Community Controlled School Boards, representing the contract schools, adopted the position that they and the BIA schools could easily unify, since they had the same (federal) funding source. This position was not endorsed by the Navajo Area School Board Association, which represented the BIA schools; they wished to remain independent of oversight authority by the Education Committee of the Navajo Nation Council (A. Barney-Nez, personal communication, August 6, 1991).

NNPSBA presented a position paper that generally supported the concept of a Navajo Department of Education, while identifying serious administrative, legal, and financial issues that needed to be resolved before such a department could become operational (Castle, Graham, & Yazzie, 1989). This position paper questioned the feasibility of implementing a Navajo Department of Education with an administrative infrastructure that lacked organizational units and professional staff for such operational functions as teacher certification, student achievement testing, and school finance. While a problem, this issue is resolvable given sufficient resources and long-term commitment. One approach being taken by the Navajo Nation to address this issue is the identification and support of key personnel within the existing Navajo Division of Education to complete graduate education degrees.

The Navajo Nation has a long-established educational trust fund, the proceeds of which are used to fund college scholarships for Navajo students. Navajo high school students graduating with a 3.0 (out of a possible 4.0) grade point average and having an ACT score of 25 or greater are awarded a Chief Manulito Scholarship of $5,000 a year for their undergraduate education. Graduating Navajo high school students with a 2.5 grade point average and an ACT score of at least 14 are usually awarded some form of a scholarship; the amount is determined by a priority list of subject areas determined to be most needed on the Navajo Nation. Recently, larger portions of the scholarship funds have been dedicated to the support of Navajos pursuing graduate-level degrees (V. Arviso, personal communication, August 15, 1991).

A preliminary master plan developed for Navajo education has suggested establishing administrative internships for key personnel of the Navajo Division of Education with state education agencies (V. Arviso, personal communication, August 15, 1991). The Navajo Nation would pay part or all of the salary and the Navajo Division of Education employee would learn how an educational unit is organized and operated. Additional benefits from this approach are the development of professional networking and personal contacts necessary for a successful transition period as a Navajo Department of Education is established and begins to assume administrative authority over existing public schools on the Navajo Nation.

As noted in the NNPSBA position paper, the proposal for a Navajo Department of Education raises several significant legal issues, particularly those related to the financing and ownership of public school facilities on the Navajo Nation (Castle et al., 1989). For example, while long-term use of the land is granted by the local Navajo chapter government, the public school buildings on the Navajo Nation are themselves financed either by P.L. 81-815 funds or by funds generated through the sale of general obligation bonds. Under provisions of ARS 15-1029, at bond maturity bondholders are guaranteed payment of school district bonds, or interest coupons, by the state of Arizona. Regarding the public schools constructed on the Navajo Nation with funds generated from general obligation bonds, who owns title to the facilities? Can title to the facilities automatically be assumed by the Navajo Nation when they implement a Navajo Department of Education? And, most important, in the event of the implementation of a Navajo Department of Education, who would be responsible for assuring payment of outstanding bonds? The legal issues raised are somewhat more complex than those of an administrative infrastructure for Navajo education, but are likewise surmountable given sufficient time and resources.

The question of adequate financial resources to fund educational programs under a Navajo Department of Education does appear to represent an insurmountable problem under existing Navajo Nation economic conditions. The Navajo tribal government reported total 1988 operating revenues of slightly more that $261 million (CANDO, 1988). Of this amount, slightly less than $73 million was budgeted by the Navajo Nation Council to fund the various departments of the Navajo tribal government, with the balance used to fund categorical programs at the chapter level (Navajo Nation, Division of Community Development, 1990). Navajo Nation Council funding for the Navajo Division of Education in 1988 was more than double the level budgeted in 1985. However, as the NNPSBA position paper noted, the $1.76 million budgeted for the Navajo Division of Education in 1988 fell far short of the $363 million maintenance and operation (M&O) expenditures that BIA, contract, and public schools reported for the same period. In fact, the entire 1988 operating revenues of the Navajo Nation represented fewer than 72% of the resources required for just the M&O budget portion of the three major educational systems operating on the Navajo Nation (Arizona Department of Education, 1990; L. Bahe, personal communication, August 8, 1991; A. Barney-Nez, personal communication, August 6, 1991; New Mexico State Department of Education, 1990).

Ft. McDowell Mohave-Apache and
Gila River Indian Communities

Two smaller tribal groups within the state of Arizona wishing to gain some degree of administrative input into the education of their children, but lacking the size, finances, and political influence of the Navajo, are the Ft. McDowell Mohave-Apache Indian Community and the Gila River Indian Community. Both of these tribal groups are smaller than the Navajo in size and are located adjacent to Phoenix. Like the Navajo, they are concerned with being able to preserve their cultural identities while at the same time preparing their children to exist successfully in a multicultural and technological environment.

However, their need is seen as more immediate because they, unlike the Navajo, do not have a large land area with relative isolation; rather, they reside in very close proximity to, and are virtually surrounded by, a very large, technologically complex non-Native American culture. The contrasts between the two cultures, and the increased growth and development on lands adjacent to their communities, are a daily reminder of their need to preserve tribal culture through their children's education.

Educational Concerns of the Ft. McDowell
Mohave-Apache Indian Community

The U.S. government legally recognized the sovereign status of the Ft. McDowell Mohave-Apache Indian Community in a treaty signed in 1936. Current tribal population is 640 members, 201 of whom are students in grades K-12; almost all of the tribal members reside on the 25,000 acres that constitute the tribal lands of the Ft. McDowell Mohave-Apache Indian Community (G. W. Bahe, vice president, Ft. McDowell Mohave-Apache Indian Community, personal communication, July 24, 1991). The relatively small size of the Ft. McDowell Mohave-Apache Indian Community, as well as extremely limited revenues, precludes any thought of establishing an independent education department under provisions of the federal Indian Self-Determination and Education Assistance Act. Currently, most Ft. McDowell children attend two different public school systems (R. Salazar, education director, Ft. McDowell Mohave-Apache Indian Community, personal communication, August 30, 1991). The remaining students attend school on the Ft. McDowell Mohave-Apache Indian Community in a branch of the Horse Mesa Accommodation School established by the Maricopa County Schools, which is governed by a county school superintendent (ARS 15-302 and 15-308).

The Ft. McDowell Mohave-Apache Indian Community appropriates slightly more than $241,000 out of a total $2 million budget for education (R. Salazar, personal communication, August 30, 1991). However, in spite of the tribal government's financial contribution, and donation of facilities on tribal lands, the governing board structure of an Arizona accommodation school has precluded the tribal government from having any meaningful voice in the administration of educational programs provided at the school.

As an alternative to the existing educational programs, members of the Education Committee of the Ft. McDowell tribal government have considered petitioning the county school superintendent, under provisions of ARS 15-443, for formation of a new common school district in Arizona's public school system. Discussions by tribal officials have included the alternatives of requesting the proposed new common school district independently or in conjunction with the Gila River Indian Community. The two Indian communities share a common culture and ancestry, and it has been suggested that by combining they could maximize their resources (G. Innis, education director, Gila River Indian Community, personal communication, August 27, 1991; R. Salazar, personal communication, August 30, 1991).

Educational Concerns of the
Gila River Indian Community

The Gila River Indian Community comprises 778,000 acres of land located south of the city of Phoenix and has a tribal enrollment of slightly fewer than 11,000 members. Tribal officials estimate that approximately 9,300, or 85%, of enrolled tribal members reside on tribal lands. Only 110 of the approximate 2,000 Gila River children attending school actually do so on tribal lands; the remainder are enrolled in 10 different public school districts (G. Innis, personal communication, August 27, 1991). In addition, a branch of the Horse Mesa Accommodation School located on the Gila River Indian Community enrolls 65 students, and a Catholic school adjacent to the accommodation school enrolls 45 students. Because of the large number of students attending school off of tribal lands, and the lack of liaison programs with some of the school districts, the tribal government seeks some means of empowerment in the development and administration of educational programs for tribal students (G. Innis, personal communication, August 27, 1991).

The Basis of Empowerment for Tribal Administration of Educational Programs

Unlike the Navajos, who have established a degree of administrative oversight, and who now seek an expanded role with the ultimate goal of establishing a tribal department of education, the two smaller tribal groups are still attempting to define their role. Lacking the size and power base necessary to establish independent tribal education systems, the Gila River and Ft. McDowell Mohave-Apache Indian Communities seek to gain empowerment by becoming part of the Arizona public school system. Clearly, the three tribal groups lack sufficient resources to implement their desired educational systems. In the case of the Navajo, the resources must be large enough to be the primary funding source for a tribal education system, while the Gila River and Ft. McDowell Mohave-Apache Indian Communities need only meet the assessed valuation requirements of ARS 15-444 to establish a public school district. Resolution of issues surrounding Indian lands (e.g., the question of ownership and the authority of tribal groups to establish taxing systems on the lands) may provide financial empowerment for tribal education programs.

As tribal governments begin to test the anomalous legal relationship that exists between them and the U.S. federal government, the courts have begun to recognize that, for the last 150 years, federal and state governments have imposed extensive power over Indian nations in violation of their sovereignty (Kronowitz, Lichtman, McSloy, & Olsen, 1987). Notably, the U.S. Supreme Court, under Chief Justice John Marshall, confirmed the concept of Indian sovereignty in relationship with the federal government in seminal cases such as *Johnson v. M'Intosh* (1823), *Cherokee Nation v. Georgia* (1831), and *Worcester v. Georgia* (1832).

Subsequently, and in sharp contrast to previous decisions, beginning with *Martin v. Waddell* (1842) and *United States v. Kagama* (1886), the U.S. Supreme Court reinterpreted the discovery doctrine as granting full title and ownership of Indian lands to the United States, leaving the Indian nations with a mere right of occupancy. This reinterpretation has become both the understanding and the cornerstone of modern federal plenary power, as evidenced by the Court's rulings in cases such as *United States v. Santa Fe Pacific R.R. Co.* (1941) and *Tee-Hit-Ton Indians v. United States* (1955). While not recognized as having ownership of the lands, tribal governments are encouraged, by provisions of the Indian Self-Determination and Education Assistance Act, to expand their authority over activities that occur on the lands. One way in which tribal governments can be seen as expanding their authority is the manner in which they assert their power of taxation based on their claims to legitimate powers as sovereign governments.

The power of taxation provides tribal governments the basis of financial empowerment for tribal education programs. Recently, the U.S. Supreme Court, in cases such as *McClanahan v. Arizona State Tax Commission* (1973) and *Mescalero Apache Tribe v. Jones* (1973), has reviewed the scope, but not the fundamental premise, of the power of Indian nations to tax activities on tribal-use, or reservation, lands. In order to empower tribal education programs in a manner consistent with the Indian Self-Determination and Education Assistance Act of 1975, and with provisions of federal treaties, the time may have come to consider the imposition of a tribal education tax on the tribal-use lands for which the federal government claims ownership.

Summary

Tribal governments have begun to view educational systems operating on tribal-use lands with increased scrutiny. Student achievement scores and other indices of educational outcome clearly show that Native American students in these educational systems are considered to be at risk. As tribal governments attempt to balance the retention of their distinct cultural identity and simultaneously prepare their youth to exist successfully in a multicultural and technological environment, the educational systems are seen as both contributors to and solutions for the problem. As a result, tribal governments are increasingly attempting to exert some form of control over the educational systems.

Definitions of the form of tribal governmental control and the
extent to which it should be implemented arc limited by issues of legal
and financial empowerment. This chapter has looked at southwestern
tribal groups to examine the problem of at-risk Native American
students. The issue of tribal empowerment, and efforts to achieve it,
has been examined from the perspective of three Arizona tribal governments. Finally, a possible solution to the problem of tribal government financial empowerment has been suggested, and the legal basis
for its implementation discussed.

References

Arizona Department of Education. (1990). *Statistical and financial data for fiscal year
1989-1990.* Phoenix: Author.
Castle, S. R., Graham, P., & Yazzie, A. (March, 1989). *Position paper of the Navajo Nation
Public School Boards Association: Navajo education 2000.* Paper presented at the Navajo
Nation Education Summit, Window Rock, Navajo Nation, AZ.
Castle, S. R., & Yazzie, A. (October, 1989). *School improvement profiling and research design.*
Paper presented at the North Central Association Commission on Schools, Navajo
Nation 1989 Fall Education Conference, Ft. Wingate.
Cherokee Nation v. Georgia, 30 U.S. 1 (1831).
Commission for Accelerating Navajo Development Opportunities (CANDO). (1988).
Navajo Nation FAX 88. Window Rock, AZ: Navajo Nation.
Johnson v. M'Intosh, 21 U.S. 543 (1823).
Kronowitz, R. S., Lichtman, J., McSloy, S. P., & Olsen, M. G. (1987). Toward consent and
cooperation: Reconsidering the political status of Indian nations. *Harvard Civil
Rights/Civil Liberties Law Review, 22,* 507-622.
Martin v. Waddell, 41 U.S. 367 (1842).
McClanahan v. Arizona State Tax Commission, 411 U.S. 173 (1973).
Mescalero Apache Tribe v. Jones, 411 U.S. 145 (1973).
Navajo Nation, Division of Community Development. (1990). *Chapter images: 1989.*
Window Rock, AZ: Author.
New Mexico State Department of Education. (1990). *The New Mexico accountability report
1989-1990.* Santa Fe: Author.
New Mexico State Department of Education. (1991). *New Mexico school district and
student achievement profiles 1989-1990.* Santa Fe: Author.
Roessel, M. (1991, June 5-11). One people, one school. *Navajo Nation Today,* pp. 8-9.
Tee-Hit-Ton Indians v. United States, 348 U.S. 272 (1955).
United States v. Kagama, 118 U.S. 375 (1886).
United States v. Santa Fe Pacific R.R. Co., 314 U.S. 339 (1941).
U.S. Census Bureau. (1980). *We, the first Americans.* Washington, DC: Government
Printing Office.
U.S. Department of Education. (1991). *Indian nations at risk: The first 500 years* (Final
report of the Indian Nations At Risk Task Force, Final Draft 6B). Washington, DC:
Author.
Worcester v. Georgia, 31 U.S. 515 (1832).

THIRTEEN

Reaching Out to Prevent Dropping Out
FINANCING PROGRAMS FOR GIFTED AT-RISK STUDENTS

JOHN R. CURLEY

There is a widespread belief that the gifted will do well in school regardless of whether their giftedness is nurtured or ignored, but this is not necessarily the case. Gifted students will underachieve and some will actually drop out when their needs are neglected or, worse, the school becomes a hostile environment for them. Many of these gifted underachievers are disadvantaged and minority students who, ironically, are most in need of programs designed to develop their abilities but all too often represent an unrealized source of human potential.

For the nation as a whole, lower levels of achievement and high dropout rates result in lower productivity and higher social costs and may presage a weakening position in the world economic system. The U.S. Department of Education (1991) has noted that "American students are at or near the back of the pack in international comparisons" and that, further, "the rest of the world is not sitting idly by, waiting for America to catch up. Serious efforts at education improvement are under way by most international competitors and trading partners" (p. 5). It clearly behooves the United States as well as all other countries to retain students in school and, by doing so, prepare to meet future international challenges in the technological, scientific, and political spheres successfully.

At-Risk Students

It is important that students from all backgrounds be actively engaged in school if they are to receive the education and training that will help them to succeed and make a contribution to society through their productive efforts. Although the overall dropout rate for grades 9-12 in the United States has ranged from 22% to 29% since 1965 (National Center for Education Statistics, 1991) one constant has been that dropout rates are strongly related to family socioeconomic status. Students who are potential dropouts due to their socioeconomic background and school experiences are often called *at risk*.

It has been noted that aggregate dropout statistics are unevenly distributed in terms of geography, race, and ethnicity (Wehlage, 1986). Nationally, the incidence of dropout by race is greatest for Native Americans, followed in order by Hispanics, blacks, whites, and Asians (Pallas, 1986). Racial minorities now represent 30% of all youth in the United States, and by the year 2010 this will increase to 37% of the total. Those minority youth who are also disadvantaged in socioeconomic terms are most at risk of school failure and of dropping out. In general, the reported statistics indicate that large urban districts have the highest dropout rates; it is no coincidence that these districts also have large percentages of disadvantaged and minority students.

The National Assessment of Educational Progress (NAEP) (1991) has reaffirmed that the type of community in which students live is often associated with achievement. Students in disadvantaged urban communities have the lowest average proficiency, and those in extremely rural areas also perform less well, on average, than students in advantaged communities. Children in many of the poorer urban and rural school districts are not afforded the same advantages in terms of course offerings, facilities and equipment, guidance, and other special support services. A positive relationship between the level of parents' education and student achievement was also reported by the NAEP, and students with two parents living in the home were found to have the highest proficiency levels across the states.

Barro and Kolstad (1987) found that while dropping out is often the result of prior disadvantages, and the frequency of dropping out declines with rising socioeconomic status, for all race/ethnic groups dropout rates also decline as school performance, based on test scores, increases. Wehlage (1986) concludes that the actual decision by an individual to drop out of school stems from "an accumulated sense of alienation" resulting from an interaction between personal background and school experiences and that the most important school-related determinants in dropping out are low expectations, low grades, and disciplinary problems, including poor attendance.

French (1981) found in a study of Pennsylvania high school dropouts that many had high IQs and that both boys and girls appeared to have poor relationships with teachers and to regard the school as not preparing students for the "real world." Whitmore (1987) cites five reasons for underachievement, among gifted students in particular: lack of motivation, poor academic preparation, lack of intellectual nurturance within the family, chronic poor health, and physical disabilities.

In recognition of the importance of positive and successful school experiences to avert dropping out, there are now many ongoing attempts to help retain the average student in school, but it may be that gifted students, particularly those from disadvantaged and minority backgrounds, are not being provided opportunities commensurate with their needs.

Dropouts in New York State

The proportion of children belonging to racial or ethnic minority groups is increasing in New York as it is nationwide: Approximately 60% of black and Hispanic students in New York State attend schools that have at least 80% minority enrollments (New York State Education Department, 1989). It has also been reported that 50% of all black children and 42% of all Hispanic children live in single-parent households and that the children from these two groups constitute 57% of the state's poor children and 54% of the near poor. A profile of school district characteristics for groups of K-12 districts in New York State with the highest and lowest dropout rates is provided in Table 13.1. New York City is not included because its large size would skew the data and render them less meaningful. However, it should be noted that New York City would place in the high dropout decile group if it were included.

Table 13.1 Profile of School District Groups With High and Low
Dropout Rates in the 1988-89 School Year

School District Group	Full Value per Student	Income Wealth per Student	Mean Enrollment	Disadvantaged Students (%)	Minority Students (%)	Students Going on to College (%)
High dropout decile	90,465	38,844	3,334	36.6	28.8	65.2
High dropout quintile	113,058	40,220	3,207	35.9	29.6	66.0
Low dropout quintile	172,352	76,065	1,925	7.6	9.4	84.0
Low dropout decile	191,564	82,486	1,645	.7	9.9	87.4

SOURCE: New York State Education Department (1989).

The four other large urban school districts of Buffalo, Rochester, Syracuse, and Yonkers are all in the quintile of districts with the highest dropout rates (Rochester and Syracuse are in the high dropout decile as well). These districts and New York City all have large percentages of disadvantaged and minority students, as indicated in Table 13.2.

Of the five New York State districts with at least 15% Native American enrollment, three were in the high dropout quintile and two of those were also in the high dropout decile. Native American, Hispanic, and immigrant students often have low English-language-proficiency, which compounds their other disadvantages.

The profile in Table 13.1 confirms that districts with high dropout rates have less wealth, are larger in size, and have greater percentages of disadvantaged and minority students than do districts with low dropout rates. Also, lower aspirations and fewer opportunities for students in high dropout districts are demonstrated by the much lower percentage of students in districts with high dropout rates who go on to college when compared with low dropout districts.

Table 13.2 Percentages of Disadvantaged and Minority Students in Large
Urban School Districts, 1988-89

School District	Disadvantaged	Black	Hispanic	Other Minority
Buffalo	68.6	48.6	7.3	2.3
New York	59.0	38.4	34.3	7.4
Rochester	52.9	54.4	13.7	2.6
Syracuse	52.2	36.2	2.8	1.8
Yonkers	42.5	27.9	28.5	2.3
Statewide	33.8	19.9	14.8	4.1

SOURCE: New York State Education Department (1989).

School districts in the quintile with the lowest dropout rates are more than 50% wealthier in property full value and almost 90% wealthier in resident income per student than districts in the high dropout quintile.

In the low dropout quintile, suburban districts predominated (67% of the group), and only 2% were urban. A third of the districts in the high dropout quintile are urban districts, which, of course, usually do have larger enrollments and larger percentages of disadvantaged and minority students.

Of the 49 K-12 school districts statewide that have a minority enrollment of 25% or more, 22 are in the high dropout quintile, and 10 of them are minority-majority (50% or more of enrollment being minority students). Of the districts in the quintile with the lowest dropout rates, 9 have minority enrollment of more than 20%, but in 6 of the 9 the dominant minority group is Asian.

Although districts with low dropout rates tend to be smaller than districts with high dropout rates, this does not mean that all small districts have low dropout rates. In fact, the quintile of districts with high dropout rates is made up predominantly (60% of the group) of small, rural districts. Southern (1981) cites the problems of rural gifted students as including community acceptance of the status quo, lower spending, and fewer students, all resulting in a more limited curriculum.

More than 35% of the students in high dropout districts are disadvantaged, while less than 8% of students in the low dropout quintile are disadvantaged (and less than 1% in the low dropout decile). In 61% of the high dropout quintile districts, more than 25% of enrollment is disadvantaged, using eligibility for free school lunch as a proxy for economic disadvantagement. Only 22% of the districts in the low dropout quintile have as many as a quarter of enrolled students living in economic disadvantagement.

In the NAEP results, New York's data basically mirrored those at the national level. These results confirm earlier reports that black and Hispanic students living in disadvantaged communities with single parents and parents with lower educational attainment levels are most apt to demonstrate low proficiency. Students in rural communities, however, were found in general to do about as well as those in advantaged communities.

Support and encouragement of learning received from parents affects both student proficiency and aspirations, and the percentage of students going on to college is 18% greater in the wealthier, low dropout quintile of districts compared with the poorer, high dropout quintile. This might be attributed in part to better preparation and guidance and to family ability and willingness to finance a college education as well as to aspirations.

Participation in Programs

In a study of high school dropouts in Iowa, Green (1962) reported that although the gifted represented only 3.5% of the dropouts, 17.6% of the gifted were dropouts. Of course, these results may not be generalizable across the nation or to the conditions of today, but, even if the gifted were to drop out at only the same rate as all other students, this is a great waste of potential that might be stemmed through well-planned programs to meet their individual needs. Programs for at-risk students in general are important, but these for the most part provide ancillary support such as guidance, health, recreation, and social services. Gifted at-risk students need academic stimulation and enrichment as well if they are to stay engaged in learning in a school setting.

The Education Amendments of 1969 (P.L. 91-230) mandated a national study of programs for the gifted and set in motion events that included (a) a review of research and literature, (b) testimony by experts on children and youth, (c) the compilation and analysis of the data that were gathered, and (d) studies of existing programs. The study disclosed "a nationwide neglect of the gifted" (Marland, 1971, p. 4), and reported that special services for the gifted produce significant outcomes, while the deprivation of such services can be detrimental to the development of the abilities and emotional well-being of these students. An astonishing 57.5% of schools surveyed for the study in 1969-70 reported having no gifted students.

Since that time, the number of states requiring school districts to provide programs for the gifted has been steadily increasing. A 1977 survey found that 37 states had statutory and administrative policies governing the education of the gifted (Grossi, 1980); of these, 9 mandated educational services for the gifted. In the others, the provision of services was permissive, with local districts having the option to provide or not provide services. By 1981, according to results of another survey, there were 17 states mandating services for the gifted (Mitchell, 1981), and by 1987, 25 were doing so (Council of State Directors of Programs for the Gifted, 1987).

Even though education of the gifted is not mandated in New York State, the number of school districts identifying and serving gifted students and the number of students being identified and served have increased markedly. From the 1981-82 to 1987-88 school years, the number of students identified and the number served in K-12 school districts, exclusive of the five largest urban districts, increased by 26.5% and 48.5%, respectively (Curley, 1991). However, many districts still do not have a program for all grade levels and some have no program at all.

It is not easy to determine in aggregated data which students, particularly in the larger urban districts, are given opportunities to participate in programs for the gifted. In those districts with multiple school sites, there could well be a disproportionate number of participating students in schools that draw students from more advantaged backgrounds. Even within individual school buildings, disadvantaged and minority students are often underrepresented. Brown (1985) has stated that differences in minority and nonminority participation in gifted programs are greatest in desegregated schools. This lack of assignment of minority students to programs for the gifted was recognized as such a widespread problem that it was included as a specific issue area in a wider study of within-school discrimination by the U.S. General Accounting Office (1991).

The variation of participation in school programs among the several student subgroups has been widely reported. Plisko and Stern (1985) note that although black and Hispanic students participate in programs for the gifted at almost half the rate of white students, the participation rate for Native Americans is even lower. According to Kirschenbaum (1988), a higher percentage of Native American students are in programs for the learning disabled than any other group. The College Entrance Examination Board (1985) found that black students are also disproportionately more likely to be enrolled in special education programs and vocational education programs, although the proportions were found to vary widely across school districts. It was further determined that even among college-bound seniors, most black students had taken less rigorous courses, and that students of low socioeconomic status and in elementary schools with predominantly minority students had less access to microcomputers. Materials and personnel resources provided to Hispanic schoolchildren have also been reported to be lower quality and less plentiful than those provided to others (Ortiz, 1988).

Identification of the Gifted

A major problem in achieving the proportionate representation of disadvantaged and minority students in programs for the gifted lies in the identification of gifted students. Disadvantaged and minority children are not well represented in programs for the gifted often because the standardized tests commonly used for identification purposes do not measure all types of intelligence, and these students may have learning, communication, and even thinking styles that are different from the norm.

In seeking to ensure that a larger and more diverse group of gifted students is served, the U.S. Office of Education has sought to encourage the use of a broad definition of *gifted* beyond intellectual ability and academic achievement, as follows:

> Gifted and talented children are those identified by professionally qualified persons who by virtue of outstanding abilities, are capable of high performance. These are children who require differentiated educational programs and/or services beyond those normally provided by the regular school program in order to realize their contribution to self and society.

Children capable of high performance include those with demonstrated achievement and/or potential ability in any of the following areas, singly or in combination:

1. general intellectual ability
2. specific academic aptitude
3. creative or productive thinking
4. leadership ability
5. visual and performing arts
6. psychomotor ability (Marland, 1971, p. 10)

This definition has been assumed to encompass a minimum of 3-5% of the total school-age population. Although the definition was later changed in the Gifted and Talented Children's Act of 1978 to exclude psychomotor ability, this broader definition was widely accepted and brought education of the gifted wider public support because a greater number of the public could identify with one or another of the abilities designated and a greater number of pupils were considered eligible to receive special education.

However, in spite of that, in a limited national survey, Hunsaker, Abeel, and Callahan (1991) found that general intelligence aptitude and academic achievement are still the two most commonly used methods for identifying gifted students, and that few districts consider the needs of limited English speakers, students of low socioeconomic status, or those with disabilities.

In New York State, school districts use various methods, either singly or in some combination, to identify gifted students and to determine admittance to programs. These include, but are not limited to, intelligence tests, standardized achievement tests, teacher ratings, parent ratings, creativity measures, and ratings by other means. These various methods if used in combination can be weighted in any way a school district chooses.

Clearly, the methods used and the weightings given have a very definite influence on what kinds of students will be identified as gifted and admitted to programs. Some students have skills and abilities that are not easily tested for or quantified, and yet may be important to a successful and productive life. When scores on standardized tests become the sole or primary criteria for admission to programs

Table 13.3 Frequencies in Use of Methods for Identification of the Gifted

Identification Method	High Dropout Decile Districts Using Identification Method (N = 61)	Low Dropout Decile Districts Using Identification Method (N = 53)
(1) Individual aptitude	31	27
(2) Group aptitude	45	39
(3) Achievement	59	48
(4) Creativity	24	20
(5) Teacher rating	56	46
(6) Parent rating	18	19
(7) Other	26	19

SOURCE: *Fact Sheet* (1989).

for the gifted, students from underserved populations are often discriminated against. Minority gifted students, especially, are more apt to be identified through the use of creativity tests, leadership scales, and parent, teacher, or peer nominations (Baldwin, 1987), although Davis and Rimm (1989) have cautioned that teacher nominations may be less useful than other measures, due to cultural bias on the part of some teachers.

The possible responses to methods for identifying gifted students and their frequency of use in the high dropout and low dropout decile groups of districts are provided in Table 13.3. In the high dropout decile group, only one district used a single method and four used only two. In the low dropout decile group, two districts used one method and two used only two methods.

Most districts (61% of those in the high dropout and 64% of those in the low dropout decile), while relying basically on standardized aptitude and achievement test scores, tempered those measures by also using at least one of the alternative methods. Teacher recommendation was the most widely used alternative method. Fewer districts attempted to measure or identify creativity or to take into account parent recommendations. Under the "other" category, districts used such methods as subject grades, peer or self-recommendation, or school committee or principal recommendation.

The high dropout decile districts identified a lower proportion of enrolled students as gifted (6.8%) and served a lower proportion

(6.3%) than did the low dropout districts (8.1% identified and 8.1% served). In most of the districts in both the high and low dropout deciles groups, a full 100% of the gifted pupils identified are served. Only five urban districts, including the two largest in the high dropout group, Rochester and Syracuse, account for almost all of the difference between the number of students identified as gifted and the number served in that group. This was true even though Rochester and Syracuse each identified lower proportions of total enrollment, 2.6% and 4.3%, respectively, than the group mean. They served an even smaller proportion of enrolled students in programs, 2.1% in Rochester, and 4.0% in Syracuse. The other three urban districts in the high dropout group each identified over 17% of enrollment as gifted and served at least 10% in programs for the gifted.

Data regarding education of the gifted for New York City are not readily available, because even though the New York City school district is a unified district with a central board of education and central administrative offices headed by a chancellor, it consists of 32 separate community districts, each of which has its own local board of education, superintendent, and budget. Any attempt to assess expenditures or educational performance in New York City would need to be conducted on a community district basis, and not all of the community districts have submitted the necessary reports to the State Education Department. Of the two remaining large city districts, Buffalo identified 5.9% of enrolled students as gifted and Yonkers 16.6%.

In a 1988 study, Aldrich reported that only 6.3% of the reporting districts in New York had programs for gifted students in grades K-12, and only 36% offered high school courses for these students. Yet 15% of districts in the decile with high dropout rates and 11% in the low dropout decile reported programs in grades K-12, and 60% of the high dropout districts had at least some course offerings to gifted students at the high school level.

In Rochester, the large urban district with the highest proportion of minority students (70%) and the highest dropout rate (14.3%), it was reported that only gifted students in grades 4-8 are served, although certainly there are students in advanced placement and other specialized courses at the secondary level. In Buffalo and Yonkers grades K-12 are served, and in Syracuse grades 1-12.

It would seem that in at least two of the large city districts, a greater percentage of enrollment might be found to be gifted and that greater efforts could be made to serve these students with programs designed to meet their special needs. These same districts have relatively higher dropout rates, suggesting a possible relationship.

However, as Richart (1987) has noted, because of limited resources, parents whose children are being served through present identification and selection practices "are understandably defending the status quo because they fear their children will be excluded if other groups, such as the disadvantaged, are included" and that a wider identification of disadvantaged gifted students requires pragmatic acknowledgment that additional resources must be found to support programs (p. 152).

Financing Programs for the Gifted

Federal funds for education of the gifted have always been limited. Programs for education of the gifted were once authorized under the old ESEA Title IVC program, the overall purpose of which was to support demonstration programs for the improvement of educational practices and under which grants were awarded to local educational agencies on a competitive basis. However, a major change in federal policy occurred under the Reagan administration with enactment of the Education Consolidation and Improvement Act of 1981. Under Chapter 2 of this act, also known as the education block grant, education of the gifted became 1 of 30 program options, and states and school districts were given discretion to choose which programs would receive funding and which would not, depending on state and local priorities.

In a national study of school district use of Chapter 2 funds over a 3-year period, it was found that 17-19% of districts used at least some Chapter 2 funds for education of the gifted (Curley, 1986). However, there was extreme variation in the amounts allocated, some districts committing almost their entire Chapter 2 allocation to programs for the gifted and others only a token amount or none.

Small amounts of funds under Title II of the Education for Economic Security Act and certain other federal programs are also used by some districts on behalf of the gifted, and a few grants (41 in FY 1990) are provided under the Jacob K. Javits Gifted and Talented Students Program.

Most of the states—45 according to a 1987 survey (Council of State Directors of Programs for the Gifted, 1987)—provide some state aid

Table 13.4 Mean Amounts of Local Funding per Student, 1988-89

	High Dropout Decile Districts (N = 61)	Low Dropout Decile Districts (N = 53)
Mean amount of local funding for gifted programs per enrolled student ($)	32.07	47.28
Mean amount of local funding per gifted student identified ($)	470.38	584.75
Mean amount of local funding for gifted student served ($)	510.49	585.01

SOURCE: *Fact Sheet* (1989).

to school districts for education of the gifted, but there is wide variety in how the funds are distributed. In some states, funds are provided through general aid or in the special aid formula. In others, funds come from separate categorical formula aid or competitive grants. Some states determine the amount of funding on a per student basis; others use instruction units or some other cost basis.

New York has a flat grant program of state aid for education of the gifted and these funds, although limited, have stimulated more widespread development of school district programs and the allocation of increasing amounts of local funds for education of the gifted (Curley, 1991). Programs for gifted students were, however, found to be funded primarily with locally allocated funds, these making up 80% of total funds for the gifted in 1987-88. High-wealth districts, many of them located in the New York City metropolitan area, had almost twice the amount of local funds as low-wealth districts and, more important, funding disparities for education of the gifted between high-wealth and low-wealth school districts in New York grew ever wider from 1981 to 1988, chiefly because high-wealth districts are able to allocate greater amounts of local funds to this program area.

Differences in locally allocated funds have also been found to exist between school districts in the decile with high dropout rates and those in the decile with low dropout rates, using data reported by school districts to the State Education Department. Districts with high dropout rates allocate far less funding per student for education of the gifted, as indicated in Table 13.4, even though virtually all of the reporting districts in this group make some commitment of locally allocated funds in support of programs for the gifted. Greater school district wealth and fiscal capacity in the low dropout districts makes possible a mean amount of funding on an enrolled student basis that is considerably more (47.4% greater) in the low dropout districts.

Districts with low dropout rates were also found to spend a mean amount that is 24.3% more for each gifted pupil identified than the high dropout districts. However, the difference in amounts of locally allocated funds spent for each pupil served in programs for the gifted is less, this being only 14.6% greater in districts with low dropout rates. This is because in the low dropout districts, a greater number of gifted students identified are also served in programs (the number served was actually numerically greater than the number identified, but not enough to make any statistical difference in the percentages identified and served as gifted in that group).

Funding Strategies for the Gifted

Federal aid for education of the gifted continues to be a very minor amount, but as an extension of the federal role of providing leadership and compiling and disseminating statistics and program information, perhaps some federal aid to the states should be provided to support the activities of coordinator positions for gifted education in each state education department.

In terms of state aid programs, categorical formula aid seems preferable to competitive grants because the element of grantsmanship is removed and all districts are assured of a consistent source of funding over time. The state aid should be distributed in inverse proportion to school district wealth, so that gifted students in poorer communities can be provided with more equitable programs. Such aid can also stimulate the allocation of greater local funds for education of the gifted.

Unfortunately, in times of fiscal constraint, funding for education for the gifted is often an early target of cutbacks in many school districts. In New York, the state has abetted this practice by allowing school districts beginning in the 1991-92 school year to consolidate state aid for the gifted with funds from several other categorical aids, if these aid programs total less than $75,000, to permit greater

Table 13.5 Local Funds for Education of the Gifted in Large City
School Districts, 1988-89

School District	Funds per Enrolled Student ($)	Funds per Student Identified as Gifted ($)	Funds per Gifted Student Served in Programs ($)
Buffalo	82.28	1,392.00	1,392.00
Rochester	32.21	1,224.43	1,564.05
Syracuse	32.09	755.20	797.06
Yonkers	4.49	27.13	27.34

SOURCE: *Fact Sheet* (1989).

flexibility in the use of the funds. One of the real benefits of the state aid program for education of the gifted has been that it focused attention on this student population. The change could all too easily result in an erosion of programs for the gifted in districts that receive small amounts of aid because the elimination of direct state aid removes this stimulus for local funding of such programs.

Even though services must still be provided to the gifted in the 340 school districts eligible to exercise this option, it is not clear at what level. Schools, especially small schools in rural areas, would be able to use funds more efficiently if they could combine resources for education of the gifted in cooperative program ventures and use technology such as interactive television to broaden the number of students who are able to participate.

As indicated in Table 13.5, because relatively fewer students are identified as gifted and served in programs, the level of local funding support is relatively high for each one identified and each one served in Rochester, Syracuse, and Buffalo. In Yonkers the amounts are low, but Yonkers also reports that a large amount ($5,634,211) of state magnet school aid is used to support programs for the gifted. Yonkers receives more of this aid, $16,500,000 in 1988-89, almost one third of the statewide total, than any other school district. If the magnet school aid dedicated to programs for the gifted were to be factored in, the amount allocated for each gifted student identified and each one served in Yonkers would, of course, be greatly increased.

Magnet schools offer themes, such as science and technology or the performing arts, and special courses of study that are designed to attract students. They also tend to exhibit many of the characteristics of effective schools, including a high level of student achievement. Although the state magnet school aid is provided primarily to assist Yonkers and other school districts in desegregation efforts (Curley, 1989), magnet schools may be a very realistic approach to dealing with a variety of issues in education, including school choice, innovative curriculum, and, of interest here, dropout prevention and providing appropriate instruction for certain gifted students. The enlistment of volunteer mentors from the school, colleges, or the community, when matched to student interests and cultural backgrounds, can additionally provide important guidance and encouragement and facilitate the provision of out-of-school activities to students from single-parent homes at low cost.

The fact that Yonkers uses a considerable portion of its magnet school aid to provide programs for the gifted illustrates the fact that the most critical funding decisions are made at the local level. Local school officials decide how much of the funds received from the federal Chapter 2 and Title II programs, from general state aid, and from local tax levies will be used to support programs for the gifted. For this reason, it is important that advocates for the gifted convince local boards of education and school administrators of the need for programs for the gifted.

Summary

There is a need for more rigorous educational efforts on the part of schools and students to enable the United States to meet the challenge of other nations in the world arena across a spectrum of competitive areas. It is in the best interests of the nation and individual students for those who are gifted to be provided educational opportunities that will promote learning and enhance opportunities for achievement. For far too many disadvantaged and minority gifted students, however, the opportunities to fulfill their potential and to succeed in life are greatly diminished by social and economic factors that put them at risk of failure and of dropping out.

School-based programs for the gifted can ameliorate socioeconomic disadvantages to some extent, but to accomplish this such programs require the equitable participation of students from disadvantaged and minority backgrounds and adequate allocation of funds. Districts with high dropout rates are typically less wealthy than those with low dropout rates. They also have higher percentages of disadvantaged and minority students, and fewer students going on to college. Since some of these school districts do not have the fiscal capacity to generate an adequate level of local funds to provide programs for the gifted, the states must do more to ensure that supplemental funds are provided and are driven to where they are most needed.

When, in 1958, the U.S. Congress in response to another international challenge enacted the National Defense Education Act to support instructional improvement in mathematics, the sciences, and foreign languages, Congressman Carl Elliott answered his own question concerning that program, "Where does the gifted student fit into this legislation?" with the statement "Any action we take to improve the quality of education for all children will greatly aid the gifted, or the academically talented" (quoted in Conant, 1958, p. 143).

Many state systems of school finance are inequitable and are currently being challenged in the courts. New or restructured state aid programs to distribute more funds to less wealthy urban and rural school districts, where dropping out is often regarded as a desirable alternative, in order to improve instruction in the sciences, mathematics, and languages, to redesign and rebuild outdated facilities, and to bring greater technological capability to poor performing schools, would directly benefit all at-risk students. Gifted at-risk students would potentially benefit all the more.

Yet, the problem of providing programs for gifted at-risk students is certainly not one that can be addressed simply by increasing funding. The use of multiple methods for identifying gifted students is necessary to ensure that underserved populations are given opportunities to participate in meaningful and challenging activities that will meet their particular needs and concomitantly provide them with more rewarding school experiences to reduce the risk of these students dropping out.

As more states mandate local educational agencies to provide services to the gifted and continue to allocate funds for that purpose, education of the gifted is not likely to be as easily overlooked or relegated to a low-priority status as in the past. Rather, education of the gifted should become an integral component of the full educational plan of school districts as they strive to meet the needs of all pupils. At the same time, programs originally or primarily designed for the gifted can be of benefit to the general school population, or such programs can be outgrowths of certain other instructional initiatives even if the requirements and experiences of gifted students are qualitatively different. The potential returns on investment in gifted at-risk students are simply too great for us to be satisfied with the status quo.

References

Aldrich, P. (1988, September). *Advocacy for gifted and talented (AGATE) testimony at the regents legislative conference*. Albany, NY.

Baldwin, A. 1987. Undiscovered diamonds. *Journal for the Education of the Gifted, 10*(4), 271-285.

Barro, S., & Kolstad, A. (1987). *Who drops out of high school: Findings from high school and beyond*. Washington, DC: U.S. Department of Education.

Brown, C. (1985). Is excellence a threat to equality? In B. Gross & R. Gross (Eds.), *The great school debate* (pp. 296-302). New York: Simon & Schuster.

College Entrance Examination Board. (1985). *Equality and excellence: The educational status of black Americans*. New York: Author.

Conant, J. (1958). *The identification and education of the academically talented student in the American secondary school*. Washington, DC: National Education Association.

Council of State Directors of Programs for the Gifted. (1987). *The 1987 state of the states gifted and talented education report*. Topeka, KS: Author.

Curley, J. (1986). *Federal education policy and the block grant*. Reston, VA: Association of School Business Officials International.

Curley, J. (1989). Financing desegregation in the Yonkers public school. *Urban Review, 21*(2), 95-109.

Curley, J. (1991). Financing programs for education of the gifted in New York State. *Journal of Education Finance, 16*, 332-347.

Davis, G., & Rimm, S. (1989). *Education of the gifted and talented*. Englewood Cliffs, NJ: Prentice-Hall.

Fact sheet on programs for the gifted, 1988-89. (1989). Submitted to the New York State Education Department.

French, J. (1981). The highly intelligent dropout. In W. Barbe & J. Renzulli (Eds.), *Psychology and education of the gifted* (pp. 492-493). New York: Irvington.

Green, D. (1962). A study of talented high school dropouts. *Vocational Guidance Quarterly, 10*, 171-172.

Grossi, J. (1980). *Model state policy, legislation and state plan toward the education of gifted and talented students: A handbook for state and local districts*. Reston, VA: Council for Exceptional Children.

Hunsaker, S., Abeel, L., & Callahan, C. (1991). *Instrument use in the identification of gifted and talented children*. Charlottesville: University of Virginia, National Research Center on the Gifted and Talented.

Kirschenbaum, R. (1988). Methods for identifying the gifted and talented American Indian student. *Journal for the Education of the Gifted, 11*(3), 57-63.

Marland, S. (1971). *Education of the gifted and talented: A report to the Congress of the United States by the U.S. Commissioner of Education.* Washington, DC: U.S. Department of Health, Education and Welfare.

Mitchell, P. (1981). *A policy maker's guide to issues in gifted and talented education.* Washington, DC: National Association of State Boards of Education.

National Assessment of Educational Progress. (1991). *NAEP 1990 assessment of the nation and the trial assessment of the states.* Washington, DC: U.S. Department of Education.

National Center for Education Statistics. (1991). *Digest of education statistics.* Washington, DC: U.S. Department of Education.

New York State Education Department. (1989). *New York: The state of learning.* Albany: Author.

Ortiz, F. (1988). Hispanic-American children's experiences in the classroom: Comparison between Hispanic and non-Hispanic children. In L. Weis (Ed.), *Class, race, and gender in American education* (pp. 74-83). Albany: State University of New York Press.

Pallas, A. (1986). School dropouts in the United States. In *The condition of education.* Washington, DC: U.S. Department of Education.

Plisko, V., & Stern, J. (1985). *The condition of education, 1985.* Washington, DC: National Center for Education Statistics.

Richart, S. (1987). Rampant problems and promising practices in the identification of disadvantaged gifted students. *Gifted Child Quarterly, 31,* 149-154.

Southern, T. (1981). The rural gifted child. *Gifted Child Quarterly, 31*(4).

U.S. Department of Education. (1991). *America 2000: An education strategy.* Washington, DC: Author.

U.S. General Accounting Office. (1991). *Within-school discrimination.* (Publication No. GAO/HRD91-85). Washington, DC: Government Printing Office.

Wehlage, G. (1986). *At-risk students and the need for high school reform.* Madison, WI: National Center on Effective Secondary Schools.

Whitmore, J. (1987). Conceptualizing the issue of underserved populations of gifted students. *Journal for the Education of the Gifted, 10*(3), 141-153.

American Education Finance Association Board of Directors, 1992-1993

OFFICERS

David H. Monk, *President*
C. Phillip Kearney, *President-Elect*
George R. Babigian, *Executive Director and Secretary/Treasurer*
Van D. Mueller, *Immediate Past President*

DIRECTORS

<table>
<tr><td>*1993 Term*</td><td>*1994 Term*</td></tr>
<tr><td>

Patricia Anthony
Debra S. Haas
David Honeyman
Anne L. Jefferson
Joel D. Sherman
</td><td>

James N. Fox
G. Alfred Hess, Jr.
Stephen B. Lawton
Mary T. Moore
Lawrence O. Picus
</td></tr>
</table>

1995 Term

William J. Fowler, Jr.
Robert D. Hickman
Mary P. McKeown
Eugene P. McLoone
Lynn M. Moak

Index